W9-BYE-469

NOT
LIGHT,
BUT
FIRE

NOT LIGHT, BUT FIRE

HOW TO LEAD MEANINGFUL RACE CONVERSATIONS IN THE CLASSROOM

MATTHEW R. KAY

STENHOUSE PUBLISHERS
PORTSMOUTH, NEW HAMPSHIRE

Stenhouse Publishers
www.stenhouse.com

Library of Congress Cataloging-in-Publication Data

Names: Kay, Matthew R., 1983- author.
Title: Not light, but fire : how to lead meaningful race conversations in the classroom / Matthew R. Kay.
Description: Portland, Maine : Stenhouse Publishers, [2018] | Includes bibliographical references.
Identifiers: LCCN 2018004786 (print) | LCCN 2018019979 (ebook) | ISBN 9781625310996 (ebook) | ISBN 9781625310989 (pbk. : alk. paper)
Subjects: LCSH: Multicultural education--United States. | United States--Race relations--Study and teaching | Group work in education. | Discussion.
Classification: LCC LC1099.3 (ebook) | LCC LC1099.3 .K39 2018 (print) | DDC 370.117--dc23
LC record available at https://lccn.loc.gov/2018004786

Book design by Blue Design (www.bluedes.com)

Manufactured in the United States of America

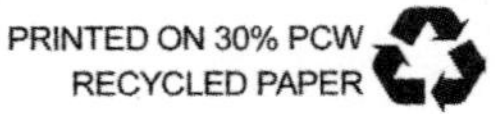

24 23 22 21 20 19 18 9 8 7 6 5 4 3 2

In loving memory of Sherrill Jones Kay,
my mother, a thirty-six-year teaching
veteran and the reason I do what I do.

"I've decided to keep you."

2/12/80 by R.C. Kay III

CONTENTS

PART 1: THE ECOSYSTEM

PART 2: A STUDY OF CONVERSATIONS

ACKNOWLEDGMENTS

I'd like to thank my wife, Cait, for providing honest, insightful, and comprehensive feedback on every draft of this book; my father, Rosamond, for the decades of mind-sharpening debate that model the discourse I want for my students; and my aunt Connie, for her unconditional love and support.

Thanks to my principal and great friend, Chris Lehmann, for all the professional opportunities that led to the writing of this book. I will always be grateful to my editor, Tori, for her patience, expertise, and encouragement.

Finally, thank you, Dia. You were a perfect gift, just in time. Daddy loves you.

INTRODUCTION

NOT LIGHT, BUT FIRE: THE CASE FOR MEANINGFUL CONVERSATIONS

Talk is cheap. We have built a mountain of clichés to say as much and a canon of stories to indict the boastful rabbits and loose lips among us. History praises Lincoln for his brevity at Gettysburg, while it forgets Edward Everett's two-hour speech that preceded it. Shakespeare made sure that Hamlet punished Polonius's sermonizing with an ignoble death-while-hiding. And lest the bard's point go unmade, the wavering prince meets his own end only after letting his righteous revenge dissolve into "words, words, words." The most garrulous among us are dismissed as weak-willed; many hate a windbag, most fear the silver-tongued. Knowing that those who "talk long" often "talk wrong," we have developed a uniquely American succinctness. We expect to be sold ideas in the time it takes to ride an elevator, and to be able to judge their merits just as quickly.

Yet, moments of racial tension scratch from us a great tolerance for empty talk. There is a certain formula a racial story can reach, some unknown combination of timing, rarity, and the notoriety of those involved that draws analysts to gravely suggest that "we need to talk about race." And then we do. A lot. With little regard for substance or coherence, we find our airwaves filled with empty rhetoric and thoughtless repetition. Consider, for example, the following race conversation from our nation's not-too-distant history. In March of 2008, ABC News unearthed some of the Reverend Jeremiah Wright's sermons, highlighting lines like, "The government gives them the drugs, builds bigger prisons, passes a three-strike law, and then wants us to sing 'God bless America.' No, no, no, not 'God bless America,' God *damn* America! That's in the Bible! For killing innocent people. God *damn* America for treating us citizens as less than human!" And this excerpt responding to 9/11 that borrows from Malcolm X's comments after the Kennedy assassination: "We have supported state terrorism against the Palestinians and black South Africans, and *now* we are indignant! Because the stuff that we have done overseas is now brought right back into our own front yard! America's chickens are coming home to roost" (Wright 2008). After trying in vain to quell the controversy about his pastor, then senator Obama was forced to deliver his celebrated More Perfect Union speech, where he acknowledged that Wright had "used incendiary language to express views that had the potential to not only widen the racial divide, but views that denigrate the greatness and the goodness of our nation." Later, Obama argued that

> we have a choice in this country. We can accept a politics that breeds division, and conflict, and cynicism. We can tackle race only as spectacle—as we did in the OJ trial—or in the wake of tragedy, as we did in the aftermath of Katrina—or as fodder for the nightly news. We can play Reverend Wright's sermons on every channel, every day and talk about them from now until the election, and make the only question in this campaign whether or not the American people think that I

somehow believe or sympathize with his most offensive words . . . or . . . (Obama 2008)

He then pivoted to a plea for post-racial populism, challenging Americans to *talk* about crumbling schools, jobs, and health care. The speech was received well enough to inspire T. Denean Sharpley-Whiting to gather a collection of scholarly essays written about it into a book titled *The Speech: Race and Barack Obama's "A More Perfect Union"* (2009). Eminent scholars such as Michael Eric Dyson and Ta-Nehisi Coates contributed. But, considering this race issue settled, the public conversation had already moved on. The issue flared back up, however, soon after our country's first black president was elected, when Harvard professor Henry Louis Gates was arrested in front of his home in Cambridge, Massachusetts. Six days later, President Obama claimed that the arresting officer had "acted stupidly," and the *call for conversation* went out again. Many of us remember the resulting "beer summit," where the involved parties talked reconciliation near the White House Rose Garden.

More recently, we have collectively held forth on the Trayvon Martin, Michael Brown, and Eric Garner decisions; riots in Baltimore; shootings in Charleston; and the burning of black churches. As supremacists march, we talk. As confederate statues come down, we talk. We tweet, we post, we meme, we chat. Our news networks cram eight analysts into eight tiny boxes, then pit them in a moderated struggle to be the most quotable.

It's not a new habit—we have always appreciated a chance to bloviate about race. In 1852, Frederick Douglass was invited to speak at Corinthian Hall by the Rochester Ladies' Anti-Slavery Association. He'd been asked to deliver an address celebrating the Fourth of July, an odd request for a man who had to steal his own freedom. Midway through his speech, he famously skewered America's preoccupation with meaningless race conversation. Specifically, Douglass critiqued our national eagerness to make theater out of the obvious, while leaving tough conversations for future generations.

Douglass, along with many abolitionists, had often been chided for the honesty and directness of his race discourse. He was told that, instead of offering fiery rebukes, he should spend more time "shedding light" on the country's race problem. That afternoon in Rochester, an exasperated Douglass finally responded, "On what branch of the subject do the people of this country need light?" He then offered up his frustrations:

> Must I undertake to prove that the slave is a man? That point is conceded already. Nobody doubts it. The slaveholders themselves acknowledge it in the enactment of laws for their government . . . It is admitted in the fact that Southern statute books are covered with enactments forbidding, under severe fines and penalties, the teaching of the slave to read or to write. When you can point to any such laws, in reference to the beasts of the field, then I may consent to argue the manhood of the slave. When the dogs in your streets, when the fowls of the air, when the cattle on your hills, when the fish of the sea, and the reptiles that crawl, shall be unable to distinguish the slave from a brute, *then* will I argue with you that the slave is a man! (Douglass 1852)

And

> Would you have me argue that man is entitled to liberty? That he is the rightful owner of his own body? You have already declared it . . . There is not a man beneath the canopy of heaven that does not know that slavery is wrong *for him*. (Douglass 1852)

Then soon after, he offered his audience a challenge: "It is not *light* that is needed, but *fire*" (Douglass 1852). Douglass knew what many are noticing now: that we never seem to graduate to the *next* conversation. The hard one. That we hide our stasis beneath puffed-up punditry and circular debate. He called for us to infuse our conversations with *fire*—to seek out and value historical context, to be driven by authentic inquiry, and above all, to be honest—both with ourselves and with those with whom we share a racial dialogue. Just as *fire* rarely passes through an environment without acting upon it, so too should our world be impacted by our students' race conversations.

This is a book for educators who want to answer Douglass's challenge: teachers who wish to tackle race conversations with more than a light show, who want something to *be different* after they and their students have wrestled the great ideas. This book does not seek to prove what has already been proven: that all students are capable of learning, that many of our students of color face considerable and purposeful inequity, that diversity is a beautiful opportunity for any teacher. It will not linger in debates about the value of student voice. It will acknowledge as fact that most educators are people of goodwill, that most of us respect the enormity of the task before us. It's directness will honor the time that educators commit to reading its pages.

Each chapter grounds itself in a dialogic tradition that understands that great learning happens when both teachers and students explore the limits of their own understanding through rigorous discussion. We have long known that students given the opportunity to speak and listen take more responsibility for their interpretations, retain these interpretations longer, and develop agility of mind. Perhaps most importantly, dialogic pedagogy disrupts the traditional classroom power dynamic, positioning school as a place where students have an equal share in their education. Students are not empowered; rather they are shown that their inherent power has been recognized—and that it matters. Well-crafted discussions build confidence, and confidence is sacred currency to students and teachers alike.

This is an action book with a movement mission. It will live in the *how* of powerful race conversations, acknowledging that the above *why* has already been addressed. It is for teachers who wish to help students develop healthy habits of both mind and discourse that will serve them for the rest of their lives. It is hard for a student to unlearn empathy, to forget discernment, to dismiss the importance of solid evidence once they've grown used to demanding it. This book acknowledges that if we are training the next generation of teachers, entertainers, lawyers, and politicians; if we are molding thoughtful citizens, wise counselors, and people of righteous passion; then our classrooms must be deliberate in their approach to conversations about race. The next generation needs to be far better at this stuff than we have been. They are coming of age in a world of artfully disguised injustices, most of which will stay both invisible and vicious if people never learn how to meaningfully discuss them.

OWNING OUR JUSTIFIABLE FEAR

During one of my graduate classes at the University of Pennsylvania, we discussed how to lead meaningful conversations about race. Our professor had pulled quotes from our responses to an online prompt, then hung them on chart paper around the classroom. We were asked to walk around, commenting on each paper with sticky notes. Itching for a fight in the way of the vaguely bored, I deliberately tried to stir up trouble with comments that seemed either superficial or untested.

One classmate claimed, with undue confidence, that most minority students were afraid to talk about race, then asked how teachers might manage this fear. To that, I scribbled

They are afraid? Says who?

This narrative of minority students afraid to discuss race didn't hold up against an avalanche of anecdotal evidence that seemed to prove otherwise. I knew my experiences were no more all-encompassing than any other teachers', but *my* minority students discussed race openly and vigorously in most of their social spaces. Their social media lit up with observations every time some racial incident hit the news. I saw nothing that would indicate timidity on the topic—yet, in progressive education circles, we seem determined to make these same students *more* comfortable discussing race. Where on earth did that idea come from?

I looked around a graduate classroom of overwhelmingly white, middle- and upper-class, well-intentioned future teachers—and I thought to myself, *Have you* asked *them if they are afraid to talk about race?* I know that if they had asked me when I was in high school, I would have answered that race talk is oxygen to black folks—breathed into our jokes, our social norms, our storytelling at family gatherings. I'd tell them how we identify strangers by race before other physical descriptions. If I was close to them, I'd add that *whiteness,* especially, occupies a special, complicated place in our dialogue. Black folks tease it in its absence, talk about it behind its back.

I'd tell them that, no, teenage me was not afraid to discuss race. I'd ask if these teachers were projecting their own fears onto me. If they were, what were *they* afraid of? Messing up? Saying the wrong things? Mishandling controversy? Letting their own bias show? All of the above? And perhaps with good reason.

CAUTIONARY TALES

Hollywood has spent decades telling teachers to ignore these fears and boldly jolt students into engagement. In the movie *Stand and Deliver* (1988), for example, teacher Jaime Escalante teases the gang members in his class by saying, "Tough guys don't do math, tough guys deep-fry chicken for a living . . . You want a wing or a leg?" In *Dangerous Minds* (1995), LouAnne Johnson tells her students that "nobody is forcing you to be here. You can stay, or you can leave . . . You either don't graduate, or you have to put up with me. It may not be a choice you like, but it is a choice." In the 2007 movie *Freedom Writers*, teacher Erin Gruwell points out the similarity between a drawing found on a student's desk and the racial caricatures central to Nazi propaganda. In the midst of the ensuing argument, she tells a boy, "You know what's going to happen when you die? You're going to rot in the ground. And people are gonna go on living. And they're gonna forget all about you. And when you rot, do you think it's going to matter whether you were an original gangster? You're dead. And nobody is going to want to remember you, because all you left behind in this world is this!" (She holds up the caricature.) All three speeches inspire immediate student breakthroughs: Escalante's "tough guy" solves a math problem, Johnson's students start thoughtfully interpreting Bob Dylan lyrics, while Gruwell's shyly ask her to explain the Holocaust.

Shocking students, of course, requires teachers to eschew students' expectations. In all three of these movies, teachers offered brutal directness—when their students, presumably, expected meekness. Hollywood's seamless execution of such techniques, and the prompt rewards that followed, caused a generation of teachers to attempt their own racial shock and awe campaigns, only to find out that it was nowhere near as easy. Or prudent. For example, look at the tenth-grade assignment from a teacher in Albany, New York, shown in Figure 0.1.

Q3 Post Assessment: Persuasive Writing

For the following assignment, you need to pretend that I am a member of the government in Nazi Germany, and you are being challenged to convince me that you are loyal to the Nazis by writing an essay convincing me that Jews are evil and the source of our problems. After viewing the videos (if they work) and reading the packet of propaganda, combine that knowledge with what you've learned in history class and through any experiences you have to complete this task.

Since this is a persuasive piece, you need to choose from the types of rhetorical arguments we covered in quarter 1, in writing your commentaries about religious freedom, freedom of religious expression, etc. Review in your notebooks the definitions for LOGOS, ETHOS, AND PATHOS. Choose which argument style will be most effective in making your point. Please remember- your life (here in Nazi Germany in the 30's) may depend on it!

Your essay must be 5 paragraphs long, with an introduction, 3 body paragraphs containing your strongest arguments, and a conclusion. You do not have a choice in your position- you must argue that Jews are evil, and use solid rationale from government propaganda to convince me of your loyalty to the Third Reich! Use the following brief outline to structure your essay appropriately, and turn in this sheet with your completed essay. This assignment will be due on WEDNESDAY, April 10.

FIGURE 0.1
Think Like a Nazi assignment

It's safe to assume that this teacher was not a Nazi, and that her intentions were neither to encourage anti-Semitism nor to recruit future skinheads. I suspect that she had opposite intentions: to have her students struggle with the absurdity of hateful thought systems—in what would seem to be a key step to dismantling them. And she likely sought to connect her students' understanding of the rhetorical devices Logos, Pathos, and Ethos to each technique's real-world exploitation in propaganda. What student would prefer arguing that *oranges are the best fruit* when they could instead engage Nazism? Yet she faced immediate resistance. One-third of the students in the class refused to write the essay. Then, in a teacher's nightmare, an irate parent fed her assignment to the local news, which quickly spread to the Associated Press, which led to national reports on CBS and CNN and articles in the *Washington Post* and *New York Times*. While none of these reports identified the teacher, all quoted Albany's superintendent Marguerite Vanden Wyngaard's response. The assignment, to her, was "completely unacceptable." She asked, "How could you ask a student to justify prejudice leading to genocide? It's an illogical leap . . . it doesn't make any sense." She allowed that the teacher probably didn't intend "to cause any insensitivities to our families of Jewish faith" (CBS6 Albany 2013). Still, the teacher would be suspended, and the superintendent would enter into conversations with the Anti-Defamation League about future sensitivity training for her staff.

Many of us would have more thoughtfully considered this assignment, but there are many ways that discussing race can get us flayed on the news. In 2014, for example, a teacher in Redmond, Washington, was working through a unit on the Industrial Revolution, and found her students having trouble understanding the cotton gin. So she brought in cotton plants, and asked her seventh graders to pull the cotton from the plant and separate the seeds. The irate mother of one black student gave her daughter permission to not do the assignment. The teacher, in a "tough love" move that seems plucked from the aforementioned "hero teacher" movies, gave her a failing grade. This student's mother took the story to the local media, which ran a segment that was picked up by the *Huffington Post*. In it, she says, "My daughter is African American, and for her to pick cotton when our grandparents were raised on a plantation to pick cotton—it's just not okay. Not okay at all." When asked for comment, the Lake Washington School District issued a written statement to remind critics that the lesson was "about the impact that the invention of the cotton gin had on the Industrial Revolution." Lake Washington, unlike Albany, apparently supported their teacher's idea, if not its execution. Still, with all of the fuss, it is not hard to imagine this teacher deciding that engaging race this sensorially is not worth the headache.

These incidents are unique only in their publicity. Every time that I facilitate a professional development workshop on how to lead meaningful race conversations, I ask if participants have similar horror stories. The question is met with a forest of hands. Some recall old episodes from their student years. Parents describe horrendous incidents from their children's classes. Colleagues share blunders that they've heard through their school's grapevine. Occasionally, brave teachers expose their own mistakes. Each time, it's painfully clear that every teacher's missteps during race conversations are magnified regardless of their intentions. The penalty for misspeaking, improper planning, or a lack of foresight can be the total loss of a teacher's moral authority. And once lost, students' respect can seem impossible to recover. No wonder my Penn classmates spoke about the prospect of race discussions with a tremble in their voices. No teacher wants to be the villain in someone else's horror story, or the fool in a dark comedy.

But we can't settle our own anxieties by passing them on to our students. If they *are* fearful, it is not a myopic fear. It is a fear just as layered as our own, ranging from mild nervousness over using the correct racial labels to those reflected in a Facebook message, sent to me by a former student on the night of the Trayvon Martin decision, that said, *I'm afraid of how bloody tonight might be*. Many realize the limits of a social media diet of out-of-context news clips and misleading memes. Many recognize that Facebook is only a place for declarations, its comment threads mostly inhospitable to probing questions. They recognize that Twitter's very nature values brevity over layered inquiry. They have a desire to wrestle with hard ideas—but instead find themselves needing to speak fast and listen hurriedly. They want the conversation to—paradoxically for such a rapid age—slow down.

If anything, I propose that we teachers are most afraid of this eagerness. In contrast to their engagement with a great many of our discussion topics, many of our students actually hold passionate opinions about race. These opinions are unpredictable, and they accompany questions that seem far outside our training. And students actually care if we get it right. This added pressure leads too many of us to think that only certain personality types—the *magic* teachers among us—are equipped to lead meaningful race conversations.

BUT IT'S NOT MAGIC

Allow me to excoriate one last "hero teacher" movie. In *The Dead Poets Society* (1989), fiery Mr. Keating asks his students to read the preface to their class textbook. There, Mr. J. Evans Pritchard, PhD, has written a guide to "Understanding Poetry," a precise metric for measuring a poem's greatness, which Keating sketches derisively on the chalkboard. Keating then whispers, "Excrement. That's what I think of Mr. J. Evans Pritchard. We're not laying pipe, we're talking about poetry . . . Now, I want you to rip out that page." Fired up by his students' minute-long assault on their textbooks, Keating delivers the movie's iconic speech: "This is a battle, a war, and the casualties may be your hearts and souls . . . In *my* class you will learn to think for yourselves again!"

Keating's diatribe implies that objective measurement is both soulless and a ridiculous way to ascertain the value of a poem—or the effectiveness of a teacher. Great teachers are, instead, born with *immeasurable, unteachable* stuff. This presumption leads many to believe that powerful classroom conversations require a Mr. Keating—iconoclastic, charismatic, blessed with a preternatural interpersonal intelligence. Teachers who do not readily identify as one of these "types"—those of us who are more quiet, less combative, more deliberative—begin to consider our conversational game to be fixed. We are either cool enough to hold great conversations or we aren't, and no amount of professional development can stretch the limits of our intuition.

But this is too simple. First, such a stance implies that Keating-types' conversational successes are due to intuition, not hard work. It ignores hours spent picking the best texts, designing the best prompts, researching the best structures, practicing the best activities, reflecting and building up both victories and failures. The more a teacher's work is ignored, the easier it is for him to ease up on the work, start slipping, and have no idea what went wrong. Furthermore, it demoralizes colleagues who yearn for their colleagues' conversational successes. This often inspires jealousies, which eventually dissolve the important connective tissue between classrooms. It's hard to collaborate through closed doors. Most importantly, such a stance stymies teacher development. We rarely work on attributes that we believe to be fixed. We invest hundreds on gym memberships because we consider our waistlines alterable. We listen to Rosetta Stone lessons because we know our brains have room for new words. The moment our deficiencies become immutable, our efforts to improve begin to wane.

Some among us do have innate conversational strengths. Yet, teachers who come to the discourse naturally can't be the only people with enough confidence to broach hard classroom discussions. Morale must be developed through a purposeful, logic-driven, *measurable* method. A reliable process that can be both applied and reflected on without magical thinking.

The chapters of Part 1 propose developing an ecosystem that can reliably support effective classroom race discussions. The first chapter describes quality relationship building, both horizontally among students and vertically with their teachers. In the second, teachers will learn which interpersonal skills are most beneficial to holding productive race conversations, and how to develop them. Chapter 3 describes the curriculum and conversational structures that are most important to sustaining the rigor, empathy, and focus that these important conversations deserve. While reading the final chapter of this section, teachers will learn how to infuse their conversations with clearly communicated purpose, so that students will not only know what's at stake, but fully understand their locus of control.

Each of the chapters of Part 2 will take a closer look at a different, specific, meaningful race conversation that I've held with my students. Most of these conversations are composites, drawing statements and exchanges from over a decade of classroom discourse. The last will be an example of what this book calls a "pop-up" conversation, one made necessary by students' concerns about current events. While I offer concrete examples throughout the book for how teachers might practice the new habits and skills described with peers before students, the epilogue proposes an approach to professional development that an entire department could adopt, so everyone can grow these skills—and confidence to not only face but embrace meaningful race conversations—together.

With earnest humility in the face of the heavy lift before us, let us begin.

PART 1

The Ecosystem

Successful race conversations depend on a very specific ecosystem. As teachers, our biggest mistake is undervaluing any of the many elements that might, on their surface, seem inconsequential—but that turn out to be vital for our discourses' survival. Without healthy classroom relationships and sound conversational structures, race conversations cannot thrive. Without honest interpersonal skill development, teachers' successes will depend more on natural personality traits, which are more unpredictable than we like to think. Finally, without clear methods of establishing purpose, students will rarely decide to invest enough mental, spiritual, and emotional energy to move any race conversation from light to fire.

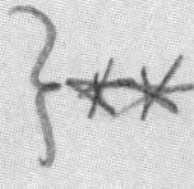

CHAPTER 1

DEMYSTIFYING THE "SAFE SPACE"

The first, and ultimately most important, magical concept to be demystified is the *safe space*. Among progressive educators, no goal is more holy. In each classroom, students are to feel comfortable enough with their various identities to be honest, open, and vulnerable. Conveniently alliterative, the term *safe space* captures our best dreams of what classrooms can be: havens; calm harbors; shelter from our students' stormy home lives, neighborhood violence, or school drama. The dream is so powerful that naming it has become a staple of our introductory spiel.

"My name is Mr. Kay, and I want you to consider this classroom a *safe space*."

This assertion is offered with a magician's *Voila!—I have said it, therefore it is so*. And with these magic words, bullies are tamed and introverts peek from their shells. We are suddenly ready to lead conversations about sensitive topics, because our students are magically now eager to take risks. If, over the course of the year, they forget our first-day pronouncement, we eagerly remind them: *Remember, everyone, this is a safe space.* After this, students who undermine such spaces are viewed as troublemakers, and to mete out appropriate discipline, we pull from our bag of behavior modification tactics. Meanwhile, familiar classroom hierarchies and interactions remain stubbornly visible—outspoken kids still dominate conversation, and students remain disagreeable when they disagree. This, of course, frustrates us. Why won't students share in our utopian vision? Did they not hear us?

They did. However, for most students, a teacher's *safe space* designation doesn't mean much. Definitions of *safety* are surprisingly varied. For some teachers, the term is used in its most literal sense—"this is *safe space*; here we don't fight each other." This makes great sense in a school in which wayward students roam the halls looking for open classroom doors to burst into and disrupt lessons, or where neighborhood kids regularly wait at the nearest subway stop, looking to jump the most vulnerable. When teachers in these environments promise a *safe space*, they might simply want their students operating a step higher on Maslow's Hierarchy of Needs. Assured that each class period won't end in a bloody nose, kids might breathe easier for an hour or so.

In less harrowing environments, however, teachers use the term to describe a sense of order: "This is a *safe space*, so everyone can focus on their work." Here, the students are safe from both distractions and surprises. Eighth graders often describe this particular safety when interviewing for a spot at my school, Science Leadership Academy (SLA). Asked to describe their ideal learning environment, more than a few answer, "*A place where all the students are sitting down, and they are quiet while the teacher is speaking. Nobody is shouting out. When the teacher tells them to do something, they do it. Nobody is acting up.*" This classic vision shows up everywhere, from "no-excuses" charters to elite magnets to public, private, and parochial schools, large and small.

Less often, and more controversially, teachers use the term to reference ideological safety: "This is a *safe space*, so your ideological comfort is valued." This definition has been red meat in political conversations among conservatives and liberals alike, especially when it comes to college classrooms. The Right rails against the encroachment of "political correctness," which is deviously softening a generation of students, while the Left caricatures its opponents as simple-minded zealots incapable of properly nurturing diverse student populations. The tension between these views especially affects conversations about race, leaving teachers to define where on the ideological comfort spectrum they'd like their classroom conversations to fall. This can be especially frustrating for students, who might find standards in their English class drastically different from those in their history class. Not to mention the yearly vertical transitions (grade to grade, school to school) that bring waves of disparate definitions of *safety* mixed in with teachers who don't bother making the claim in the first place.

It's not just that students must decipher what a teacher means when they claim "safe space." They must also shoulder an unannounced burden: responsibility over their classmates. Schooling is an individual exercise. Most of its incentives, from kindergarten through graduate school, are individualized (e.g., glossy stickers, grades, scholarships, internships, jobs). Collaboration is generally the least valued and most haphazardly executed aspect of teachers' pedagogy, and some entire schools are being built around individualization and specialization. When we then ask students to, in effect, be their brother's keeper, many understandably have no idea what comes next. And this is where we, as teachers, must have more to offer than a day-one "abracadabra!"

In order to nurture hard conversations about race, first we must commit to *building* conversational safe spaces, not merely *declaring* them. The foundation of such spaces is listening. When facilitating professional development sessions, I often ask teachers to describe a moment when they felt truly listened to. How did they know that the listening was authentic? *Eye contact*, *patience*, *engagement*, *focus*. How did that moment make them feel? *Valued*, *important*, *safe*. I share with these colleagues my own listening Mount Rushmore: the minister at my old church, who always looked the smallest children directly in the eye; the head football coach at West Chester University, who, beyond all reason, allowed a lowly student assistant to break down film; and my wife, who never tires of follow-up questions. Without prompting, colleagues often share moments when they were not listened to, and how it made them feel. *Ignored, unimportant, unsafe.* It stands to reason then, that we should create a culture of *listening*—an act that can be broken into discrete, practicable, and measurable skills.

This is the first of many times in this book where I'll offer an approach that is by no means a panacea. Teachers, as some of the most creative people on earth, can create listening activities that fit their own style and pedagogical vision. I share only what has worked for me, hoping simply to shift the *safe space* conversation from the realm of magical thinking to a more practical skills-based approach. Before I do so, however, there is one key understanding: Students and teachers might spend their entire lives learning how to listen. It is one of our hardest self-improvement missions, and can be the most costly—ask family and relationship counselors. We must understand this, and orient our approach to student discipline accordingly. Students learning how to listen to one another might show the same symptoms of those who are "being bad." But when we manage both issues equally, we scuttle students' opportunities to develop key listening skills. We can no more punish our way into a conversational safe space than we can conjure one from thin air—so we must instruct where we used to admonish, encourage where we used to excoriate, and carefully track what we used to ignore.

In my classroom, the conversational safe space is established with three discussion guidelines: Listen patiently, listen actively, and police your voice. After their introduction, each is practiced explicitly over the first few weeks—a period of time that I like to think of as a conversational "training camp." This camp works as an extended norming that I reference for the rest of the year.

LISTEN PATIENTLY

The more we care about a topic of conversation, the more we rush to speak. The less we care, the less we feel obligated to pay attention to conversational partners who do. In both instances, we often fail to show others that we are listening patiently to them. This display is important, as people cannot access your brain to measure your level of focus. Social cues are necessary to show people they have our attention.

Practicing this skill requires a shift. Normally, after a teacher calls on a student to speak, we give most of our attention to the respondent. We shift our attention away only when someone else calls out, or behaves in some way that we deem disrespectful. But to help students listen patiently, we must invest considerable focus on the students who are *not* speaking. And in doing so, offer some rules: First, *hands should not be raised while someone is still talking*. When a teacher calls on one student to speak, the rest of the hands in the room have to go down. Any student who does otherwise is communicating to everyone in the room that they don't care about the person who is still talking. That raised (and sometimes *waving*) arm is saying, "I wish you would *shut up!* I have my own thing to say!" This behavior sparks an unnecessary rush for respondents, causing them to speak as if trying to squeeze comments in under the wire, before their teacher dumps them for the other raised hands.

Second, listening patiently means that students should never be interrupted. This is not new. Many teachers have variations of "one voice at a time." The problem is that too many of us frame the rule as more disciplinary necessity than skill development. Students who have an impulse to interrupt each other care deeply about what is being discussed—this is a win! Calling out signals impatience, not meanness. Something in the student's brain is boiling, and the lid couldn't hold it, but students must be taught that (1) their big *eureka* might be influenced by what is currently being said, and (2) patient listening is transactional—and when they speak, they will want their classmates to keep the lid on too. (This is more difficult when students come from environments that define safety as *students are quiet*. Dialogic classrooms offer so much new stimuli that it's easy to get wired. Also, students might not trust that they'll ever get a turn, so they try to squeeze their points in before the teacher shuts down the conversation.) We don't interrupt for any reason, including affirmations and agreements, both of which still have the unintended effect of drawing focus from the speaker.

Beyond these nonnegotiable rules, there are countless suggestions. Try for eye contact. Try nodding. Try smiling. Try pursing your lips in thought. Students should reflect on what they appreciate from a listener and try to mimic those behaviors when someone else is speaking. Regardless of whether or not they are in doubt, they should ask each other if they feel "listened to."

Over the first few days of school, and often afterward, I offer various scenarios to illustrate the importance of listening patiently. One student raises his hand, and I ask others to wave theirs while she speaks. *How does that make you feel?* As a student speaks, I constantly interrupt him with seeming affirmations. "Uh-huh, yeah, uh-huh, yes, I know! Right??" *How does that make you feel?* A student pauses to gather her thoughts, and I step in with, "That reminds me of . . ." *How does that make you feel?* Throughout these scenarios, I pepper personal stories. For instance, as a stutterer, I've always hated interruptions, especially the last sort, where people would step in to help me finish, but would instead fling my conversation far from the thread I was trying to follow. "I was going to get there!" I tell students, "if you would have just let me finish."

A commitment to the language of *listening patiently* drastically impacts not just students' peer-to-peer interaction, but our core relationship with students. Consider the following classroom scenarios:

(A)

Mike (interrupting Joe, a classmate)**:** *Yo! That same thing happened to me yesterday when . . .*

Mr. Kay (frustrated)**:** *One voice! You've got to stop interrupting!*

Mike (equally frustrated, whispering to a classmate)**:** *Told you Mr. Kay doesn't like me.*

(B)

Mike (interrupting Joe, a classmate)**:** *Yo! That same thing happened to me yesterday when . . .*

Mr. Kay (smiling, holding up a placating hand)**:** *Patience, man! Listen to Joe—he's making a good point! Tell your story in a bit.*

Mike: *Oh, my bad, Joe.*

In the second scenario, Mike's enthusiasm has survived the exchange. The teacher's choice to not be adversarial means that we might actually get to hear Mike's story, as he won't be too resentful to share it. Also, notice how in the second example, Mike is more likely to acknowledge Joe, whom he may have unintentionally annoyed with his zeal. Both students are likely to leave this exchange feeling listened to.

LISTEN ACTIVELY

Let's continue from the second classroom example in the previous section. Mike, in this moment, has just been reminded to listen patiently to his classmates. He may be tempted to ask, "Why?" The answer is too often, "To be respectful" or "Because calling out is bad." The ideal answer should be, "*Joe's ideas are worthwhile to everyone in the classroom community.*"

Each idea can inspire another, can inform, can be the reason that no two classroom conversations are exactly the same. As such, ideas should not just be shared, but built on. In order to build, ideas must be actively collected before they dissipate. Toward this end, we must design structures that require students to engage each other's ideas and *listen actively*. In my class, this means notebooks, where students are encouraged to write down classmates' comments that intrigue them. Student teachers, or occasionally student volunteers, do the same on the whiteboard. Notice how, in Figure 1.1, my student volunteer has cited her classmates' contributions about Chapter 9 of *Lord of the Flies* by putting names next to each comment. Students eventually are encouraged to cite each other in essays as reliable sources, as fellow experts, when such citations are appropriate.

As teachers, we can offer just as much praise to students who thoughtfully build on classmates' ideas as we offer to those who say cool things. In the early days of a school year, I like to follow the thread of a conversation, maybe even illustrate it on the board: "Joe said _______, which inspired Mike to tell this story, which Marcia thought related to this character in the play. After she made this connection, Tanya told us about this book she read that seems to back up Joe's thesis. I love the way you all are building." After a few examples of this, students find themselves eager to cite each other. I teach them transitional language, my favorite being a simple "Building on [classmate's name]'s point . . ." By the middle of the year, I can tell

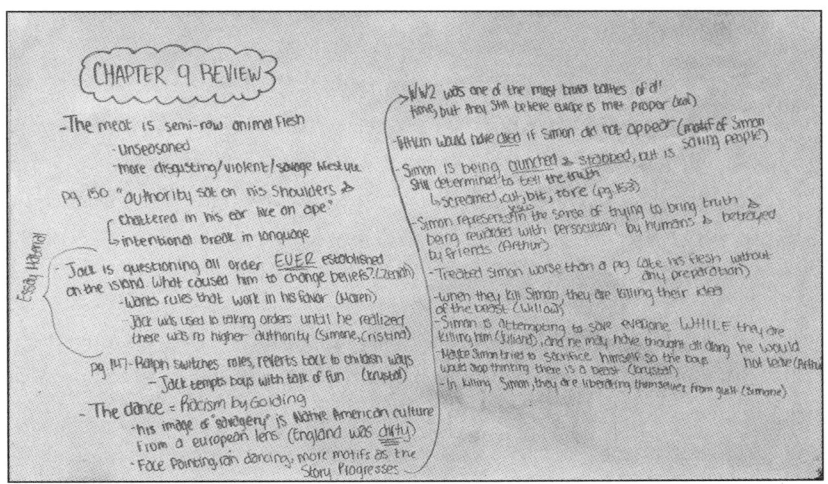

FIGURE 1.1
Students track interesting comments from their classmates so they can later cite each other in essays. See names in parentheses next to comments.

how well my students are listening actively by how often the comments appear daisy-chained together by citation. Of course, I must also model appreciation for the original speaker, working hard to extrapolate points they might not be clearly articulating. This type of synthesis and modeling does require a lot of mental energy from the teacher, but it's work that transfers in a fairly short time.

Consider the following scene, which demonstrates one student's comment with two teacher responses:

> **Joe:** (recovering from Mike's interruption)**:** *Um . . . yeah, I was saying that when Troy uses the N-word in* Fences, *it's different from when white people use it. Well, it's the same sometimes when he's yelling at his son. He wants to make him feel bad. Like white people do when they say it sometimes. But when he's talking to Bono, because that's his best friend, the N-word is saying something else. It's saying, we are real tight, you know?*
>
> **(Response A)**
>
> **Mr. Kay** (turns to next raised hand)**:** *Good point.*

(Response B)

Mr. Kay (pausing reflectively to show patience)**:** *That makes sense! So people use the N-word for different reasons—but you are telling me that it can actually make people feel a sense of intimacy with their friends? That's . . . interesting.* (Turning to his classmates.) *Joe says that the N-word can make people feel close to each other. Has anyone else seen this?*

This redirection, when properly executed, makes listening actively contagious. The trick is to never stop redirecting and to ceaselessly praise students for citing each other. Great discussions become self-rejuvenating creatures, truly student-centered events that rarely repeat themselves—even when the text being discussed is the same year after year. In addition, students don't feel just safe, but also important. And smart. This makes it more likely that they will speak again.

POLICE YOUR VOICE

The focus shifts here, but still places listening at the forefront. If your classmates have to listen both patiently and actively to you, you must make it easier for them to do so by *policing your voice*. The teacher is no longer the prime audience, a fact that I make clear to students by pointing to their classmates and saying, "Speak to them." Early on in the school year, I constantly nudge my students to turn their faces away from me when answering a question, looking instead at peers. The reminder is gentle, and often excited, as if I am trying to say, *What you are saying is too good for just me to hear. Let's get everyone else in on this stuff!* Classmates are often surprised to have a speaker address comments to the larger group. Many perk up immediately because they are used to one-on-one student/teacher exchanges that they'd felt free to check out of. This encourages the golden moment: when a student, without teacher prompting, asks classmates for their opinions on an issue. Whenever I hear this, I know they are nearly ready to keep each other safe during meaningful race conversations.

The second part of policing your voice is understanding that students (and teachers) should speak succinctly. This means that, as a speaker, you are humbly aware of how much space you are taking up at any given moment. Class time is limited. Students should not speak forever; they should not repeat themselves or deliver sermonettes. Transgressions happen. Our students are young, impulsive, and, we hope, impassioned. But there are ways to redirect that build community and respect instead of just shutting kids down. Consider the two following scenarios:

(A)

Maria: *That reminds me of when . . .* (A two-minute, quasi-related story follows.)

Mr. Kay (visibly annoyed, cutting the student off at the first opportunity)**:** *Yes, but we are talking about . . . and please let other people talk.*

Maria (equally annoyed, whispering to a classmate)**:** *He's always cutting me off!*

(B)

Maria: *That reminds me of when . . . (A two-minute, quasi-related story follows.)*

Mr. Kay: *That's a great point! I didn't even see it like that before . . . Quick thing . . . Let's remember to police our voices, right?*

Maria (sheepishly)**:** *Oh, my bad, y'all!*

As with the previous situations, option B removes multiple layers of unnecessary disciplinary tension. A teacher now has the language to say, *I appreciate that you care enough to speak passionately in my class. Thank you for being awake! However, I need you to realize that other people are also awake, and they deserve the opportunity to speak as well.* This particular interaction, however, requires an extra step. It helps to pull Maria aside after class to introduce her to (or remind her of) strategies for being succinct. She could consider pausing before she speaks to gather her thoughts so that she gets right to the important parts. She could work with me to build a reliable structure for her comments, like the one that career coach Lea McLeod published in her article "3 Smart Ways to Keep Yourself from Rambling" called P-R-E-S. (First, state your *Point*—the main idea, then your *Reason*—why you think so, then an *Example*—the evidence that backs you up, then offer *Summary*—restate your main idea.) There are many strategies out there. After this initial conversation, it's important to follow up with Maria, praising small successes with whatever strategy she's decided to try.

A final, important note: We should acknowledge that a student who seems to ramble or have trouble following a conversational thread may have social anxiety or another learning difficulty. If you notice this happening frequently, be sure to bring in the rest of the student's support team, just to double-check that the student is getting the needed supports.

PRACTICE LISTENING

Patient listening, active listening, and policing your voice establish a good conversational foundation for the heavy stuff. But introducing the skills isn't enough; they must be framed and practiced. For me, there is the aforementioned "training camp" period. During the first few weeks of class, my students hold many practice conversations, in both large- and small-group settings, after which we reflect, not on the topic but on how well we listened to each other. Over the year, we openly try to climb from level to level in each skill. For example:

Listen Patiently

Beginner: Students no longer interrupt each other / raise their hands / talk while others are talking.

Advanced: Students exhibit good nonverbal "I am listening thoughtfully to you" behaviors.

Listen Actively

Beginner: Students reference each other's comments in their own.

Advanced: Students follow up that reference with a high-order question to their classmates that pushes the conversation forward.

Police Your Voice

Beginner: Students don't ramble on or stray far off topic when called on.

Advanced: Students apply public speaking techniques of projection, articulation, etc., when speaking in class. They follow up by asking classmates if they were clear.

And just as our students need to practice, so do we. Over our careers, many of us have developed instinctive overreactions to students' listening mistakes. Not to mention how often we find ourselves lacking the same listening skills we're trying to teach. How patient are we? My biggest problem is an instinct to interrupt students. It comes from a good place—I am eager to encourage. But that doesn't matter. I also have trouble policing my voice, especially when the subject is something I know more about than my students. The best and worst thing about practicing these skills with students is that they have the language to call me on my own mistakes. Yet, their doing so is evidence that I'm that much closer to my ultimate goal—*safety*. My students know that their ideas are the sacred currency of our classroom, and that they will be received with a purposeful and structured empathy. Only from here can we can move to meaningful conversations about race.

HOUSE TALK

Students might not be as afraid to discuss race as we often make them out to be, but this does not mean that they are eager to do so with *us*. Consider the following: I run an after-school poetry club. The first few minutes of every meeting are normally set aside for unstructured conversation because it gives exhausted students a chance to unwind after a long school day and to build community with each other. I sit with them but generally keep my mouth shut, unless I'm directly asked to participate. In the fall of 2014 one of these conversations took an intriguing turn. One student had just left a class where they'd discussed that summer's protests in Ferguson, Missouri, which flared after the fatal shooting of Michael Brown, a young black man, by a white police officer, Darren Wilson. Apparently, one of her classmates had made a statement about the protesters that she'd found inappropriate. She became frustrated when her teacher didn't "step in," and she aired these grievances in poetry club. Her fellow poets shared similar stories, some dating back to middle school. Over the next few minutes, two camps formed: students annoyed about having to discuss the protests in a diverse environment, especially in conversations facilitated by white teachers, and students of all colors who were frustrated by the lack of Ferguson conversations in their classes.

I pointed out the obvious conundrum. I asked our young poets, *What's a white teacher to do?* According to these students, white teachers were supposed to avoid discussing the Ferguson protests with students of color—an act that opened them to harsh criticism from the same minority students they were trying not to offend. A poet in the latter camp shrugged, then explained that the protests were monopolizing their social media, which made images from Ferguson constantly top-of-mind. Their school subjects seemed trite by comparison, and they appreciated that their teachers wanted to directly address the elephant in the room.

A poet in the former camp offered a quick rebuttal to this cliché. "I don't want to talk about Ferguson with white people. No matter how liberal they are, it's still going to be just . . . academic for them. But it's our actual lives. We really have to *be* black when this stuff is going on. I don't have the energy to explain my emotions every time a teacher decides to talk about race." There was near-universal agreement, and the implications of her comment were not lost on me. Listening, as emphasized in the last section, is already hard. But it takes even more effort to both listen *and* to be heard when your conversational partners (or facilitators) don't have the same emotional sensitivities, investment, or cultural background. This exertion tempts minorities to just keep their mouths shut, rather than enter into exchanges that would otherwise sap their energy.

This debate, I told them, made me think of something. When I was growing up, my parents used the term *house talk* to label conversations that I was not to share with anyone else. This term implied that people outside of our family wouldn't understand, and involving them would annoyingly complicate things—or cause actual trouble. I asked this latter group of student-poets if they felt that race conversations were better kept as house talk. When they agreed, I asked them to explain. Interestingly, a white poet spoke first, sharing that during such conversations, she was often wary of offending classmates of color—not because she disagreed with them, but because she wasn't always as articulate as she wanted to be. There seemed to be a thousand ways to be misinterpreted. Ask a question the wrong way and one might be chastised for one's ignorance. Disagree with a minor point, and one might be charged with leveling "microaggressions." Occasionally, it seemed that her expected job was only to absorb the anger and frustrations of her classmates.

One of their fellow poets, a black boy, answered this by sharing how he felt the need to soften such anger as to not offend well-meaning white classmates or teachers. After prodding, he admitted that he also was inclined to disguise his strong disinterest in the empathetic anger of white allies and pretend that it just doesn't frustrate him. At this, some admitted that, when tensions are highest—as they'd been during the height of the summer's protests—it's sometimes hard to look a white person in the face, even when that person is smiling.

This last bit was rough to hear, a brutal honesty that was followed by silence. As I figured out where to go next, a few parallels came to mind. First, I considered classroom conversations about street harassment. By the time many of my female students reach ninth grade, too many of them have been repeatedly called the foulest words in the ugliest manner possible by complete strangers. In my role as mentor, I rail against this and do my best to affirm my female students when I can. However, I am not a woman, and as such, I recognize that I might look and sound like the man who tried to touch them this morning on the way to school. It would be hubris for me to expect every girl to feel comfortable sharing their anger, embarrassment, or shame with me. What is academic to me is visceral to them. At certain times, some would rather discuss their frustrations with a woman, who might better understand the violence of being objectified, the fear of late nights and lonely street corners. It's equally understandable if these girls don't want to deal with the annoyance of reassuring male classmates who might answer "Not All Men" to their protestations.

As the seconds ticked away, I thought about how often I had mishandled race conversations that I couldn't viscerally identify with. A few years earlier, I had been teaching Markus Zusak's *The Book Thief*. For this unit, I'd wanted students to engage the countless propaganda tools used by Nazis during the Holocaust. Early in the text, the protagonist has to attend the BDM (the Hitler Youth for Girls), which inspired me to find out how adults tailored their propaganda to influence young girls. If I found primary sources, my students could then analyze their use of propaganda techniques. A quick Google search turned up a collection of anti-Semitic children's fables called *Der Giftpilz*, which begins with a famous story called "The Poisonous Mushroom." In the tale, Jewish citizens are compared to mushrooms that appear harmless, but are capable of killing little boys and girls who can't distinguish them from less evil vegetables.

I ordered it. For a teacher who had just spent a unit having students analyze and create allegories, it was a gold mine. Eighteen illustrated stories laying out the structure and intentions of anti-Semitism. When I showed it to my students, I haphazardly voiced my history-nerd enthusiasm. My exact words may have been, "This is a *beautiful* thing!" The kids giggled—all but one, Adam, who raised his hand to say, "Beautiful?" His great-grandparents, he told me, had escaped the Holocaust. I apologized immediately, though the import of my recklessness came at me in waves. How could I even make this mistake? I organize trips to the Holocaust Museum in Washington, DC, every year, and I have invited survivors to talk to my classes. I make certain to frame our Holocaust studies around resistance so as to not make the genocide just about victimhood. Every step of the unit planning is thoughtful, meant to respect the varied humanity of everyone who experienced the era's trauma. Yet, I was still capable of such a terrific blunder, one that I would be considerably less likely to make if I were Jewish, and not merely a well-meaning black ally.

In tough times, minority communities often believe that we're all we've got, so we more thoroughly invest in each other's well-being. Our struggles directly, and maybe even subconsciously, influence the language we use with each other. (This became mortifyingly clear during the more publicized police shootings, as I noticed black students leaving each other with a handshake and a reminder to "stay safe.") With this in mind, it should be easy to understand why minority students might prefer to discuss racial issues only within an intimate community of shared experiences. However, daily cultural exchange with students from different races has duped many teachers into assuming an intimacy that does not exist. We reason that since students from different backgrounds are comfortable discussing occasional racial topics with us, they are automatically eager to join us in "unpacking" their deepest racial anxieties, anger, and confusion.

Yet there has always been a difference between collegial banter and house talk, between the water cooler and the dining-room table. It is dangerous to invite ourselves to the latter because we are tolerated at the former. We must, if we value our students' right to determine healthy relationships, never accept invitations unless they have been proffered. We must, through earnest humility, earn our seats. Just as we cannot conjure *safe spaces* from midair, we should not expect the familial intimacy, vulnerability, and forgiveness needed for meaningful race conversations to emerge from traditional classroom relationships.

To this point, we teachers have to honestly measure our classroom relationships. A good place to start is to reflect on our classrooms' stated and implied priorities. Familial intimacy depends on both parties feeling like a priority to the other. We do not tend to feel close to those who continually treat us like afterthoughts. To preserve our emotional well-being, healthy people draw specific parameters around these relationships, saving our vulnerability for those to whom we are the greatest priority. This extends to the classroom, where most students consider their teachers only tangentially invested in their lives beyond their academic performance. Traditional classroom conversations rarely trouble this perception, as most of the discourse is directly related to course content. Notre Dame's former vice president for public relations James W. Frick famously claimed, "Don't tell me what your priorities are. Tell me how you spend your money and I'll tell you what they are." It is the same, with a slight variation, for teachers: Allot more time for a particular activity, and that is what students will think you value most. By this reasonable metric, students generally understand our course content to be the most important subject in the room. So while students may believe that we mean them no active harm, and that we would generally prefer that they were happy, their personal lives rarely feel like *a priority*.

This is problematic when it comes to discussions of race, where teachers suddenly find themselves asking students to pry open wounds; be honest about fears, hopes, and anger; and mine their own lives instead of assigned texts for source material. Teachers here break a tacit agreement to keep our class conversations detached. This paradigm can be changed, but only through the effort and practice of building genuine *house talk* relationships. As before, I acknowledge that teachers are beyond capable of creating their own structures and activities that fit both their students' needs and their personal pedagogy. I only share what has worked in my classroom. There, we practice three activities that I've seen build trust and community, so that conversations in our space are akin to house talk: Burn Five Minutes, Good News, and High-Grade Compliments.

Burn Five Minutes

I'll never be able to allot more time for discussing students' personal lives than I allot for our subject matter. Doing so would be both irresponsible and disrespectful of my mission as a teacher. But I *can* shift our schedule so that I engage kids as humans *before* I engage them as students. If you ever visit the beginning of my class, you are likely to find me sitting on my stool in the front of the room, already teasing a young Giants fan about her football loyalties. After that, maybe I'll ask another student's opinion of a television show from the night before, or a news event, or something that has been going on at school. Most of my students enter the classroom to find me already engaged in conversation with their peers. When I notice that most of them are in place, I'll pivot to the entire class to bring them into the informal chat. If I can think of a funny story, I'll tell it. Sometimes I'll ask them about a current event—usually something silly, like "Who watched [whatever TV show is currently hot] last night?" or perhaps something more serious. The students weigh in for a few minutes, and then we transition into the day's academic conversations.

It all lasts five minutes. Occasionally three, or seven, or ten. I try not to check my watch. (Though of course, I preemptively adjust this activity to make room for what I have planned that day.) After a few days of this, students begin to initiate informal conversations with me. I do this for two reasons. First, to acknowledge that students are thinking people who hold opinions independent of my curriculum. Second, to show that I do too. Teachers know that when our students see us in the outside world, they often express astonishment at our most mundane humanity: *You shop here too? You like fruit-flavored cereal?* We laugh. Do they think we plug ourselves into our classroom walls when they leave? Of course we have favorite cereals! Just like we have favorite TV shows and books, movies, and albums. When I open up class with these conversations, just about every day, I acknowledge that neither student nor teacher powers down when we leave the classroom. I show that I find them worthy enough to warrant five minutes speaking as equals. (At the beginning of class, no less. Consider the difference between an athlete being asked to start a game and being invited to play in "garbage time" at the end when the outcome is obvious. That's the difference between starting class with informal conversation and mopping up extra minutes with it.)

This time commitment is minimal, until one steps back and considers that five minutes a day becomes nearly two hours of informal chatter over the course of a month. This banking of conversational democracy buttresses all other classroom dialogue—students can take more risks, and our classroom culture can survive more mistakes, because students are less likely to consider our respect for their opinions either disingenuous or capricious. We build with them every day, and not just about things that they will eventually be graded on.

Good News

I owe the following two activities to the genius of my former colleague and good friend Zac Chase, the coauthor of *Building School 2.0* (Lehmann and Chase 2015). I noticed that Zac, too, used informal conversations with his students to show how much he valued their opinions. But Chase's students seemed so much closer to each other than mine. You could feel it walking into his classroom. I wanted to find out why.

Zac takes the same five-minute allotment and asks students to share any good things that might be going on in their lives, an activity he calls simply Good News. Zac noticed that people are naturally quicker to share negative ideas and reluctant to share good news. Yet there is a strange intimacy to sharing good news; asking someone to join you in celebration takes a degree of trust that they will be happy for you. He managed it beautifully. Students raised their hands, and when called on, they stood and shared something good. The students spoke directly to their classmates, and their classmates asked questions.

I have since put my own touch on the activity, framing it as a way to practice our three discussion skills. While someone is sharing, the students must *listen patiently*. Their questions must show that they have been *listening actively*. The presenters must *police their voices*. For the same reasons that I burn the first five minutes of each class, every Monday begins with good news. Students often request a quick Good News session at any point in the week, and if the schedule permits, I allow for it.

After a short time, students begin to follow one another's narratives. They want to know how their classmate's martial arts tournament went, if someone's grandmother is feeling better, whether another's mother has had the baby yet. Dancers learn that a fellow classmate dances, too. A web of connections forms across the room. Students celebrate with each other across all manner of cultural boundaries—some recount a weekend with their church's youth group, while others share their excitement about the upcoming Eid holiday. They ask each other about how fasting works at Ramadan. One student shares that his father will soon be coming home from prison. Another shares that she hasn't skipped a meal in the past two days. My personal favorite moment was when a student shared the good news that his mixtape had finally "dropped," to which at least four classmates turned to me and shouted, "You have to hear it, Kay."

Fifteen minutes of a Good News activity, once a week, is an investment of one hour per month. This hour of building a classroom community helps the students to celebrate the best of each other's cultures. It lays the foundation of empathy that the heavier conversations depend on.

High-Grade Compliments

One of the best gifts we can give one another is a genuine compliment. With it, we can redirect the momentum of someone's day. Compliments are an underutilized superpower, one of the most reliable ways to make a person feel valued. If someone compliments your smile, for example, it's harder to walk past a mirror that day without flashing it. If someone compliments your style, that time you spent choosing your outfit this morning feels validated—no matter how much you pretend to have just "thrown something together." When peers or colleagues compliment your approach to a problem, you feel more confident approaching another. We gravitate toward people who are not only paying us close attention, but also genuinely appreciating what they see.

Think about how it feels when someone pays you a compliment that acknowledges your efforts, especially after some heavy lifting. I ask students to remember the many times they have done more than their share of the work for a group project. Often, even if they don't admit it, they are hurt when their partners don't express appreciation for their contributions. This can be especially stinging after offering contributions they didn't have to offer in the first place: times they helped a friend understand a particularly difficult math concept; times they stepped in after seeing a classmate bullied. Though many students have been taught to let unselfish acts be their own reward, a sincere *thank you*, followed by an earnest compliment, mends the natural resentment that may emerge eventually from feeling unappreciated. Over time, this resentment can sneakily become toxic, eventually discouraging students from attempting the riskier acts of tolerance, humility, or coalition building. All of these behaviors are necessary for meaningful conversations about race.

Compliments, like shared good news and prioritized unstructured chats, can be a pillar of teachers' house talk culture. Zac Chase celebrated what he called "high-grade compliments." In a 2011 blog post, he describes the term:

> The difference between a high-grade compliment and a low- or medium-grade compliment is the focus on complimenting who you see a person as being—the best parts of that character my mom was always so concerned with building.
>
> A low-grade compliment might be something like, "I like that shirt," or "Your hair looks nice." Physical attributes, but still things that accessorize a person physically.
>
> A medium-grade compliment might be something like, "You have a nice smile," or "You've got a great sense of humor." Sometimes still physical attributes, but closer to who people are or who they present themselves as.

> A high-grade compliment says, "I see you. I appreciate you. And here are some of the reasons why." (Chase 2011)

Inspired by Chase's work, I have brought High-Grade Compliments to my classes. Here's what the activity looks like: Once every few months, and before big holiday breaks, we dedicate twenty minutes to students' giving each other high-grade compliments (see Figure 1.2). The first time any of my classes tries it, I describe the rationale that introduced this section, explaining how compliments benefit community building. I give concrete rules for complimenting, some of which I have students write on the board:

1. **Proximity is important.** I ask students to sit down across from the recipient, eye-to-eye. They may not stand over a seated classmate; their body language must communicate being equal and patient. I have them think about how, as younger children, they probably liked it when adults squatted down to their level to address them. Imagine a weary parent sitting in a daughter's tiny chair for a tea party. At times, I mention my father, who, in his role as a deacon, often has to make hospital visits. He makes a point of never standing over someone, but always pulling up a chair and sitting as close to level as he can with his host.
2. **Speak earnestly.** A thoughtful compliment is strangely intimate, and to minimize this feeling, some students tend to fall back into the safety of teasing. For example, a student might say, "You always listen to me. Well, when you are not being a jerk." In other settings, this would not be a problem—I assure students that teasing is my "love language." During a high-grade compliment, however, the recipient may have made themselves too vulnerable to properly deflect sharp language. For however long you compliment someone, you must mean exactly what you say.
3. **It's not about you.** The intimacy of an earnest compliment persuades some students to hide behind self-effacement. A compliment might start with, "I love having you in my math groups. You help me on my projects when nobody else does."

This is good. But then the student might launch into a story describing how they have always struggled with math, ever since the third grade when they had this mean teacher . . . and three minutes later, everyone has forgotten that the soliloquy started with a compliment. I tell the students, "It is not about *you*. It is about *them*. Don't get their hopes up, then steal their moment."

4. **Everyone loves a compliment.** The need to feel appreciated is human, as is the desire to be celebrated for one's contributions. I tell students after introducing the activity, "That person you are thinking about, right now. *Yes*, *that* person. They are sitting there hoping that someone says something nice about them right now. Ignore their averted eyes, and know that any cool-kid smirks are fraudulent. They want to hear what you have to say."

Some teachers prefer to let students silently draft their compliments first. I allow two minutes of silent reflection before the activity begins, so that my students may gather their thoughts. When we are ready, I choose a student and give a genuine compliment. I make a point to

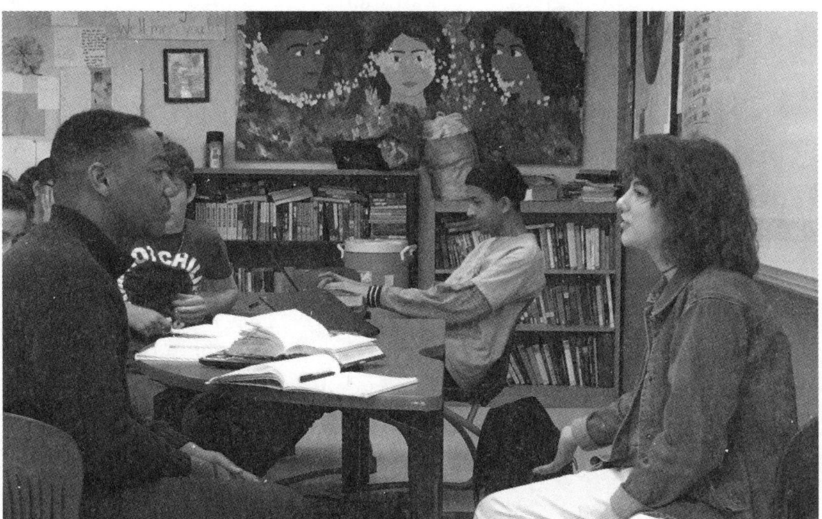

FIGURE 1.2
Sophomore Juliana compliments her classmate Horace, telling him that he has "a really admirable drive in life," and that she appreciates how hard he works to achieve his goals.

offer something beyond a surface compliment. For example, instead of saying, *Your sense of style is really on point. You really have a one-of-a-kind swagger*, I might say, *I've always noticed your incredible sense of style. I love how you embrace your uniqueness. But what's really impressive is how you always celebrate everyone else's individuality too! I see you trying to make it okay for everyone to be themselves, which is so important at this school.* This sort of compliment doesn't just model the activity (and make a student feel good), but also sets the tone for the stuff that our community finds worthy of complimenting.

I then ask for volunteers. Sometimes I have to wait around for hands, and the room takes on the reflective feel of a Quaker meeting. Eventually, when I get my first volunteer, I ask him to walk over to a classmate, sit down, and deliver the compliment. At times, I have worried that some students will never receive a compliment. But every year I notice that students begin to seek out their quieter, less social classmates, or the ones who always seem to be in trouble. This could be because I seek out these same students to model the activity, but it's also because delivering honest, authentic, well-articulated compliments becomes valued as a talent, and the kids want to show off. And how great is that? Students *want* to be the kindest kid in class. However, every teacher is capable of tweaking the activity to fit their students' needs. Just be certain that after these modifications, students are still being earnest. It works only if the compliments aren't canned.

Before moving from this activity, I must acknowledge an easily overlooked point. Teachers might assume, as I did, that all of our coaching should be focused on the giver of the compliment. In a 2016 blog on the topic, Zac Chase gave us one last job:

> What [students] struggled with—to the development of deep blushing, nervous smiles, and an inability to hold eye contact—was hearing someone else call out how they made our classroom a better place.
>
> It's why I added coaching on the receiving of compliments to the process. The rule was simple, "Really listen to what they are saying and then say, 'Thank you'."

> School, life, and any number of outside forces had tuned them into hearing criticism from others, and even accepting it. And while critique has its place in the building of better ideas and examining beliefs, it shouldn't be our default when people start to talk about us or our work. Living in the belief that the world wants you to know what's wrong with what you've built doesn't lend itself well to inspiring the building of new things. (Chase 2016)

- - -

In committing to all three of these activities, I invest just under two and a half hours a month preparing and maintaining a healthy classroom culture. That's around 12 percent of my class time—a significant statement to my students about my values. These activities can be modified, rejected, or used to inspire brand-new approaches. As the most creative people on earth, teachers are best equipped to design activities that fit their students' temperaments and situations. But however varied the activities may be, the root understanding must be the same: Students pay close attention to how we allot our time. We value what we make time for. Garbage is saved for "garbage time." If all of our nonacademic conversations with students happen in "garbage time," or not at all, it is understandably healthy of them to maintain thick walls around their vulnerability. It is understandably healthy of them to trust only those who consider them a priority. It is understandably healthy of them to distrust teachers who are eager to walk them through hot-button racial land mines, but don't know about their dance recital or new business, or if they won their football game. We may not always be invited to engage in house talk, but our odds increase once we create an environment of humility and genuine interest in each other's lives and passions. This is the sort of real safe space I try to build in my classroom, a not-so-magical notion that has opened the door to rich and meaningful race conversations—and deep, empathetic learning.

Professional Practice

Often, the safety of classroom spaces directly mirrors the safety that teachers feel in their own meeting rooms and staff lounges. As professionals, we quickly become inured to not being listened to—by our bosses, by our colleagues, by our students' parents, by the greater community, by the politicians who are supposed to represent us. Knowingly or not, we pass these frustrations on to our students. We might even consider the culture of *not listening* to be the unforgiving "real world" that we're meant to prepare students for. To change this dynamic, it makes sense to reimagine how we, as adults, listen to each other. During staff meetings and professional development, the norms of listening patiently, listening actively, and policing our voices should be both agreed on and practiced.

Perhaps the easiest shift is the incorporation of Good News and High-Grade Compliments activities into our time together. Staff meetings are considerably more tolerable when they begin with colleagues sharing the good things going on in their lives. And with all that teachers go through, we need affirmation and appreciation as much as our students do. Every compliment has the potential to chip away at the rivalries and dissension that, when unchecked, breed an unproductive negativity among colleagues.

Finally, some of these activities might require coordination between colleagues. The effect of high-grade compliments, for example, might be compromised if students do the activity in multiple classes the same week. There is only so much good news that students can share on any given day. Consider developing a schedule with colleagues. Or, even better, work together to design and thoughtfully implement your own new, fresh house talk activities.

CHAPTER 2

DEVELOPING YOUR "TALKING GAME"

Safe classroom communities, once established, need to be maintained, much like cars, which need periodic oil checks and tire rotations. Too often, after the first tune-up, we take our students immediately on the road, driving them forward from conversation to conversation, ignoring all manner of flashing indicators and follow-up maintenance, until we eventually find ourselves stranded by the roadside with a broken-down community. As we try making the repairs, we recall the warning rattles and verbal potholes we ignored, and we promise to take better care of our classroom culture next time.

I have been there as often as anyone else . . . noticing that students who seemed at first to care deeply about each other are now rolling their eyes at one another's good news, are regularly interrupting, are inserting below-breath snark and open sarcasm into our conversations. I notice that the elastic house talk boundaries have begun to shrink into racial and cultural islands. In these moments, it's easy to blame the kids, their families, any of the usual suspects, but it's imperative to ask myself, *When's the last time I took our classroom culture to the shop?* More often than not, I realize that I have let the daily grind of quizzes, the pressure to have adequate coverage, the distractions of being an athletic director, stresses in my personal life, and myriad other concerns keep me from strengthening and sustaining my classroom community. I will have forgotten to chat informally with the kids, rushed good news, and slipped lazily into disciplinary language instead of skill-based coaching. I will have continually put off high-grade compliments, so they seem like an afterthought, or worse, a nuisance. And now our classroom community sits at the edge of some interstate, steam pouring from under the hood. I'm stranded miles from being able to meaningfully discuss literary symbolism, much less race.

When this happens, I've got to recommit to the community-building activities described in the previous chapter and seek out new and better ones. As long as too much time hasn't passed, and the foundation was patiently set, students tend to settle back into form soon enough.

Dialogic teachers need to examine their own interpersonal strengths, thoughtfully acknowledging and working on their weaknesses. This is difficult. Many of us went into teaching with a hardened image of ourselves as deft discussion leaders. We imagine ourselves in front of our classrooms, smiling as we direct our students' conversations with such facility that the quiet students always find their voices. In this projection, we are warm, funny, and engaging. "Troubled" students do not misbehave because they do not want to; they are entranced with the vigor of the dialogue, the brilliance of their classmates, and our own intoxicating passion. This self-image is healthy, as far as it helps us to view ourselves as essentially interesting, compassionate, and *necessary*. Yet, we must eventually graduate from this comforting vision and commit to more honest, grounded self-assessment.

I've learned that even though students can feel both safe among *and* valued by their peers, teachers can find potentially powerful race conversations undermined by their own undeveloped interpersonal skills. Many have rightfully argued that a self-assessment should begin with teachers reflecting on how their own racial experiences influence their ability to hear and properly respond to other perspectives. Chapter 4 of Glenn E.

Singleton and Curtis Linton's *Courageous Conversations About Race* (2006) describes this idea:

> In terms of our own racial experience, we may have a limited understanding not only of the lives of people of a different race, but even of how our own personal racial identities impact our own lives. White people struggle to recognize that they have a racialized existence and that their color, indeed, affords them privilege and opportunity in our society. Likewise, people of color may distrust the motives of White people collectively, without actually discussing this distrust with individual White people in their lives. To develop racial consciousness is to address our assumptions and build our funds of knowledge. This will allow us to live more authentically within our own racial experience and deal more honestly with the existence of others. (56)

Mary Dilg, in *Race and Culture in the Classroom* (1999), uses this initial examination to advocate a sharper look at our curriculum:

> We and the students must work to overcome the prejudices—in part linked to our identities—that accompany us to the group. The open and supportive nature of the forum depends in large part on the extent to which we teachers and the students are able to put aside actively our own destructive biases.
>
> As teachers, we encourage an atmosphere of open questioning, and we understand that questions may well and indeed should, for the sake of broader exploration, be turned upon us and our choices. The process of teaching across lines of cultural identities becomes part of the focus of the inquiry; that is, the students may explore or scrutinize the joys and challenges inherent in that process. This makes for layers of learning, since students are learning about the process of teaching and learning as well as the subject matter of that teaching or learning. The result of such exploration led one young White woman to

> remark at the end of the course one year, "When I get a text now, I'm going to say: Who wrote this? What's being included and what's being left out?" Inherent in this young woman's observation is not only a critical examination of a text, but by extension, a questioning of the process by which the text was selected . . . Her question is a question about power, authority, point of view, pedagogy, inclusion, and exclusion—as each relates, in part, to cultural identity. (78)

Without a doubt, we should take the advice of both of these texts. Meaningful race conversations depend on teachers understanding the implications of their own racial and cultural perspectives. And few such conversations are inspired if our curriculum does not have multifaceted diversity. I recommend these books, and encourage teachers to take on such reflections. Equally important, however, is an honest assessment of a teacher's ability to actually *facilitate* the discussions. Mel Silberman and Freda Hansburg's book *PeopleSmart* (2000) distills interpersonal intelligence into eight discrete skills, three of which I find especially relevant to dialogic teachers: expressing yourself clearly, resolving conflict, and shifting gears.

EXPRESSING YOURSELF CLEARLY: MINDFUL ORIENTATION AND THOUGHTFUL SUMMARY

I, like many teachers, have a couple of students who religiously ask, "What are we doing today?" as they walk into the classroom. My natural instinct is to respond with teasing or sarcasm; my personal favorites are "Learning!" or "Trying to take over the world." While not especially harmful, this instinct to be evasive belies an underlying complication: I enjoy surprising my students. I rely on their amazement when I spring unexpected discussion prompts. This habit can quickly become a staple of dialogic curriculum, especially because, at times, students seem to really appreciate the roller-coaster feel of certain conversations. What complicates the analogy, however, is that when people board a roller coaster, they generally know exactly what they are getting into.

Silberman and Hansburg (2000) distrust the idea of surprises. Instead, the authors ask us to patiently *orient* our conversational partners to what we are about to discuss, so that they might brace themselves for upcoming turbulence. We are all familiar with orientation: Most of us have been told that we "need to sit down . . ." or warned that we're "not going to believe . . ." The former allows us to settle into our minds' emotional and spiritual cushions, to grab hold of something solid. Whatever is about to happen will require more than our normal allotment of attention; it is likely to engage parts of our psyche that we hold sacred: our sense of safety, our belief system, our schedule. The first verbal orientation means that whatever else we had planned to do this day is about to lose its comparative value. The latter orientation prepares us for excitement, prompts us to reach for the popcorn and kick back. Our stress level drops proportionally, our mood and focus regulate so that we can engage with whatever follows in a light spirit.

Orienting students to a racial conversation is a tricky business that requires careful balance. If a teacher is too heavy-handed, he risks provoking a *you need to sit down* response, where many students either sink deeper into the seats and prepare to cry, or prepare themselves to operate as if under threat—to fight or fly, to forcefully mark out their territory. There is also the temptation to disengage entirely. Furthermore, the teacher risks the students' accusation of crying wolf if the conversation does not match the anticipated level of heaviness. Students may think that the teacher has no sense of perspective, is overly dramatic, with an inflated sense of her own importance. Teachers get to oversell the orientation only a few times before such an assessment becomes permanent. However, the opposite is also true: If a teacher undersells the orientation, or worse, does not offer one, we get incidents like the cotton-picking lesson debacle from the introduction. Students and parents may think that a teacher is dismissing the importance of the racial conversation or is insensitive, or God forbid, they could even transfer their worst assumptions to the closest authority, believing, for instance, that a well-meaning teacher *is a racist*.

To strike the right balance, we must try to understand the intersection of our students' histories and the exchange of ideas they are about to engage in. One way to do this is to acknowledge aloud—and express clearly—our own experience with what we're about to discuss. For example, every year

I try to hold a conversation with my students the week before Columbus Day about the Native American genocide. We read the introduction to Howard Zinn's *People's History of the United States* (1980), which first describes Columbus's attitude, as depicted in his journal, toward the Arawak natives that he encounters in the Bahama Islands:

> They . . . brought us parrots and balls of cotton and spears and many other things, which they exchanged for the glass beads and hawks' bells. They willingly traded everything they owned . . . They were well-built, with good bodies and handsome features . . . They do not bear arms, and do not know them, for I showed them a sword, they took it by the edge and cut themselves out of ignorance. They have no iron. Their spears are made of cane . . . They would make fine servants . . . With fifty men we could subjugate them all and make them do whatever we want. (1)

In later pages, Zinn describes Columbus's savage tactics when the Arawaks did not prove easily subjugated:

> In the province of Cicao on Haiti, where he and his men imagined huge gold fields to exist, they ordered all persons fourteen years or older to collect a certain quantity of gold every three months. When they brought it, they were given copper tokens to hang around their necks. Indians found without a copper token had their hands cut off and bled to death. (4)

After reading the excerpts, I prompt students to journal about their feelings on the national holiday. Over the course of my career, I've noticed that more of my ninth graders know something of Christopher Columbus's brutality, but few have been sufficiently exposed to the details. I orient the students to the excerpt and conversation first by acknowledging that some of them may have already learned that Columbus was a brutal murderer and slaver, but I also ask them to recognize that some of their classmates may not have learned this. I share that, in elementary school, I'd learned that Columbus was a great explorer who sought to prove that he would not sail off the edge of the earth if he sailed west in the *Niña*, *Pinta*, and *Santa Maria*. I learned that he arrived in what he thought was India, then went back to Spain to share that the world was indeed round, and that without Columbus, we would all still think that the world was like a great flat table. I share that I learned that Columbus was a great teacher to Indians, but admitted I don't remember as much detail about that part; most of that understanding comes from the illustrations in picture books. I remember from my textbooks a big white man in metal armor, and a lot of barely clothed Indians.

This orientation removes a lot of pressure from students who have not learned it any differently from how I did. It positions me not as an intimidating authority about to publicly expose their ignorance, but as a fellow traveler, someone who has also been exposed to the myth. Conversely, students who have had a more progressive education (or who have read more broadly on their own) usually nod, as if saying that they too recognize this version of the Columbus story as a partial truth, at best, or maybe even as a lie. This orientation affords every student their dignity, positing that everyone in the room is smart enough to handle the truth. Then, through text and discussion, we seek to tease out that truth.

Silberman and Hansburg argue that conversations beginning with mindful *orientation* should end with effective *summary*. The key decisions, agreements, and action items should be discussed as the classroom dialogue draws to a close. We often forget to do this, especially if the conversation has gone well, which tempts us to milk the last drops from it before the bell rings. The more rigorous the discussion, the more kids desire a defined sense of what has been accomplished.

Over the years, I have developed the habit of summarizing as comments happen, usually with a healthy dose of compliments: "I just heard Mike say _______, which seems to be a brilliant take on _______. Did I get you right, Mike? Yes? Okay. But if that is so, doesn't that mean _______?" After another few students weigh in, it's time for a summary of the exchange: "We've got something good going on here. Mike said _______, which seemed to mean _______, which Dayonna really didn't seem to agree with because of _______. Is this what everyone is hearing? Or did I get it all wrong?" Here we have not only an opportunity for the students to organize their thoughts, but a reminder of their power to correct me.

Before we move on from *expressing ourselves clearly*, we should mention Silberman and Hansburg's reminder to "talk straight" (59). It is easy for teachers to forget to provide clear delineations between fact and their opinions. We teachers tend to be naturally declarative speakers who feel strongly about the topics we're discussing. Most of our students have come from classroom cultures that emphasize the inherent *rightness* of teachers' statements. This status quo is persistent, so if Mrs. Robinson feels a certain way about the efficacy of building a wall on the United States' southern border, her students are likely to think she wants them to consider her opinion gospel. If Mr. Taylor feels a certain way about reparations, students might consider those who disagree to be somehow wrong, at least in academic discourse.

In response, some argue that teachers should hide their opinions in student-centered academic discourse. They argue that we should act only as facilitators, burying our voices so as to not become a "sage on the stage." While I have seen this done masterfully, I believe this stance to be an overreaction. We should never forfeit the right to be scholars in our own discussions. In fact, the more we do the work to build the classroom culture described earlier in Chapter 1, the more the students will be interested in our contribution as their companions in the conversation. When a conversation gets good and hot, my students often grow irritated and ask, "But Mr. Kay, what do *you* think?" The temptation to wave it off and pivot back to their opinions is both real and understandable, but I've realized that doing so is paradoxically dismissive of their voices. They have clearly *expressed a need*, and such a pivot communicates that I do not find this *need* important. Furthermore, when teachers participate in the conversation, we signal that it is okay to have a personal stake in the exchange of ideas. I love when one of my students says, "You are so hype!" When I am passionate about my opinions, I establish our classroom as a place where it is okay to be a nerd. Anyone who works with teenagers recognizes "cool kid" syndrome—the stylized academic apathy that we know to be paper-thin. "Hypeness" over our own ideas has the ability to redefine *cool kid* to mean "passionate scholar."

To "talk straight," teachers need to qualify our beliefs by calling them what they are: our beliefs. Then we can always offer an invitation to disagree, or better yet, invite students to find holes in our arguments. One of my favorite classroom questions is "Does this hold water?" I ask my students this with exaggerated sincerity, even a touch of vulnerability, as if asking them to weigh my idea on their much truer scale. Here the students learn (1) that criticism should be humbly sought, (2) that it is okay to (respectfully) disagree with a person with perceived authority, and (3) that we can express ideas before they are fully formed. It doesn't take long before kids begin to say, "I don't know if this *holds water*, but . . ." or, "Good point, but I think that you are forgetting . . ." With this language, students find themselves more prepared to handle larger disagreements.

RESOLVING CONFLICT: NOT LETTING THE "FIGHT" BECOME A DISTRACTION

You don't quite know how it happened, but all heck just broke loose. One of your students compared Rachel Dolezal's "plight" as a white woman who had been fraudulently claiming to be black throughout her adulthood to the struggles that transgender folks often endure. Someone took exception, and lofted a grenadelike accusation of transphobia, which, as expected, shattered the class into self-righteous fragments. Students are shouting, some are crying, and you are pretty sure that someone just whispered a homophobic slur. Turns out it wasn't imagined, because the perceived target just jumped from his seat to challenge a classmate to "say it to my face." Laughing kids have their cell phones out to catch the melee on video. You, the well-meaning teacher, had been feeling good about this conversation. Now you are just hoping to stay out of the newspapers.

Certain moments test our most fragile truces. Let's say you have spent months building community among students with gang affiliations. Or you are at a school that has recently had an influx of immigrants, and you've spent a year wrestling with the community's tensions. Perhaps the complication isn't diversity, but a deadening sameness: Your students are all from the same conservative suburb, the same low-income housing project, the same rural outpost, the same big-city liberal enclave. Since they agree on most issues, your students work themselves up to great fits of passion over seemingly unsubstantial details.

Occasionally we can sense an approaching conflict and resolve it before much damage is done. Consider the Columbus conversation from the last section: In a recent iteration, one of my freshmen said, "Yes, what he did was bad. But it really needed to happen . . . We needed to clear the land for white people." The air was sucked from the room. My student teacher looked at me with her mouth an O, her eyes darting around. She probably saw no fewer than nine students partially raise their hands, only to remember our rule to wait until the speaker finishes speaking. A room full of faces contorted in anger. In the silence, the student continued, "If that horrible stuff hadn't happened, America couldn't be America and we wouldn't be here." I nodded, while a senior who hangs out in the back of my classroom shook her head. The speaker finished unsteadily, "It was bad, though. But I think that's why we celebrate it."

I waited a beat. Certain that he was done, I smiled. Then I put on a deliberate "thoughtful face," my head tilted, eyes rolled up, fingers rubbing my goatee, biting my lip as if chewing on his idea. The tension in the room eased. Working with little kids in my church's nursery program had taught me that after taking a tumble, they usually look up at the nearest adult with eyes that ask, *Am I hurt?* At this, a veteran would either smile or briskly shake her head *No*. And off the toddler would go. Students often have the same instinct, especially after developing a trusting relationship with a teacher. The combination of *listen patiently* and my thoughtful pause headed off the initial, "Was that racist? Is this going to be ugly?" I asked him if his comment was meant to communicate how America could not have followed the same historical trajectory if not for European colonization.

"Yes!" he said gratefully, nodding, and cutting eyes to his classmates.

"And are you arguing that America is unconsciously celebrating *that*, the birth of our nation—not anything specific about Columbus's actions? That's what *I'm* hearing."

"Yes! That's what I meant. I didn't mean to be . . . to sound . . . Yes, that's what I meant." And off we went, debating his considerably less offensively worded, yet still significantly controversial thesis. However, I know that we can't always snatch back the initiative before an explosion.

This is made scarier because, as professionals, we have been consistently trained in classroom management, not *conflict* management. The former is a code word for discipline, a way to get young humans to behave like students. The latter is a considerably more complex blend of art and skill, the stuff of boardrooms and State Departments. It deals more with the great collision of ideas, the harnessing of friction so that it ignites something useful. Many of us entered the classroom with a *classroom management* mandate to keep the peace at all costs. If we are not careful, such a mandate can dupe us into forgetting that great ideas are volatile. Race ideas, doubly so. So if we wish to create a dialogic curriculum that engages race, it stands to reason that our students' opinions will eventually clash. We should be ready to thrive in these moments.

First, we must recognize that conflict is often a *result* of great curriculum design. In the aforementioned situation, students *cared passionately* about what was being discussed. That is a great victory, for race conversations are often about freedom, opportunity, and justice—visceral, emotional concepts that should feel as urgent as they are. In fact, we should be worried if our race conversations never cause conflict; this is a sign that we might only be skimming inch-deep into the complexities, not challenging our students' intellect. Students should be pushed to recognize that conflict is good for learning. It means we are awake, that we care—and should we handle conflict well, we will all be a little wiser.

What does it mean to handle conflict well? Silberman and Hansburg argue that more destructive conflicts arise when "two parties perceive their interests as incompatible" (2000, 149). Such cases often cause "zero-sum games" —defined by *Webster's Dictionary* as "situations in which one person or group can win something only by causing another person or group to lose." To illustrate this idea, the authors offer an example of two people running to catch the last taxi on a rainy day. The winner gets a dry ride to her destination, the loser gets soaked waiting for another ride. Knowing this, the runners are tempted to trip each other up, push each other down, or worse. In mismanaged classroom conflicts, students find themselves racing each other for their teacher's approval. Or their classmates' esteem. Believing that there can be only one winner, they often battle each other with misguided ferocity. Teachers encourage these habits when they either explicitly or implicitly declare winners. When students continually "lose," what they often lose is confidence, or they develop resentment toward their teacher and classmates. Habitual "winners" might eventually seek approval instead of welcoming scrutiny. When expressing their ideas, they might value palatability over truth.

In the face of conflicting ideas, we must send the message that our approval is not the goal. Growth is the goal, and conflict strips good ideas of the fluff that holds them back. I ask students to consider the example of pruning: A sharp knife saves a plant from diseased limbs and corrects irregular root behavior, both of which hinder the development of fruit. Conflicting ideas in the classroom are wonderful pruning opportunities. There are many ways for teachers to get this point across, but it begins with stating it plainly and often. *And it's important to anticipate which conversations must be oriented with a focus on impending conflicts.* While doing so, we can remind students that they are joining what is usually a long-established debate. Throughout history, smart people have stood on both sides of the same issues that our students currently disagree on—and through passionate debate, have pushed each other to greatness.

Of course, this will not always be enough. Issues of race are intensely personal, and we cannot expect our students to always keep their cool. Silberman and Hansburg tell us that when this happens, we must first *surface the conflict*—defined as identifying "the category of conflict involved in a specific situation, [making] it easier to frame the problem in a neutral, mutual, and descriptive way" (2000, 149). In order to do so, they cite the work of Dr. Jean Lebedun, author of *Managing Workplace Conflict* (1998), to categorize four different types of conflict:

1. Over Facts or Data
2. Over Process or Methods
3. Over Purposes
4. Over Values

It is important for teachers to recognize what sort of conflict we are dealing with. Each requires a slightly different approach, but most can be effectively managed. We must then help students come to the same realization—and then encourage them to begin calling each conflict what it is. To see how this works, let's imagine a hypothetical conversation about Michelle Alexander's *The New Jim Crow* (2010). Student Lisa passionately rejects the author's basic premise, arguing that the justice system does not imprison African American men at a higher rate. She has plenty of anecdotal evidence: She is white, and her father is in jail; her black aunt is a judge and her white uncle is a police officer, and both are kind nonracists who give back to the community and believe in the system. In Lisa's opinion, the teacher is unfairly proselytizing his political beliefs, and her classmates are maligning her very real cultural experience. Some classmates push back with vague charges of ignorance, which she doesn't appreciate, so she answers by calling them gullible.

This is, of course, a *facts/data* conflict. These are tricky, because Lisa is factually incorrect. According to Alexander, one in fourteen African American men were behind bars in 2006, while with white men it was 1:106 (2010, 100). This statistic, and many like it, should prove Alexander's thesis worthy of at least a hearing. Lisa's personal perspective is clouding her ability to give it one. Her classmates realize this. However, in wrestling with the resulting tension, the teacher must not alienate Lisa. If she feels *wrong*, she might feel attacked, which will prompt her to either shut down or escalate. Strangely, some well-intentioned teachers view the former as a victory. It never is. The troublesome idea was not defeated, the student was. Instead, we should emphasize that focusing on numbers does not invalidate anyone's individual experience. In this regard, Lisa is correct. Her anecdotal experiences with the justice system are valid, as are Alexander's macro-statistics.

This conversation naturally steps to a loaded question: *Are more African Americans in jail because they commit more crimes?* Lisa, placated for the moment, asks this to her classmates. The teacher steps in with more of Alexander's statistics, this time a 2000 study by the National Institute of Drug Abuse claiming that white students use cocaine at seven times the rate of black students, crack at eight times the rate of black students, and heroin at seven times the rate of black students (2010, 99). The teacher adds that according to a National Household Survey on Drug Abuse, white students are more than a third more likely to have sold illegal drugs than black students (99). Kyle asks the teacher to back up the slide show for a second. After staring at it, he whispers quizzically, "*Students*?" His classmates don't realize his point, so he continues with, "Students where? College students? How do they know? If I was in college, I wouldn't go around telling people that I use crack." Someone else in the class interjects, "Especially if I was black!" to general laughter. Pressed to explain, the student adds, "I don't mean to be smart. I'm just saying that black kids aren't rich. Their parents would be pissed if they screwed up their shot at college. White kids might not care." This exchange seems to offend some students in the class. Managing the ensuing dispute, the teacher warns against stereotyping—but first she publicly surfaces Kyle's challenge to Alexander as a *process/methods* conflict. Both Kyle and his classmate have offered worthwhile observations. In challenging the validity of Alexander's statistics, they have given their classmates a beautiful opportunity for deeper inquiry. An entire project could bloom from such questioning.

This incident also presents an example of a *purposes* conflict. Kyle's classmate who interjected, "Especially if I was black!" is a classroom comedian. It is important to remember the saying á la Ecclesiastes that there is "a time to weep and a time to laugh." Students react differently to the inherent tension of race conversations. Some feel that such situations need laughter, so they'll add jokes; some classmates, who think the dialogue needs gravity, might be offended by the humorous tone and word selection. Neither instinct is inherently wrong, and both need occasional validation. In the scenario, the jokester's initial *purpose* for the outburst was to make his classmates smile. By calmly surfacing this, and giving him the space to explain himself, the teacher has protected the student from unnecessary accusations of racism. The focus has remained on Kyle's challenge. Of course, teachers can add a reminder to the classroom comedian that now might not be the time for jokes. I've done this often.

Eventually, the students must contend with Alexander's central thesis: that the prison-industrial complex has become the moral equivalent of Jim Crow. In order for this parallel to be true, the prison system's oppression must be *purposeful*—a contention that one student, Robin, is not willing to accept. Robin does not deny the arrest or conviction data, nor does she think that plea deals and mandatory minimums are justly handled. She doesn't think convicted felons should have to "check the box" upon leaving prison, and she certainly doesn't believe that these people should lose the right to vote. Yet, Robin remains unconvinced that what walks, quacks, and smells like a duck is, in fact, *a duck*. She attributes racial disparities to coincidence and unreflective policy. Raised to value personal responsibility, Robin is skeptical of any excuses that rob people of their agency. In Alexander's thesis, she sees a harmful conspiracy theory, aimed at eroding minority communities' trust in the justice system.

Derek sees something else. His mother teaches history at an Afrocentric middle school, while his father is a social worker who works with families in one of the rougher parts of the city. They have raised him to treat the police with respectful wariness; to assume an intention to harm, an eagerness to frame, a callous disregard for his future. Now, Alexander's thesis rings true to the bottom of his gut. When he hears Robin's assertions, he finds himself inexplicably angry. She sounds like every conservative voice his parents warned him about. He immediately accuses her of being "part of the problem." She, of course, does not like this at all. The teacher justly reprimands Derek for the personal attack, and he grudgingly apologizes, but the exchange has prompted the other students to take sides—and the teacher can feel the conversation melting into a petty argument.

This is what Silberman and Hansburg might call a *values* conflict, the most difficult of the four to navigate. Robin and Derek (and the other students who joined the fray) have differing core *values*, and neither of them is likely to change their minds over the course of a half-hour class discussion. Here the teacher faces the biggest temptation to either explicitly or implicitly declare a zero-sum winner. She might favor Derek, who, despite his inelegant presentation, seems to have *gotten the point* of the lesson. Or, she might favor the more articulate Robin, whose mind seems to have been more stretched by the conversation. Even if the teacher remembers not to take sides, she might resign herself to the role of referee, with her only job the calling of fouls instead of working to ensure constructive debate. Surfacing a *values* conflict involves acknowledging the obvious impasse. Students must see that we have recognized the stalemate, and that reaching it wasn't the endgame. If they don't, some will actually begin to consider their classroom environment less safe: *This teacher just wants us to argue. She must have forgotten that I have a life outside of her classroom. I have to spend the rest of my day with these people.* Though we like to think of today's students as impulsive, the interconnectedness of social media has actually triggered an incongruous hesitation. Sharing one's opinion has always been risky business, but now one stray comment might get a student filleted throughout their entire social network. The safest thing for students to do is to (1) keep their mouths shut or (2) choose the winning side—determined by the teacher, the popular kids, or whoever seems angriest at the time.

This stalemate, like many other *values* conflicts, presents an opportunity. After surfacing it, it's critical that the teacher immediately push students to the middle of the Venn diagram: where they agree. Derek and Robin disagree on the baseline intentions of the justice system. They disagree on where minority communities should place their trust. There are likely countless other cultural understandings on which they come down on opposite sides, as well. Yet, despite all their disagreement, they do agree that black and brown people are catching a raw deal from law enforcement. This, arguably, is Alexander's most salient point. From this, both students can generate win-win solutions—the kind that safely invite their classmates to "keep playing."

Silberman and Hansburg argue passionately for the "climate of mutual interest," where people "negotiate differences side-by-side, rather than head-to-head" (2000, 155). This is often a key difference between Frederick Douglass's "light" and "fire." The former pits two unlistening parties against each other in a showy contest over minutiae, whereas win-win, side-by-side scenarios can launch students into the creation of solutions—a task that thoroughly respects their intelligence. Derek and Robin (and their classmates) grow when they are forced to operate at the same disequilibrium. Nobody knows the answers, but they can figure them out together—and here's where the most meaningful work begins.

We can "agree to disagree." We can "disagree without being disagreeable." Our conversational conflicts can be managed when these statements are no longer clichés but understandings that are readily cultivated and actively worked toward. This, like all the other conflict management strategies, leans heavily on the work described in the first chapter of this book. If the students have not built up a classroom community, they will never let a teacher push them to the center of the Venn diagram. It is far easier for them to assume the worst about each other, as is constantly modeled by an adult world that craves flat characters spewing straw-man tactics.

SHIFTING GEARS: THE UNPREDICTABILITY OF STUDENT DISCUSSION

Military analogies are naturally troubling when applied to human relationships. Our partners, neighbors, colleagues, and students are not enemies, and framing them as such is rarely productive. Still, I like to modify Helmuth von Moltke's famous reminder that *no battle plan survives contact with the enemy* for the classroom. When we replace *battle* with *discussion*, then *enemy* with *students*, we come close to the candor required to be a dialogic teacher: *No discussion plan survives contact with the students.*

We must examine our relationship to the inherent unpredictability of student discussion. Sports video games famously rate players' attributes on a hundred-point scale, one of which is often *agility*. We might ask ourselves, *What is our agility rating? Can we stop a conversation on a dime and run it in an entirely different direction? Can we operate well in a completely unplanned-for moment, finding our next points in real time? When our students ask an unexpected question, is our first instinct to answer it? Or do we feel comfortable using our discussion time to guide them through real-time research?*

In one of my earlier hypothetical examples, I created a student from an Afrocentric charter school. This was inspired by a real-life discussion in my classroom at the beginning of my teaching career. I had this immensely talented freshman student in my English class who had come to Science Leadership Academy from an Afrocentric elementary school. She did not speak up much in class, as I expect she had never been in class with more than a few white classmates—which might have unnerved her. However, she showed all the signs of being plugged into every conversation, and as the community was built, her participation grew. Toward the end of the school year, I usually lead a rhetoric unit, with one of the skills being the recognition of propaganda techniques. I cited Hitler's propaganda during the Holocaust. The connections were clear and the discussion rolled on—until this young woman raised her hand to say, "What are you all talking about?" I looked at her, expecting to check her for making an inappropriate joke. She wasn't joking. "I don't know what you all are talking about." Some of her classmates chuckled, then grew silent. I asked her if she knew what the Holocaust was, and she anxiously replied, "No."

When asked to explain herself, she shared that at her previous school, the humanities classes had taught only world events that involved the African diaspora. She had been finding things out all year, but nothing like this. *Had Germans actually killed six million Jewish people because a leader told them to? Why Jews? How did he tell them to do it? Why didn't anyone try to stop him?* Her classmates were amused, but remained respectful as she fired question after question. Many students were eager to provide answers. My teacher-mental-math told me that if I did not redirect back to propaganda soon, we would lose the focus of the day, but I could feel an even more necessary discussion brewing. I could tell that my students felt it, too. After waiting for the current speaker to finish talking, I asked everyone why they thought their classmate's previous school would choose not to teach students about the Holocaust.

A wonderful conversation followed about the merits and challenges of both Eurocentric and Afrocentric curricula. We discussed the need to make space for the too-often-ignored voices in history, while we imagined different ways that schools should balance the content. By the time the class period ended, each of my students had reflected deeply on many of the curricular decisions that their previous teachers and schools had made. Some were newly appreciative, most were unsettled. A couple were angry, resenting a culture of teachers lying by omission. Still more felt called to analyze our own school's curriculum. It was a good day, even though we never did get to my planned rhetoric lesson.

This is an example of *agility,* which I believe to be different from *flexibility*. When teachers are being flexible, they see the many different ways to reach a preset goal. They balance different learning styles, hands and feet prying open and propping multiple windows for as long as possible. They are conversant in the kids' language. These are the teachers who connect Shakespeare and hip-hop, the ones who use rides on public transportation to teach the laws of physics. They openly value the end over the means; as long as the students "get it," these teachers are rightfully satisfied. Flexibility is, of course, linked to our resilience. It allows us to withstand the thousand microfailures that naturally accompany any attempt at holding the attention of thirty-two teenagers. When we are at our most flexible, we are unfazed by students' silence, knowing that all of our prompts are not as interesting as we think them to be. We know that there is always another way to get to the goal.

Agility, on the other hand, is the ability to direct the discourse when it goes in a thoroughly unanticipated direction. In the given example, the young woman had ripped open a massive wound that completely dwarfed the importance of my intended goals—something that happens often during meaningful conversations about race. She was brave (or flabbergasted) enough to share an ignorance that must have been embarrassing. Once shared, her question floated above the students' heads, visible to all, waiting to be acknowledged. Many of the biggest frustrations that my students have shared involve the perception that their teacher has ignored a blatantly hovering question. When we do so, our students think that the planned arc of discussion is more important to us than real-time student voices. Sometimes it is. But we have only a few times to do this before our students lose incentive to do anything but attempt to guess what the authority wants them to say. In other words, students will grow wary of sharing the real-life connections that pop into their heads, for in a teacher's redirection they see swift repudiation.

Here I must lean on my principal and mentor, Chris Lehmann, who regularly reminds us that we should teach "students, not subjects." When introducing ourselves, teachers in our school are discouraged from saying, "I teach English." Instead, we are encouraged to say, "I teach *my students* English." When teachers take this stance, students are reassured that *they* are the most important people in the room. Their ideas, their passions, their growth points. When students sense that their teacher has taken this stance, they are more likely to feel encouraged to contribute in-progress ideas and their most vulnerable questions. Perhaps most important, they might feel free to be swept away by the excitement of an unanticipated thread. If a teacher has enough agility to keep up, they can spark habits of inquiry that lead students to lifelong scholarship.

Professional Practice

Silberman and Hansburg tell us to *express ourselves clearly*, *resolve conflicts*, and *shift gears*. Regardless of how thoughtful our curriculum may be, it will fall short of its potential if we do not both recognize and develop these three areas. As noted previously, it is hard for dialogic teachers to admit any deficiencies in our communication skills. Criticism of this particular flaw strikes a little too close to our core identities, especially when the feedback comes from a student or colleague. We can be corrected on our curriculum, our assessment strategies, our classroom management—but woe to anybody who implies that we don't know how to speak to kids. Even our administrators shy away from this line of critique. They figure that either we have it or we don't, and if we don't, we aren't too interested in having that pointed out. In other words, we are not encouraged to reflect, so our interpersonal skills stagnate.

Philadelphians of a certain age remember basketball star Allen Iverson's public aversion to practice. Blessed with preternatural speed and springy athleticism, he thought it enough that he played "every game like it was [his] last." Though listed at only a bony 165 pounds throughout his career, he religiously avoided weight training, dismissing concerns about his health with statements like, "If I build myself up, and get a whole lot of muscles . . . are y'all going to give me the MVP? I've [already] been the MVP, bony as [heck]" (Kauffman 2002). When pressed to justify his dismissive attitude toward skill development, he often reminded the excoriating media of his multiple scoring titles. His career, of course, was a Shakespearean tragedy; his body collapsed beneath him, and his fixed mind-set made it hard for his teams to rise above runner-up status. We dialogic teachers must understand that heart is not enough. We must honestly measure our interpersonal skill deficits, and be brave enough to receive criticism about them. Then we must practice until these deficits become strengths. Following are some professional development ideas for any community of like-minded dialogic educators:

EXPRESSING OURSELVES CLEARLY

1. Grab a polarizing article from the morning's news. Read it thoroughly. Working with a colleague, take turns orienting each other to your articles. Try to anticipate what information might need to be frontloaded, what gaps might need to be patched up, what higher-order questions must be asked to prime students for learning. Then try again with progressively more abstract or controversial articles. Eventually try something involving race.

2. Choose an interesting movie or news clip. Deliver a two-minute "elevator pitch" to sell the clip's importance to a group of two or three colleagues. After watching the clip, ask your colleagues to suggest approaches that would have better piqued their interests. Give everyone a turn, then progress to more abstract or controversial clips.

3. At the end of each department meeting, have a different colleague (not just the chairperson or department head) summarize the conversation from their perspective, highlighting the key points, acknowledging the areas where closure has not yet been reached. End by sharing and agreeing to any action items that may have been discussed.

4. To work on *talking straight*, return to the article or clip from the first two activities. After sharing the artifact, tell your colleagues how you feel about it. Ask your colleagues to report back to you about (1) your delineation between facts and opinion, and (2) how openly you make space for skepticism.

RESOLVING CONFLICT

The following activities involve the creation of imaginary case studies. The more we perform thought experiments, the easier it will be to recognize and navigate similar conflicts in our real-world classrooms.

1. As I do for this chapter, try to write sample scenarios of the four types of conflicts. They do not have to be inspired by classroom situations that you've experienced. They can be your assessment of political news stories or personal family disputes. Even while acknowledging the complexity of the conflict, identify if it is ultimately over *Facts or Data*, *Process or Methods*, *Purposes*, or *Values*. After doing so, share each scenario with your colleagues. Do they agree with your assessment of the situation? If they do, what would be possible solutions to the conflicts?
2. Do the same surfacing activity with any of the classroom conflicts you've witnessed over the past year. Be wary of easy answers: Some of us have grown used to blaming kids' special needs, their academic gaps, their parents, their "attitudes," etc. While sometimes the causes of conflicts are that easy to identify, often they are not.
3. Practice pushing both sides of a hypothetical classroom values conflict to the middle of its Venn diagram. Acknowledge what students are unlikely to agree on. Then describe where they can be challenged to work together.

SHIFTING GEARS

1. Examine a primary or supplementary resource that you plan to discuss with students. While acknowledging your main prompts for discussing this text, list as many *other* meaningful discussion prompts as possible. If this text were situated in a different unit, how might it be used? If you were teaching a different population of students, what

might you emphasize? At our best, we can see as many potential angles as possible. If the conversation strays from our thread, we might not feel as much pressure to force our students back onto the track.

2. An important variation of this activity: When preparing for a conversation, list potential student gaps that might force you to be agile. *What if they don't know about this? How might I react?*

3. A second variation: When preparing for a conversation, list potential student interest points that you might not have anticipated. For example, in the Holocaust propaganda conversation, students might become oddly excited about a connection between a propaganda technique and a popular ad campaign. This interest, if enough students in the community share it, could lead to a fruitful, worthwhile dialogue that the teacher didn't anticipate.

CHAPTER 3

STRUCTURING YOUR DIALOGIC CURRICULUM

If we have done the community-building work of the first chapter, and have committed to the ongoing self-assessment and skills development of the second, we are finally in a place where we can consider leading meaningful race conversations with our students. It starts by recognizing the different basic forms of classroom conversation, all of which are mandated by most English language arts standards around the United States: *whole-class discussion*, *small learning community*, and *one-on-one conversation.*

THE ROLE OF WHOLE-CLASS DISCUSSION

Whole-class discussion is the most recognizable form of class discussion. In its traditional form, the teacher offers a prompt, asks the students what they feel about it, then calls on students as hands are raised. Students share their opinions, usually about the class text, sometimes about an outside source. Traditionally, teachers emphasize that one voice speaks at a time. The commonly recognized victories occur (1) when a student who normally doesn't participate raises his hand, (2) when a student connects the text to a previous discussion or outside source, or (3) when a student appears to thoughtfully connect the text to their lives.

Whole-class discussion allows the teacher to maintain control over the room. We know this because even though students are welcome to address the entire community, we are usually their targeted audience. Our voice is heard after most student comments, usually as commentary on what students have just said. These intervals offer a chance for praise, critique, discipline, or redirection. This teacher-student-teacher rhythm has been ingrained enough to make any disruptions in the pattern feel monumental. Students feel off balance if the teacher rarely weighs in, since they've been trained to hunt for *right* answers, while each consecutive student comment can make their teacher feel like they are riding coach on a plane that they've been trained to fly. The fewer the teacher interruptions, the greater the disequilibrium for both parties.

Whole class, like whole grain, is a staple for long-lasting energy. The teacher's position as a focal point allows us to set and maintain a lively conversational tone. When the energy level gets low during whole class, a savvy teacher might crack a timely joke or reconnect the students through a clever analogy. The three listening skills discussed in Chapter 1 (listen patiently, listen actively, and police your voice) can be introduced and modeled in a whole-class format. Their importance is enforced under the teacher's direct supervision—mistakes corrected and successes celebrated. Whole-class discussion establishes a teacher's expectations, not just for the discussion, but for the overall classroom culture.

When sifting through my own practice in order to write this book, I realized that teachers rarely ask students how they feel about the different methods we faithfully employ during whole class. So I asked one of my students, Lotus, if I could interview her on the topic. Lotus was one of the most selectively quiet students I ever taught. In two years as a student in my dialogic classroom, she got straight As—without *once* raising her hand in a whole-class discussion. Interestingly, she was also one of my slam poets, a league all-star and captain by her senior year. So not only could she speak, but she voluntarily did so both eloquently and with great passion, in front of far greater crowds than my thirty-two-student classroom. She didn't disappoint, first sharing her opinions on teachers who call on her even though she didn't raise her hand:

> Going to a class with a teacher that frequently cold-calls students is like preparing for war. My heart rate accelerates and I break out in a cold sweat, even before the teacher asks a question and/or opens up the class for discussion—even before walking into the room, quite honestly. I am constantly fighting myself to stay in my seat, instead of making an exit by way of "going to the bathroom" or whatever excuse will get me out of the classroom and out of the pool of victims that the teacher is at leisure to call on at any moment.
>
> A justification for cold calling may be that the teacher wishes to get everyone thinking about the question posed. They may reason with themselves that, because students don't know who will be called on, we will all be trying to find an answer, and therefore we are all engaged, all learning, and all gaining more from the class than if we were allowed to sit in silence through their class. Wrong. Instead of being able to focus on the question at hand, the vast majority of my attention is focused on how much I do not want to be called on. Instead of the more confident and well-thought-out response that I'm able to give when I choose to raise my hand in class, being put on the spot when I am cold-called causes me to say anything at all that will end the misery of being the center of attention, whether that is something I truly believe or not. In most cases when this happens, I am giving short, sloppy answers because I am too nervous for anything else.
>
> Being in a classroom with a teacher who conducts their [whole-class] conversations this way makes me uncommunicative, not only in words but also in manner. I try to stay as expressionless as possible to avoid being "analyzed" (and therefore called on). I try to stay easy to glance over and forget about. I become more rigid and uncomfortable as a means of

> protecting myself, instead of feeling like I can communicate freely as I would in healthy conversation.

As a stutterer, I distinctly remember the horror of the cold call. If I was not currently raising my hand, it was because I was not ready to speak. I probably had gathered neither my thoughts nor my breath—and was about to embarrass myself with a halting Porky Pig impersonation. I never understood why my teachers did not get this. Nor did I understand my teachers' fascination with "participation points," about which Lotus had this to share:

> When teachers instill participation points, it is not only failing to encourage me to participate more verbally, but is also conditioning me to set lower expectations for myself because those critical points will be docked from my grade on the grounds that I don't speak up enough in class. *But, my own fear of public speaking is stronger than my fear of failure in any particular class, and, this being the case, my resolve stays strong.* Unfortunately, because of this, I have learned to expect failure. It is a fact that I will always have in the back of my head when completing homework, when sitting in class, when creating projects, that my highest grade will always be several points below the students who are more extroverted. No matter how well I do in every other aspect, no matter if I go above and beyond every other student in projects, essays, and classroom activities, there's something about voicing my thoughts in front of the class that teachers so value that it makes them ignore everything else I may have done exceedingly well in.

At the other extreme was Zoey, perhaps the most verbose student I've ever taught. While still considering Lotus's description of how distracting she finds the prospect of being cold-called in whole class, I asked Zoey to describe her thoughts when well-meaning teachers counseled her to speak less, ostensibly to make room for introverts like Lotus.

Zoey: *I think, OK, I'm going to zone in, I'm going to try to be quiet, I'll be strategic with raising my hand. I'm going to try to be quiet in class, I'm going to focus. And then I forget. Or I would remember but I don't have the same passion, enough for me to commit to it. The passion always fades away.*

Me: *The passion for staying quiet?*

Zoey: *I'll have a goal. Like I'll think,* Me and my teacher are at a great place. It would help her and help me, and would show that I'm more respectful . . . It would make my parents happy, it would make me happy—supposedly . . . *Then the passion dies down.*

In their reflections, both students considered not only what their teachers were trying to accomplish in whole class, but how students on the other side of the spectrum seemed to be reacting to the teachers' methods. Lotus said the following about verbose classmates like Zoey, which puts in mind the zero-sum situations described in the last chapter:

> Constantly hushing the children who are eager to speak their mind can be damaging. Teachers do not always realize the effect they have on their students, or how much power we give them, but when a teacher tells their student that they talk too much, too often, or simply ignore their perpetually raised hand, it's personal. It's saying to the student, *What you have to say isn't worth hearing,* that it doesn't matter, or is worth less than the rest of their classmates' thoughts. Conversely, the quieter students are shaking in their chairs, hoping and praying that the teacher's eyes land on someone else. It encourages an unhealthy competitive mentality and "it's either me or you" way of thinking, so that students don't think to gain success by building each other up, but instead by tearing one another down.

Conversely, Zoey had this to say about more reluctant participants in whole class:

> There were some times when my teachers would be, like, "You get to talk whenever you want." And that's when they go wrong. Classmates would tell me that they think, *I don't have to participate now, because Zoey's talking. She has to do all the work.* And I would be thinking, *I like talking, but that's not cool. That's not the point.*

These interview snippets show the often unacknowledged complexity of whole-class discussions. We sometimes fail to reflect on the efficacy of our decisions—I for one have grown increasingly hesitant to call on students who have not raised their hands, just because they seem to be looking at me. I would imagine that none of Lotus's teachers intended to inspire her to "stay as expressionless as possible" or try to be "easy to glance over and forget about." They probably meant for their cold calling to inspire the opposite. I certainly don't want my students' minds occupied by either hoping they don't get called on, or in Zoey's case, "zoning in" on being quiet. As a structure, whole class works only if we make the time to check in with students to see how *they* are processing our choices, not just how well we imagine things are going.

This whole-class complexity has special significance for race conversations, especially those sparked by heavier prompts—those that require more than a normal measure of vulnerability, emotional awareness, or intellectual disequilibrium. As a general rule, the heavier the prompt, the more time students should be given to reflect before or while being asked to speak before a large group of peers. Students have varying levels of sensitivity to the social consequences of their comments—and at the very least, we want them to feel like they are opting into public declarations. To cold-call a student like Lotus might feel generally jarring, but to surprisingly force her to hold forth on affirmative action or cultural appropriation might feel, to her, especially violent.

Conversely, we should reflect on the pressures that we place on the most verbose students in whole class. A familiar approach is to pull them aside to compliment their "leadership potential," then measure them against higher "leadership" expectations. First, this is a false equivalency. Just because a student likes to speak doesn't mean they are a natural leader. Such an idea privileges charisma over pragmatism, patience, and many other leadership qualities. Second, when held to these new standards, verbose students are often expected to check friends and classmates when they speak out of turn. When race conversations cause conflict, as explored in Chapter 2, these students find themselves deputized as their teacher's enforcers: *Why didn't you tell your classmate to settle down? You're supposed to be a leader! People follow you.* This can have major consequences when we consider two of the more common racial dynamics: minority students being asked to protect a white teacher's authority and white students being expected to discipline minority classmates.

Another famous whole-class faux pas affects both introverted and extroverted students alike: asking minority students to speak for other members of their race. When leading professional development sessions in school environments that have few students of color, teachers often ask me how they might make their few minority students more comfortable during race discussions. My first answer is usually, "Don't ask them to give their classmates *a minority perspective*." This request need not be explicitly asked to be inappropriate. Many times, it's just an unduly inquisitive first glance at the minority student every time a racial topic is brought up. It's even more troublesome if teachers treat minority students as if their job is to lend credence to a teacher's controversial opinions about race issues. Teachers tokenize minority students when they publicly ask for validation. The pressures of such tokenism are annoying: First, because teachers are the clear authority in the classroom, students are pressured to agree with us. If they choose to withhold validation, and are subsequently proven wrong, their embarrassment is their race's embarrassment. Second, tokenism heightens social tensions among students. As we well know, racial experiences are not monolithic, which means one student of color might feel rightfully miffed when her classmate is held up as a global representation.

Nobody benefits from this one-opinion-fits-all stance, especially majority students, who already face enough temptation to stereotype.

THE ROLE OF THE SMALL LEARNING COMMUNITY

The small learning community, or SLC, is, by definition, a group of students who meet regularly for academic purposes. These small groups can work on projects and serve as teams for class activities, but here, I focus on their usefulness in discussions. In my class, I follow what I've started calling the Olympia Academy model, after reading Walter Isaacson's lovely biography on Albert Einstein (2008). In the text, Isaacson describes a period in Einstein's early adulthood when he would regularly meet with fellow scientists to play around and talk physics. Here, Isaacson describes how they first got together:

> Maurice Solovine, a Romanian studying philosophy at the University of Bern, bought a newspaper while on a stroll one day during Easter vacation of 1902 and noticed Einstein's advertisement offering tutorials in physics. A dapper dilettante with close-cropped hair and a raffish goatee, Solovine was four years older than Einstein, but he had yet to decide whether he wanted to be a philosopher, a physicist, or something else. So he went to the address, rang the bell, and a moment later a loud voice thundered, "In here!" Einstein made an immediate impression. . . . Their first discussion lasted almost two hours, after which Einstein followed Solovine into the street, where they talked for a half-hour more. They agreed to meet the next day. At the third session, Einstein announced that conversing freely was more fun than tutoring for pay. "You don't have to be tutored in physics," he said. "Just come see me when you want and I will be glad to talk with you." They decided to read the great thinkers together and then discuss their ideas. Their sessions were joined by Conrad Habicht, a banker's son and former student of mathematics at the Zurich Polytechnic. Poking a little fun at pompous scholarly societies, they dubbed themselves the

> Olympia Academy. Einstein, even though he was the youngest, was designated the president, and Solovine prepared a certificate with a drawing of an Einstein bust in profile beneath a string of sausages. "A man perfectly and clearly erudite, imbued with exquisite, subtle and elegant knowledge, steeped in the revolutionary science of the cosmos," the dedication declared. (80)

Their playfulness did not end with satirical certificates:

> After their discussions, which could last all night, Einstein would sometimes play the violin and, in the summertime, they occasionally climbed a mountain on the outskirts of Bern to watch the sunrise. "The sight of the twinkling stars made a strong impression on us and led to discussions of astronomy," Solovine recalled. "We would marvel at the sun as it came slowly toward the horizon and finally appeared in all of its splendor to bathe the Alps in a mystic rose." Then they would wait for the mountain cafe to open so they could drink dark coffee before hiking down to start work.
>
> Solovine once skipped a session scheduled for his apartment because he was enticed instead to a concert by a Czech quartet. As a peace offering he left behind, as his note written in Latin proclaimed, "hard boiled eggs and a salutation." Einstein and Habicht, knowing how much Solovine hated tobacco, took revenge by smoking pipes and cigars in Solovine's room and piling his furniture and dishes on the bed. "Thick smoke and a salutation," they wrote in Latin. Solovine says he was "almost overwhelmed" by the fumes when he returned. "I thought I would suffocate. I opened the window wide and began to remove from the bed the mound of things that reached almost to the ceiling." (80–81)

After reading this, I was struck by the juxtaposition of theoretical physics, cheap wine, practical jokes, and stargazing. If this kind of learning community could inspire an Einstein, why shouldn't my students be encouraged to create one for themselves? I looked back at the text for clues on how to reimagine traditional SLCs as true Olympia Academies. First, I noticed that Einstein decided that his transactional relationship with his client got in the way; he wanted to speak with Solovine without the distractions of money and payment. This made me think about grades, still the ultimate currency in schools. To what degree do grades poison "small-group" dynamics? To what degree do they inspire what Lotus called "unhealthy" conversations where students don't feel like they can "communicate freely"? How often do kids get to just kick around ideas in small groups—without a group project or presentation to create, or participation points to accrue? Then, I noticed how the Olympia Academy's lack of a true authority figure led to an environment where *any* passionate discussion thread could be followed. I asked, *How often can students chase their own lines of inquiry without a teacher hovering to redirect them? How often have I unintentionally cautioned them against "marveling at the sun"—or in a classroom sense, discussing something that they personally found cool, challenging, or beautiful?* I noticed, in the same vein, how playful the Olympia Academy was. While I don't want my students playing pranks on each other, I did wonder how often they learned that discussions could be playful.

My answer to this was to create small learning communities that I've called *pods*. (The semantic change was inspired by the number of students who, when asked, told me they hated working in "groups.") These pods consist of four to six students. The pod groupings are randomly generated by my grade book during the first marking period and picked by members of my teaching team in later quarters. Students meet in pods often, usually with a mandate to discuss either our class text or a prompt. I rarely, if ever, assign grades to any of their pod activities. The students understand that teacher interruptions will be few. They can feel my presence as I float around the room, but they also know that most of the time I am not within earshot.

This means sacrificing the sense of control I feel in whole-class discussions. Not only am I no longer the intended target of most student comments, but I don't even hear most of them. I cannot redirect unless I happen to be standing right by the group. Inevitably, my students will chase a conversational point that I would have deemed inconsequential. They will even use pod time to discuss matters that have nothing to do with the class; they will gossip, tell jokes, talk about their next class or the one they just left. Overhearing snippets of this can send any teacher cascading into self-doubt: *How long have they been talking about this? Did I just waste the last twenty minutes?* From here, the temptation to return to whole class is great. But then I think of the students like Lotus, who would surely return to the periphery if thirty more voices were to reenter the conversation.

For any Olympia Academy–modeled small learning community to work, teachers ultimately must make peace with their students' distractibility. It can be mitigated. Taking advantage of the smartphones that most of my students bring to class, I sometimes require students to record important pod conversations and send them to me. I openly admit that I will not be listening to the entire conversation (with seven-plus pods per class, that would take hours), but I promise to periodically peruse them. (Students have always had trouble imagining what teachers do in their free time, so I'm sure that some of them think that I have nothing better to do than take detailed notes on every second of their recordings! Some of them drop little "Easter eggs" for me to discover—small jokes—and the entire class enjoys when I mention them the next day in class to show proof of my listening.)

Some teachers assign roles to their students that encourage accountability. Each role can have some deliverable artifact to be handed in to the teacher and graded. For language arts teachers, this often appears in literature circles, with their Discussion Leaders, Illustrators, Literary Luminaries, Reporters, Summarizers, and Investigators. Even with this, we teachers cannot track every word spoken—and we must not concentrate our efforts on finding ways to do so. Creative energy should be spent discovering fresh methods of encouraging the students to hold *themselves* accountable. This means that we prioritize time for them to reflect on their conversations. Then we must allow them to get back into the SLCs to practice any adjustments made after their reflection.

In SLC conversations, ideas can bounce around like atoms in a tight space, leading to a kinetic heat that can be especially scary when the topic is race. With the teacher not hovering, the kids can freely deal in stereotypes and half logic. They can use hurtful slurs, intentionally or otherwise. Natural tangents can lead them right into zero-sum situations, where only one student can "win." These battles can simmer until an explosion finally calls them to the teacher's attention. We fear that this might happen too late to avoid damage to our classroom culture. Even when the teacher arrives, we don't know how the conversation got to this point, so we might be unsure how to "fix" the situation.

On the other hand, hovering teachers make students nervous. With no "expert" nearby to correct incomplete thoughts, students are more likely to share them—feeling that, unlike their teacher, classmates will not be accessing a vast store of as-yet-unlearned information. Also, when skirmishes erupt, students are saved from a teacher's overreactions; they are often capable of working things out on their own. We don't know all of the kids' relationships, nor do we usually have the closest grip on their cultural references. This combination sometimes makes us hypersensitive to (and instinctively punitive toward) any jokes or references that we consider inappropriate. There is nothing wrong with this in whole class; after all, we are responsible for establishing the acceptable language of academic discourse. However, in the more informal Olympia Academy, ideas are king. As long as ideas are expressed in an understood language of respect, it's all good. In small groups, it's good for students to speak in their own language, and not spend as much energy checking themselves for the right scholarly words. Remember, according to Isaacson, the name *Olympia Academy* was a dig at pompous scholarly societies. Taking oneself too seriously inhibits thought—something that we should remember when designing our own small learning communities for conversation.

THE ROLE OF ONE-ON-ONE CONVERSATION

The deepest immersion into ideas comes from one-on-one conversation. With fewer diluting voices, the one-on-one exchange of ideas is most concentrated. Of all the conversational structures, this is the most intimate environment for students to ask each other questions. In the other two structures, there is an audience to every exchange—an intimidatingly large one in whole class, a more intimate one in the small learning community—but in this last structure, nobody is ever just watching. Individual students have the time to ask follow-up questions until they understand. An additional benefit: The absence of a Greek chorus provides little incentive for students to grandstand.

Teachers can participate in one-on-one conversations with students with many of the same benefits. Students are honored when their teacher takes the time to sit next to them and converse. This intimacy can be jarring to students who have never had the opportunity to privately bounce ideas off their teacher. If the teacher avoids the temptation to make these close conversations a display of their superior knowledge, there is a great opportunity for students to build their confidence. How often in our lives do we have the chance to privately discuss a subject with someone we consider to be the ultimate authority? Many of our students position us as experts. Even a thirty-second stop-in at a student's desk to ask, "I hear what everybody says, but what do you think?" can be seismic in the development of a student's confidence.

Of course, in one-on-one, shy students find themselves wedged between silence and their partner's voice. The lack of an alternative option has the potential to increase anxiety. Also, when engaged in a one-on-one with a student, even the most seasoned teacher has nearly no idea what everybody else is talking about. Accountability systems for one-on-one are the most difficult to create. And when we teachers stop next to a student for thirty seconds, we might have our back to the majority of the class—and splitting our attention brings all of its attendant apprehension. Should any conflict arise, we have absolutely no idea how it started. With more high-needs populations, the students might even be in physical danger when a teacher narrows his focus to one student. Fights break out. Students leave the room. No structure is more dependent on classroom culture than the one-on-one conversation.

Yet no other structure can be more beneficial in growing classroom culture. At the secondary school level, interpersonal relationships are essential to discourse. Sustained one-on-one conversations strengthen the network of interpersonal relationships that the other two structures rely on. The inability of students to hide forces many students to engage a secret scholarly self that would have otherwise been buried under voices like Zoey's.

CONVERSATIONAL PACKAGES: MIX IT UP!

All three structures—whole-class discussions, small learning communities, and one-on-one conversations—have specific variations. For example, the Socratic Seminar is an interesting form of whole class, while concentric circles and gallery walks are ways to get in some one-on-one work. English teacher and blogger Sarah Brown Wessling and others suggest spicing up SLCs by having some students rotate to the neighboring small group after a set amount of time, while others stay still. The digital age allows students to contribute to an ongoing conversation through Twitter or other chatting software that can be projected for the entire class to read while still discussing verbally. Or we can lean on the classic think-pair-share, a hearty blend of one-on-one and whole class that gives every student a chance to practice before sharing thoughts publicly. The possibilities are endless, with new adaptations being piloted and published every day.

There isn't one right structure for meaningful race conversations. We should all create a bag of structural variations that fit both our personal vision and our students' situations. Much like sports coaches who are devotees of certain "packages" of strategies (the 3-4 defense, the Princeton offense, the forecheck), dialogic teachers should develop their own conversational "package." This provides accessibility for the teacher and security for the students. Imagine the kids saying, "Oh, *think-pair-share*! Nice call, Coach! I was worried that you would go Socratic Seminar on that one. That would have been rough."

The real challenge is committing to *use* our conversational package once it has been thoughtfully created (or expanded). How many of us have brought back a new conversational structure from a professional development day—an article or book—or after visiting a colleague's classroom? If it works, we use it for a few days, or even attach it as an activity for a specific unit. *This worked great with* To Kill a Mockingbird. *I've got to try it again the next time I teach that!* This compartmentalization costs our students a great deal because perfectly good tools stay in the box until "next year" or only when doing a certain activity.

An even bigger problem than unnecessary compartmentalization is the failure to diversify our conversational tools. We must commit to blending effective whole-class, SLC, and one-on-one conversations into *every* unit. If we fail to consistently make time for SLC and one-on-one, all of our students might not benefit. And forcing them to speak might require the punitive extrinsic methods that so discouraged Lotus—discussion points, public shaming, and cold calling. If we swing the other way and fail to consistently make time for whole-class conversation, our communities might never coalesce.

For example, dialogic teachers often make a big deal out of permanently shifting students from sitting in rows to sitting in groups. This shift, instead of being viewed as only one of many valuable structures, is viewed as a community-building panacea. However, when a teacher doesn't vary the conversational package, these small groups can quickly become the only communities that students are invested in. I have seen this cause unnecessary classroom discipline issues: Students are strangely punished for conversing with the humans sitting directly in front of their faces, as if doing otherwise would be unnatural. (This punishment is especially odd after we've just asked students to wrestle with topics within these small groups.) Stagnancy blunts much of the structure's potential.

Instead of all ideas remaining in a small community, students need to present their SLC-seasoned ideas to the whole class. This is publishing—a chance for kids to recognize what other groups' processes have produced. This not only builds the entire-class community, but specifically reminds students that their group wasn't the only group to have kicked around some good ideas. As an added bonus, a return to whole class gives teachers a natural opportunity to not only remind our students about discussion rules, but to guide them through reflection on their conversational processes.

Most important, diversifying the three structures also allows for intuitive *state changes*, which Jerry Evanski defines as "a change in a student's thoughts, feelings, or physiology" in his book *Classroom Activators* (2009, xiv). We must never fail to realize that our students are normally trapped in their seats. They do not share our freedom of movement. In most of our classrooms, they have to ask for permission to relieve themselves, to stand when their legs go numb, to check any message that vibrates in their pocket. If sleepy, they cannot rest; if hungry, they cannot eat. While in our classrooms, they live by our leave. Most of them will never return to such a state after leaving secondary school. If they do, it will be in either prison or the military. This knowledge humbles me. It is a punch to the gut that makes regular state changes not just the mark of good pedagogy, but a true measure of selflessness and empathy. Blending conversational tools gives students a chance to move, physically and mentally. Doing it regularly assures them that we teachers consider this a priority.

MORE THAN A PROBLEM

After committing to both reflecting on and varying our conversational packages, we must next consider our approach to selecting content. What race subjects should our students be engaging? Which stories should be told? Which histories examined? Considering this book's chief assertion—there is a difference between "light" and "fire," between empty and meaningful—how do teachers pick the proper fuel for their students' race discourse?

In answering this challenge, we should begin by considering W. E. B Du Bois's lament in *The Souls of Black Folk:*

> Between me and the other world there is ever an unasked question: unasked by some through feelings of delicacy; by others through the difficulty of rightly framing it. All, nevertheless, flutter round it . . . *How does it feel to be a problem?* (2014, 4)

I've heard many students complain that when a class discusses race, the lens is always overcoming discrimination, violence, or other systemic oppression. My senior African American Lit students once asked why their previous schooling hadn't allowed them to discuss the intricacies of jazz and hip-hop, black cuisine, and the Black Arts Movement. Why hadn't they ever discussed anything beautiful about being black? My Latino and Asian students faced an even stricter narrowing of available discussion topics. Essentially, how come minority cultures were *always* discussed in relation to white oppression? Why was blackness always presented as *a problem*? Their questions soured my stomach, for I had planned a semester of inspirational Black People Overcoming White Oppression conversations, fueled solely by canonical black texts of the same theme. Apparently, my students found this repetition either emotionally draining, if they chose to invest in the conversations, or boring, if they did not. The former might, for a short while, have the symptoms of success—facing stubborn racism *is* draining to anyone with a heightened moral sensitivity. But meaningful discourse requires energy, and if students are preemptively exhausted by the mere mention of race, they are likely to be less patient with each other and less willing to take the risks necessary for meaningful race discourse. A curriculum that bases *all* race scholarship on minorities' pain also runs the risk of celebrating that pain, sometimes to the point of dismissing every other aspect of their cultures.

Thus, when considering the fodder for race discussions, it is essential to ask the following questions: (1) How can I make room for conversations that explore the many facets of minority culture? and (2) How can I encourage my students to be reasonable and deliberative while engaging controversial subject matter?

AVOIDING THE JEFFERSONIAN DISMISSAL

In his 1785 *Notes on the State of Virginia*, Thomas Jefferson spices up pages of pseudoscientific racism with an odd aesthetic criticism: "Misery is often the parent of the most affecting touches in poetry—among the Blacks is Misery enough, God knows, but no Poetry"(147). Desperate to prove the sinister thesis that blacks are inferior, Jefferson renders them flat characters, defined entirely by their struggles. This willfully incomplete picture of black people gave a generation of whites an authoritative excuse for racism.

When choosing the fuel for our classroom race conversations, we should take care not to unintentionally continue Jefferson's legacy of flattening minority narratives. Yes, the relationship between races is often exploitive and abusive, and these relationships should be discussed with honesty and directness, but we should push, with equal energy, against the trend to make struggle-against-white-people stories the *only* stories we discuss. ELA teachers, for instance, should consider introducing students to Walter Mosley's fun Easy Rawlins murder mysteries, Octavia Butler's science fiction, or Chimamanda Ngozi Adichie's *Americanah* or *Half of a Yellow Sun*. These texts not only present a more layered idea of race and culture, but they might also start students toward having authentic interest in important subjects that we might otherwise find hard to get them excited about. For example, as a young child, reading Robert Lipsyte's Contender series first got me interested in boxing, and, due to repeated references in the book, caused a lifelong fascination with Muhammad Ali. This, consequently, sparked a curiosity about Malcolm X, which eventually inspired an authentic interest in the Civil Rights movement.

And even when struggle against white supremacy is apparent, and must be highlighted, such as in August Wilson's *Fences* or Lorraine Hansberry's *A Raisin in the Sun*, we should not forget the benefits of other lenses. Both kinds of texts present the opportunity for students to discuss the dynamics of the black family, and the complicated roles that gender, religion, and recreation play in black identity, aspiration, and relationships. These supplementary themes can be highlighted through careful engagement of supporting sources—nearly every example in this book will heavily involve such sources. Ultimately, through class conversation, our students should engage the totality of racial experience. People of color are much more than our relationships with white people—a point that, while vital for both diverse classrooms and those that consist mainly of students of color, is also important for homogeneously white classrooms. In such isolation, these students have little contact with minorities that might round out their racial perceptions. Race discussion that is *solely* racism-centered, for them especially, runs the risk of habituating the Jeffersonian dismissal.

ENGAGING CONTROVERSIES

Many of our most challenging race conversations will ask students to engage and, if necessary, *debate* controversies. The biggest race controversies involve racism. Not about whether racism is wrong—this, thankfully, has become a generally closed subject—but about what counts as racist, what it has caused, and what, if anything, should be done about it. While teachers may have to work hard to find texts that meet the previous section's challenge of engaging race *without* highlighting racism, plenty of texts that *do* highlight racism have already been accepted as curriculum-worthy. For me, this meant reading and discussing Mildred D. Taylor's *Roll of Thunder, Hear My Cry* and its two sequels as a youngster, followed by *To Kill a Mockingbird* in middle school and *The Adventures of Huckleberry Finn* in high school. This established teaching-youth-about-racism canon has clear literary merits and limitations that become clearer as time passes—the prevalence of "white saviors" for instance—but, taken as a whole, these books are classics for a reason and can be valuable fuel for meaningful race conversations.

When planning curriculum meant to engage race controversies, a teacher's first question shouldn't be which text to teach. It should be, *What kind of scholar do I want to help mold?* Followed closely by, *What kind of citizenship do I hope to encourage?* In their book *The Case for Contention: Teaching Controversial Issues in American Schools* (2017), Jonathan Zimmerman and Emily Robertson offer two answers, inspired by the political philosophy of John Rawls. First, students should be *reasonable*, defined as "willing to honor fair principles of social cooperation even on occasions when the results do not advance their own interests" (60). In doing so, students should be able to "recognize that citizens may sometimes disagree, even without anyone being biased, ignorant of the facts, or selfish" (60). Next, and more important, students should be *deliberative*. According to Zimmerman and Robertson, "effective deliberators should be able to construct sound arguments for their positions, but should also be open to changing their views when confronted with better arguments" (61).

These goals have clear benefits. If, for instance, our race discussions encourage *reasonableness*, students might be able to recognize racial, economic, and gender-based privileges—the denial of which might be fueled by hyperfocused self-interest. They might also be less inclined to automatically disparage those who disagree with them in order to avoid engaging uncomfortable ideas. Students must be able to sublimate their most immediate interests for the sake of a greater mission. Any study of justice movements shows how easily meaningful work can be undone by the egos and inflexibility of otherwise good people. When our race discussions thoughtfully encourage *deliberation*, students learn how to organize arguments—then how to clearly communicate with diverse audiences. Deliberative students are better equipped to serve their own passions because they don't just seek to shut down those who disagree. Instead, they care about—then work hard toward—*convincing* both their ideological opponents and witnesses who've yet to make up their minds. Inversely,

Zimmerman and Robinson claim that deliberative students "must learn why a well-reasoned argument is different from a mere expression of opinion, and hence that some interpretations miss the mark. Students must learn that one's opinion can be wrong" (51).

If we want to develop reasonable and deliberative scholars (and citizens), our approach to controversial race discussions can help us get there. These two goals should inspire focused examination of our discussion activities. If we want to encourage deliberation, for instance, we should ask ourselves how often we give students the opportunity—and permission—to be *convinced*. So many of our traditional ways of dealing with controversial issues in the classroom involve students trying to convince *others*. We set up formal debates and host classroom trials, both of which are quite useful in helping students develop "an array of skills and dispositions embodying the ability to formulate and evaluate arguments" which Zimmerman and Robertson argue fosters students' "capacities for rational thought and action" (59). While this development is important, if we *always* position our students to be on the offensive, and base most of our incentives (grades, teacher praise, and so on) on winning, we condition our students to never acknowledge better arguments. I, for one, have often counseled students to not "lose focus" and to stick to their claim, regardless of what an opponent says. This stubbornness is supported by traditional thesis essays, which often reward dogged focus on a single argument: We teach students to point out the other side's flaws while ignoring its merits. This stance unintentionally mirrors many of the inflexible adult behaviors that so frustrate us.

Consider the Think Like a Nazi assignment from this book's introduction. The teacher's written instructions made clear how little deliberation was valued. Students were instructed to play a flatly anti-Semitic character, focused on proving that "Jews are evil and the source of [their] problems." Strangely, students were then encouraged to combine their knowledge of propaganda skills with "any experiences [they have had] to complete this task." *What* experience? Did this thesis's inflexible lens require so much fidelity that students needed to carry it to their real-life cross-cultural relationships? Ratcheting up the urgency, the assignment then encouraged students to remember that "your live[s] (here in Nazi Germany in the '30s) may depend on it!" Then, a few lines down, "You do not have a choice in your position—you must argue that Jews are evil, and use solid rationale from government propaganda to convince me of your loyalty to the Third Reich!" There is no "solid rationale" for anti-Semitism. But even if this teacher had not offered this ridiculous implication, she would have been undone by a vigorous effort to counsel students away from deliberation. This teacher apparently found it vital that students practice being intractable in the face of controversy.

My ninth-grade class includes a rhetoric unit, through which I try to encourage a more deliberative stance. In the unit, students learn how to recognize rhetorical devices (logos, pathos, and ethos) and then how to best use them to convince an audience. When introducing logos, we spend a few days discussing the prevalence of logical fallacies, and how they are often wielded as intentional tricks. Many students are eager to learn the structure of argumentation, how solid premises can be built up, while faulty premises leave arguments vulnerable to collapse. When discussing Straw Man, they call out, "My mom does that!" or "I'm going to come clean; I do that to my little brother all the time." They wince when I show them politicians using Post Hoc or Slippery Slope reasoning to justify controversial proposals. They giggle when I show these same politicians using Glittering Generalities to describe whichever slice of America is being courted at the moment. Newly aware of the prevalence of Red Herrings, they hunt for them doggedly, like younger kids seeking Easter eggs. The final project asks them to write a persuasive speech and record it as a podcast with accompanying images. Students are encouraged to write about their passions—as long as they focus on persuading an audience. They bring me potential topics for approval, and most seem refreshed by my generous acceptances.

Students' giddiness fades quickly, however, when they review the project's rubric. Twenty percent of their grade depends on their ability to construct an argument without employing logical fallacies—even unintentionally. This requirement drives students to tease out their arguments, deliberating in pods to check for faulty premises. During these conversations, and through conducting research, students often realize that they've been relying on unsound logic. They then ask for permission to tweak their approach or even to switch sides. One year, a Jewish student began the process blaming Palestinians for the violence in the West Bank and advocating for their total removal. During a week's worth of conversations, he continually picked at his argument, testing each premise and unearthing fallacies. At the end, he told me simply that, while his opinion had not fully changed, he was now aware of more complexity. He was worried that his speech could no longer advocate for any specific action, as he didn't know enough to do so. I offered the chance to add an addendum to his speech, explaining how his argument had shifted through deliberation and careful research. It was one of the best projects in his class.

One of the key frustrations about most controversial race conversations is that they so rarely initiate change. This, certainly, was Frederick Douglass's concern when addressing that 1852 convention, and likely inspired his *fire* metaphor. Too often, all sides of a race issue settle comfortably into their respective corners, unwilling to listen actively to the other side, slow to examine both the soundness of their logic and the effectiveness of their argumentation. This encourages the celebration of (and in some cases, an addiction to) meaningless victories. Our curriculum counters this momentum when it gives students the permission, encouragement, and space to practice deliberation. Students must know that they can have strong convictions, and yet remain open to making adjustments when exposed to better arguments. This habit will prepare them to mindfully engage a lifetime of race controversies, while perhaps finally putting some of the oldest ones to bed.

THREADED CONVERSATIONS

A few years ago, an alumnus gave me a picture to place on my classroom desk. In it, a smiling student sits with her hand raised, beneath a caption with a slightly modified Maya Angelou quote: "At the end of the day she won't remember what you said or did, but she will remember how you made her feel." As the message is a reminder to always show my students empathy, I chose to display it. However, on sight, the words cut two ways. If my students are destined to forget all of our well-designed conversations, what am I even doing up there? The words ring true—I am hard-pressed to remember *any* classroom discussions from one of the best secondary educations that Philadelphia could offer.

We want our students to remember our race conversations, just as I am certain an engineer wants her drawbridge to still be passable fifty years from now. The ideas we choose to wrestle with should have the same permanence as vocabulary and grammar rules, as the "hard" sciences, as mathematical formulas. We hope our students never lose the ability to blend figurative language tools from our writing workshops into wonderful pieces of expression—their wedding vows, their elevator pitches, the eulogies written for lifelong friends. Our race conversations should be just as enduring.

For this to happen, we must adopt a threaded approach to unit planning. A *thread* is a clear connection between a main theme and every conversation that follows. This can take many forms. At Science Leadership Academy, every year has a theme across all subjects: ninth grade is Identity, tenth is Systems, eleventh is Change, and twelfth is Creation. All but senior year have corresponding gradewide Essential Questions:

Ninth Grade: Identity

Who am I?

How do I interact with my environment?

How does the environment affect me?

Tenth Grade: Systems

How are systems created and defined?

How do systems shape the world?

What is the role of the individual in systems?

Eleventh Grade: Change

What causes systemic and individual change?

What is the role of the individual in creating and sustaining change?

What is the relationship between the self and a changing world?

This approach invites all our students to see their education as a purposeful thing. For my freshmen, the connections can be mind-blowing; they ask me, "Wait . . . we're talking about that in algebra. Do you talk to Mrs. Giorgio?" They look around as if realizing that their teachers are involved in some great conspiracy. When everything is clicking, we no longer ask our students to compartmentalize ideas. In the fifty-fourth thesis of *Building School 2.0*, Chris Lehmann argues that classes should be "lenses, not silos." The latter leads to "a rigidity of thought," whereas the former encourages students to "ask real questions and solve real problems" (Lehmann and Chase 2015, 155).

If your school has not tried gradewide themes and/or essential questions, encourage your leadership to try them. In the meantime, I recommend introducing a yearlong conversational thread to your classroom. If chosen properly, the overarching theme can provide comfort and stability for the students, a reassurance that race issues aren't being introduced haphazardly.

For instance, imagine a conversational thread that seeks to understand the roots of different cultural beauty standards, held during a unit on the *Autobiography of Malcolm X*. When leading such a conversation, I might orient with a video clip from Chris Rock's movie *Good Hair* (2009) that explains the lengths that black women go through to "process" their hair. (I have found that a considerable number of my white students are not familiar with what their black classmates go through to get their hair to lie straight.) After the orientation chat (and with the projector still fired up), I might move to the opening scene of *Malcolm X*, where Denzel Washington acts out a good approximation of Malcolm surviving searing congolene burns. The kids would laugh, as always. We might move from there to reading the section of the text where Malcolm describes this first "conk":

> The congolene turned pale-yellowish. "Feel the jar," Shorty said. I cupped my hand against the outside, and snatched it away. "Damn right, it's hot, that's the lye," he said. "So you know it's going to burn when I comb it in—it burns bad. But the longer you can stand it, the straighter the hair." He made me sit down, and he tied the string of the new rubber apron tightly around my neck, and combed up my bush of hair. Then, from the big

vaseline jar, he took a handful and massaged it hard all through my hair and into the scalp. He also thickly vaselined my neck, ears and forehead. "When I get to washing out your head, be sure to tell me anywhere you feel any little stinging," Shorty warned me, washing his hands, then pulling on the rubber gloves, and tying on his own rubber apron. "You always got to remember that any congolene left in burns a sore into your head."

The congolene just felt warm when Shorty started combing it in. But then my head caught fire. I gritted my teeth and tried to pull the sides of the kitchen table together. The comb felt as if it was raking my skin off. My eyes watered, my nose was running. I couldn't stand it any longer; I bolted to the washbasin. I was cursing Shorty with every name I could think of when he got the spray going and started soap lathering my head. He lathered and spray-rinsed, lathered and spray-rinsed, maybe ten or twelve times, each time gradually closing the hot-water faucet, until the rinse was cold, and that helped some.

"You feel any stinging spots?"

"No," I managed to say. My knees were trembling.

"Sit back down, then. I think we got it all out okay." The flame came back as Shorty, with a thick towel, started drying my head, rubbing hard.

"Easy, man, easy!" I kept shouting.

"The first time's always worst. You get used to it better before long. You took it real good, homeboy. You got a good conk." When Shorty let me stand up and see in the mirror, my hair hung down in limp, damp strings. My scalp still flamed, but not as badly; I could bear it. He draped the towel around my shoulders, over my rubber apron, and began again vaselining my hair. I could feel him combing, straight back, first the big comb, then the fine-tooth one. Then, he was using a razor, very delicately, on the back of my neck. Then, finally, shaping the

> sideburns. My first view in the mirror blotted out the hurting. I'd seen some pretty conks, but when it's the first time, on your own head, the transformation, after the lifetime of kinks, is staggering. The mirror reflected Shorty behind me. We both were grinning and sweating. And on top of my head was this thick, smooth sheen of shining red hair—real red—as straight as any white man's. (X and Haley 2007, 55)

From there, we might move to his analysis of the moment:

> How ridiculous I was! Stupid enough to stand there simply lost in admiration of my hair now looking "white," reflected in the mirror in Shorty's room. I vowed that I'd never again be without a conk, and I never was for many years . . . This was my first really big step toward self-degradation: when I endured all of that pain, literally burning my flesh to have it look like a white man's hair. I had joined that multitude of Negro men and women in America who are brainwashed into believing that the black people are "inferior"—and white people "superior"—that they will even violate and mutilate their God-created bodies to try to look "pretty" by white standards. (X and Haley 2007, 56)

From this, I might ask the students to evaluate Malcolm's thesis that black people distort and damage their bodies only because they have adopted a Eurocentric standard of beauty. The kids would weigh this a little bit until one of them reliably mentioned the role of media in transmitting beauty standards. From here, I would have to feel out where the kids wanted to go. Perhaps a pod breakout session where students are challenged to craft an answer to Malcolm's 1962 Los Angeles speech by the same name that asks blacks, among other things, "Who taught you to hate yourself?" Perhaps, if the community is strong, a series of one-on-one conversations about how individual students developed their self-image. Or I could keep it whole class and ask them to make sense of the complexity of the magazine cover shown in Figure 3.1, then debate whether our society has grown since its 1966 publication in *Ebony* magazine.

This would be a quality discussion on its own, or as part of an ongoing classroom theme of understanding the cultural roots of beauty. A good day. Yet, as a part of a yearlong exploration of identity, it has greater potential to be remembered. Let's say these same students have, in previous classes, recently discussed the disturbing trend of young girls asking YouTube audiences to evaluate their prettiness. And earlier than that, they had written memoir vignettes about some form of cultural influence on their identity. By the time they reach this Malcolm X excerpt, the ground will have already been softened. The students will recognize that this very personal line of questioning was not the result of some educator's 7:00 a.m. brainburst. And since more students trust that we are "going somewhere," more of them might commit themselves to the exercise.

While *agility* is crucial in our instruction, we must not appear *haphazard*, especially when asking students to analyze their own experience alongside a text. Every time we ask students to share personal information, it is helpful

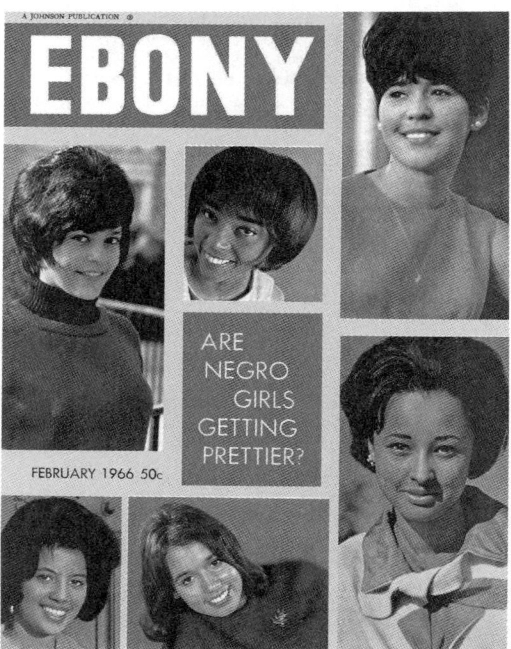

FIGURE 3.1
I collect any source that might spark an interesting conversation about our current thread, like this *Ebony* magazine cover from 1966.

to imagine their much younger selves offering us some handmade holiday gift. In such a situation, all of us know to be generous with our gratitude, accepting our scribbly drawing or misshapen clay mug with full knowledge of the moment's significance. Most times we display the youngster's gift prominently, making it clear that we value it just as much as (or even more than) expensive "adult" gifts. We tell our spouses and anybody within earshot to come and take a look at what the child has given us. The more we do this, the more likely it is that the child will continue offering us their creative best. Our adoration must be predictable. And we must be sensitive to our students' vulnerability.

In my early career, I tried a few of the more unpredictable sharing activities. I crafted a version of the Privilege Walk that I'd seen in the movie *Freedom Writers*. My students lined up facing each other, then were asked to step out of the line if different statements applied to them. Some of the heavier ones were as follows:

> If you've lost a loved one to gang violence
>
> If your ancestors came to the United States by force
>
> If you believe that you were *denied employment* because of your race, gender, or ethnicity
>
> If you were embarrassed about your clothes or house while growing up
>
> If you were raised in a single-parent household
>
> If your parents or guardians attended college

The appeal is obvious. Theoretically, the students are shocked into a place of empathy; there are tears and declarations of newfound openness. From a teacher's perspective, this is another good day. When I did a similar activity with my students during a freshman drama class, one of my colleagues visited the classroom. Kids were crying. I felt proud of myself. Afterward, my colleague earnestly asked, "Is that what you wanted?" The gravity of this question brought me some harsh realizations: *You have all the power in this situation. They did not choose to come to your class; they did not choose to participate in this activity. Even though you publicly gave them the option to not react to the questions, you've spent half a year persuading them to trust you. They might be accessing something depressing that they have purposely locked away. Your only certification is in teaching students English. If this haphazard situation makes some trauma bubble up, you have no training in how to deal with it. Just who exactly do you think you are?*

The problem wasn't the activity, it was the lack of a contextualizing thread and a sequentially developed understanding. Students came to the class expecting improvisation games, only to be smacked by a very public therapy session run by a neophyte. The Malcolm X example, while less jarring, poses the same problem: Many of our students are at the age when poor self-image is particularly prevalent. While a majority of my students might experience a healthy disequilibrium through this discussion, some might suffer a punch in the gut that feels oddly personal. This pain from the blow can cause double vision: A student ends up seeing the teacher as calloused or, in some situations, blithely racist. Worse, the shock caused by haphazard conversations often causes student expressions that can *look* like breakthroughs, as in my drama episode, but may not be. After doing the community-building work described in Chapter 1, we can think so much of our classroom communities that every show of raw vulnerability is regarded as evidence of progress. *They are crying, so I'm good.* This inch-deep Hollywood metric has more potential to feed our egos than help our students.

Here's an example from my classroom for readers to consider. Knowing that SLA's gradewide theme for sophomores is Systems, my English classes begin the year with an examination of societal order by discussing its absence in *Lord of the Flies*. From there, we move to a conversation on the philosophy of human behavior by reading the theories of Locke, Hobbes, Hume, and Voltaire. This is connected to a series of activities that engage constitutional law, culminating in mock Supreme Court rulings on student-created cases that try to "break" the Bill of Rights. This leads to conversations about Hitler's Germany as represented in *The Book Thief*—specifically, the relationship between propaganda and censorship in repressive governments. In the latter third of the book, the theme switches to our human tendencies to resist oppression. From here, we move to

Native Son and many conversations about the distressed within a system, one of which I describe in Chapter 7. Finally, we wrap up the year with a speech-writing unit that invites students to use new rhetorical devices to present their own theories about the role of the individual within the system. Race is never shoehorned into a discussion without proper context. The sequence's power (and scholarly community) grows from an always-developing understanding, not a single *shock and awe* moment. From philosophies about human nature to government to propaganda to agency to rhetoric, the complexities of race are never flattened.

Race issues are *human* issues, and a threaded approach makes it easier for us to avoid segregating them into a silo, which might diminish their value. Imagine a unit that discusses antebellum slavery not in isolation, but as a lens through which to discuss our human capacity for both cruelty and resistance. In it, a teacher might access a wealth of outside resources, from the Stanley Milgram and Stanford prison experiments to violent social media videos. An African American Literature class might visit the Holocaust Museum in Washington, DC, while still reading excerpts from slave narratives. A nonthreaded approach, if a teacher is not careful, might end up offering students considerably fewer avenues of inquiry. Also, if we are teaching in a diverse environment, our students who identify as neither black nor white might not feel welcome to publicly relate their experiences. Oftentimes, I will have Asian or Latino students express frustration at the constant black/white dichotomy of race discussions. They have grown used to keeping their opinions to themselves, denying their classmates vital perspectives. I have had West African students who grew up in refugee camps. We've taught descendants of both victims of the Cambodian genocide *and* the Khmer Rouge. We do not benefit from their silence.

In addition, if we are not careful, a nonthreaded approach might encourage a Jeffersonian dismissal of minority cultures. For a few conversations—often during one month—we duck into slavery, or Jim Crow, or the Holocaust, or police brutality, or any other contemporary hot-button racial topic—then when we've established the good guys and bad guys, and just how horrible it was or is, we let it go. For these situations to have value, they must be presented in their larger human context. *I do not call for indirectness.* Quite the opposite: I argue that our students should be talking race *all year*, as a part of a curriculum that views race relations as human issues and as one of our most powerful and relevant analytical lenses. These conversations should provide no hiding place for groups that have historically been disengaged or threatened into silence.

Consider the following example from my unit on Octavia Butler's *Kindred*. This text follows Dana, a twentieth-century black woman, as she time-travels to the antebellum South. Midway through the text, her white husband, Kevin, accidentally joins her journey to an ancestor's plantation. In order to manage suspicion, Dana pretends to be his slave. This, of course, stresses the relationship, as Dana and Kevin experience vastly different levels of brutality and subjugation. At one point, the two stroll through the fields and witness a group of enslaved children playing at auctioning each other off:

> "Now here a likely wench," called the boy on the stump. He gestured toward the girl who stood slightly behind him. "She cook and wash and iron. Come here, gal. Let the folks see you." He drew the girl up beside him. "She young and strong," he continued. "She worth plenty money. Two hundred dollars. Who bid two hundred dollars?"
>
> The little girl turned to frown at him. "I'm worth more than two hundred dollars, Sammy!" she protested. "You sold Martha for five hundred dollars!"
>
> "You shut your mouth," said the boy. "You ain't supposed to say nothing. When Marse Tom bought Mama and me, we didn't say nothing." (2009, 99)

After seeing that this scene upset Dana, Kevin tries to reassure her that they are stuck "in the middle of history," and that they "can't change it." She responds with, "But I can't close my eyes."

A dialogic teacher might guide her students through this scene by focusing on the brutal economics of slavery. They might start with an outside source that depicts the dehumanizing spectacle of slave auctions—perhaps a section from Solomon Northup's primary slave narrative, *Twelve Years a Slave*. Students might compare it with similar depictions in another fictionalized account, maybe Lawrence Hill's *Book of Negroes*. Both have accessible film adaptations, and after watching them, the students could tackle a question like

How did a dominant culture grow so numb to seeing such an inhumane spectacle?

Without a doubt, this approach would net a powerful few days of conversation. Yet, in addition to the previous approach, the *Kindred* excerpt *begs* to be examined *thematically*. First, there is the gamesmanship of the slave children that Dana finds so objectionable. Students might be encouraged to reflect on situations where humans play at their own subjugation. For example, I describe for my students a popular game from my childhood called "catch a girl, freak a girl," which consisted of boys chasing their female classmates in the schoolyard until one could be tackled. After catching a girl, a boy would mime a sex act against their prone body. The boy would then sprint away to find another target. Victims would eventually be tallied to find a winner. Every year, to this day, some of my students have recognized some version of this game from their elementary days. We discuss how play like this is emblematic of our nation's rape culture.

After adding their own troubling games to a class list, the students wrestle with the following question: *Why do humans play at their own destruction? Is it appropriate to do so? What are the real-life consequences of such play?* Every student is encouraged to reflect on their complicity. Some, like me, played in the past. Some darkly admit to playing still. Many have watched and said nothing, while a few heroes have habitually shut such games down. Some remember being the bully, some the victim, while others question the appropriateness of such labels. The students often bridge to a discussion of violence in video games, while I offer a comparison to misogynistic lyrics in hip-hop. This threaded approach to *Kindred* recognizes that the text offers three available perspectives: troubled Dana, apathetic Kevin, and the enslaved children. The dialogic teacher's challenge is to invite each student into any of the available characters' shoes. From here, students might converse in a spirit of personal investment.

THE PREACHER'S DILEMMA, PART 1

Ultimately, dialogic teachers face a *preacher's dilemma:* We see meaningful connections between often-archaic texts and our students' very modern lives; our mission is to make these connections clear without boring our students into inattention or complacency. When discussing historical injustice, this personal engagement becomes even more important: As many students as possible must recognize the thread between yesterday's crimes and the world they currently inhabit. In the aforementioned *Kindred* example, the teacher wanted to ask, *How* did *a dominant culture grow so numb to seeing such an inhumane spectacle?* But we still *are*. Brutality is not just something that was ignored in the antebellum South. When students are invited to discuss their own numbness to brutal games—and see what they have in common with generations of silent bystanders—the conversation is likely to *mean something* to them. Students can also see *themselves* as both the auctioneers and the enslaved.

There are other thematic approaches to the *Kindred* excerpt. A teacher could ask her students to explore the theme of family—more specifically, the stresses that oppression places on family units. The enslaved children in the excerpt speak about their families being separated. Students could be asked to consider stresses that have been placed on their own family units. They could debate the assertion that an unfair justice system is to blame for the number of single-parent households in low-income minority neighborhoods. Then, perhaps the class could consider possible connections between the historical slave trade and the purported dissolution of the black family. Or perhaps the teacher would rather focus on the protagonist and her husband, as Dana and Kevin's interracial marriage makes it harder for them to support each other. Students could share moments in which they have had trouble communicating empathy across cultural boundaries.

So how do we know which thematic lenses will spark the best conversation? Better question: How well do we know our students? The relationship-building work discussed in Chapter 1 has just as much importance to winning the preacher's dilemma as it does to building safe spaces for our students. Our young scholars are the most important target of our own inquiry. We do not ask them questions only to make them feel important. We also seek to learn their interests, the natural lenses *they* are likely to bring to a text. For example, during the lead-up to the 2016 presidential election, students were interested in Donald Trump's presidential race. Students across the political spectrum recognized that they were coming of age at a potential turning point in the nation's history—and they were eager to explore what that meant. This provided a smorgasbord of themes that held most of my students' interest. The nature of presidential power. Our susceptibility to coded racist language. Voter outrage at the status quo. All of these themes made easy marriages with our school's themes for ninth and tenth grades (Identity, Systems) and the gradewide Essential Questions. They played equally well with the three Essential Questions from my *Kindred* unit plan:

How does environment affect the way we see ourselves or behave?

What affects our sensitivity levels to abuses/words/ideas?

What is the relationship between who we are and society's expectations for us?

When preparing for a discussion about the *Kindred* excerpt, an additional approach could be to reexamine the enslaved children's interaction ("You shut your mouth," said the boy. "You ain't supposed to say nothing. When Marse Tom bought Mama and me, we didn't say nothing.") through the lens of partisan politics. How often are people advised not to express their confusion, frustration, or disillusionment with those in power? Or with any harmful aspect of the status quo? The students could wrestle with writers who have asked why African Americans have retained such unwavering loyalty to the modern Democratic party. Or, the students could debate Martin Luther King Jr.'s assertion at the conclusion of the Selma to Montgomery march that the elite classes intentionally feed racism to poor white people as a substitute for answering their questions about poverty:

> If it may be said of the slavery era that the white man took the world and gave the Negro Jesus, then it may be said of the

> Reconstruction era that the southern aristocracy took the world and gave the poor white man Jim Crow . . . And when his wrinkled stomach cried out for the food that his empty pockets could not provide, he ate Jim Crow, a psychological bird that told him that no matter how bad off he was, at least he was a white man, better than the black man . . . And when his undernourished children cried out for the necessities that his low wages could not provide, he showed them the Jim Crow signs on the buses and in the stores, on the streets and in the public buildings. And his children, too, learned to feed upon Jim Crow, their last outpost of psychological oblivion. (1965)

Taking either track, students will be able to engage their own personal interest in the presidential election. When they go home and watch TV, it will be difficult for them to absorb a campaign commercial without remembering our class discussion. It will seep into their dialogue with peer groups and families. Guiding students to such analytical leaps might even inspire them to make similar leaps when crafting unique projects. To be remembered, a discussion must have such utility.

BEWARE FEBRUARY SOUP

A siloed focus often lies to students about the availability of easy answers. The bad guys are often distant, the victims are always clear, the struggle is mostly superficial, the solutions are glaringly obvious. This approach leads to what I call *February Soup*—a bland, scattered morass that most curricula mistake for sound multicultural education. After twelve years of February Soup conversations, students are apt to think that Martin Luther King freed the slaves with the "I Have a Dream" speech. He was assisted by both Harriet Tubman and Rosa Parks, who ended all segregation when she refused to give up her seat on the bus. Then there are the legendary names whom we've separated from their vibrant stories—Sojourner Truth, W. E. B. Du Bois, Booker T. Washington—all people whom students vaguely recognize as people who did something good way back in what my students too-often call "Racism Times." There are many ways to avoid February Soup, but I'll focus on two: student inquiry and seeking the hard problem.

Use Student Inquiry to Ensure Dynamic Conversational Roles

A few weeks before I drafted this chapter, Dallas, an often-quiet sophomore, approached me after class. She thanked me, explaining that she felt honored that I had taken the past two days to explore a point about gender in *The Book Thief*. A few years prior, another sophomore had noticed that the relationship between the text's preteen protagonist, Liesel, and Max, a Jewish refugee ten years her senior, appeared quasiromantic. This, to me, was ridiculous, but I put it out to the students. Nearly half of my students agreed! Since that moment, I've brought it up whenever we reach that part of the book. This year, during this conversation, Dallas expressed frustration over my discussion prompt. According to Dallas, we were questioning the relationship only because Liesel is a girl and our American society is overly eager to sexualize young girls. This struck me as profound, so the next day I tabled my planned thread (the ethics of violent resistance) to debate Dallas's thesis. We tried to find examples of hypersexualized younger girls in media, from Juliet Capulet to Princess Jasmine. I took the same track with my other sophomore class, owning that we were taking a detour inspired by one of their fellow students.

For those two days, Dallas was cast in the unfamiliar role of lead scholar. It was an unexpected abdication of her teacher's power to choose our conversational focus. This was her reason for gratitude. It was one thing for her to be included in classwide general compliments: "You are all so smart!" "I appreciate the way you all are wrestling with this idea!" and so on. It was another thing to have one's thesis singled out, praised, and lifted up for deep analysis *by* the teacher, *for* the community. On the surface, this might seem like the *student empowerment* that people seek from dialogic instruction. That phrase, however, is grossly misleading. We do not give our students power. They have it—and have been using it for as long as they've been holding conversations. Generations of classroom cultures have been pruning their power, developing their power, and (both consciously and unconsciously) *suppressing* their power. Student power is an active thing, turned back on in the hallways after leaving our classrooms—and behind our backs on the cell phones that we ban.

Students should be encouraged to let private inquiries drive them to new roles in the classroom. The varying conversational packages help this because smaller groups allow students to design their own discourse as a teacher might during whole class. The responsibilities of a *planning* role encourage students to engage areas of their brains responsible for anticipation and empathy. Students are no longer merely communicating their responses to a teacher; they now must organize a line of inquiry that might spark their classmates' deliberations. When a teacher has modeled a *threaded* approach to discussing race issues, he or she models a particular kind of scholarship for students, one that they will mimic when taking on their own discussion-planning roles. This process makes ideas more likely to occupy their own space in students' minds, and not be blended casually into February Soup.

Seek the Hard Problem to Inspire Unpredictable Exchanges

Every dialogic teacher has felt the sting of a "wasted" conversation. To us, the text is exhilarating, while our students find it underwhelming. Why are their souls not stirred when they hear Frederick Douglass's oratory? How do they not appreciate Thurgood Marshall's brilliance or Medgar Evers's bravery? We grow even more exasperated when our students appear bored during discussions about *right now* issues: trickle-down economics, the prison complex, or even the inequities found in the very same school system that is currently underfunding their education. Reflecting on this, we often come to one of two conclusions:

1. *Something is wrong with these kids. If only they were not so distracted by their technology. If only their previous school/teacher had prepared them. If only they were more curious, more intelligent, more disciplined, they would recognize the importance of this race discussion.*

2. *We do not speak their language. Perhaps our age, our economic class, or our own cultural upbringing has made it more difficult to*

effectively communicate a particular race conversation's relevance to our students' lives.

Neither of these conclusions is automatically wrong. The first (minus its dismissive tone) acknowledges the reality of our kids' attention spans, the occasional harm done by prior education, their still-developing scholarly habits, even their natural aptitude and processing ability. The second may very well be true, especially in circumstances where the students are considerably younger, or from a vastly different cultural background. Still, both conclusions often lead to stagnation—because we let this deficit model limit our imagination and resilience. The battle against distractions will always be there, and despite our best efforts to stay cool, every year widens the gap between our students' cultures and our own.

Honest reflection might take us to an uncomfortable third conclusion: The failed race conversation was boring because we underestimated our students' intelligence. Since we did not openly challenge students to tackle any *hard problems*, they chose not to invest much analytical and emotional energy in the dialogue. Students feel they can safely allocate most of their attention elsewhere without missing much, operating in what appears to us a "low-power mode." From a student's perspective, the teacher seems to be spending a lot of energy proving that $2 + 2 = 4$ and is unfairly expecting his students to be moved by such a conclusion.

Again, we should remember Du Bois, and avoid making *all* of our race conversations about race problems. But when we do decide to go there, let's not tarry long in the simple stuff on the way to finding a hard problem. For example, after reading Wil Haygood's *Showdown* (2016), we teachers might be fascinated enough by the life of Thurgood Marshall to offer our students a series of discussion prompts about the first African American Supreme Court justice. Instinctively, we might focus on the obstacles that Marshall had to overcome during his confirmation hearings. The approach of notorious racist senator Strom Thurmond toward Marshall might provide a good launching point, since Thurmond pulled out nearly every trick in a segregationist playbook to make Marshall look like a fool. Haygood describes an example:

> THURMOND: Do you know who drafted the 13th amendment to the U.S. Constitution?
>
> The Young Turks—[Ted] Kennedy, Tydings, Hart—could not believe it. Such a question was eerily reminiscent of the questions southern voting registrars had been asking blacks for decades: How many marbles in this jar? How many judges are in the state of Mississippi? How many dots on the state map of Georgia? [Black prospective voters] were, of course, turned away when they couldn't provide the answers. (247)

According to the transcript, Strom Thurmond did not let up with the vagaries, offering up the following gibberish as a question:

> THURMOND: Do you agree with an article by Prof. Alfred Avins in the Cornell Law Quarterly of 1964 that the provision against involuntary servitude in the 13th amendment prevents either Federal or State legislation which requires any person to render personal services to any other private person, whether the refusal to render such services is motivated by racial or religious discrimination or for any other reason, and if you do not agree with this view, why do you think that the provision against involuntary servitude does not forbid legislation requiring personal services? (248)

Seeing this, we might feel inspired to have our students examine the history of Jim Crow voting laws. They could comb through a list of bizarre and impossible questions asked of black people who desired to vote in the South. They could watch the opening of the 2014 movie *Selma*, where an African American woman is turned away at the registrar's office. Since this is still living history, it might be possible to find an elder willing to share her experiences. After considering these sources, students might compare Jim Crow practices with the debate over modern voter ID laws. Is the Left being hyperbolic in the comparison? Are the laws evidence of the Right's obsession with voter suppression? This is a debate that our students can easily access, combing the Internet for speeches and interviews from politicians on both sides of the issue. These opinions can be evaluated, sided with, or argued against, and it all would be a valuable time.

Yet, the Marshall hearings illustrate a much more intractable hard problem, one that could inspire a considerably more interesting conversation: *How should Marshall, or anyone else in such a situation, respond to Thurmond-esque bigotry? When facing a powerful racial majority who can either allow or retard a well-deserved advancement depending mostly on whether a minority keeps their cool—should minorities "keep it real" by speaking up?* There seem to be two approaches. The first could be called the Jackie Robinson approach, named after the famous temper-suppressing challenge given to Robinson by Dodgers manager Branch Rickey, as quoted in the 2013 movie *42*:

> **Rickey:** I know you're a good ballplayer. What I don't know is whether you have the guts.
>
> **Robinson:** Mr. Rickey, are you looking for a Negro who is afraid to fight back?
>
> **Rickey:** Robinson, I'm looking for a ballplayer with guts enough not to fight back.

This approach expands a traditionally understood meaning of "guts." Robinson's contemporaries seem to agree that he had a relatively short fuse, yet he could not afford to explode when facing verbal abuse, death threats, opponents spiking him, or an opposing team's fans releasing black cats onto the field to mock his efforts. His bravery would have to be the show-the-other-cheek variety, the symbolic sort that separates the February Pantheon (Robinson, Martin Luther King Jr., Rosa Parks) from February's Forgotten (Marcus Garvey, Huey Newton). After reading another excerpt from Haygood's book, our students would realize that Thurgood Marshall, like Jackie Robinson, was unquestionably brave by all measures symbolic or otherwise. His multiple trips South, first to research the conditions of segregated schools, and then to litigate civil rights cases before hostile juries, nearly cost him his life. No amount of Strom Thurmond patronization could be as threatening as the time Marshall was nearly lynched by a police-assisted Tennessee posse:

> "We have got to arrest you for drunken driving," one of the men said to Marshall, who quickly protested that he had not been drinking. Nevertheless, he was arrested and placed inside a sheriff's car with four armed men. Marshall's cohorts were told to drive on to Nashville. Looby, Weaver, and Raymond stood in shock as the car with Marshall inside vanished. When they saw it turn off the main road onto a side road, they gave pursuit: they imagined Thurgood Marshall was going to be lynched. The brazen pursuit seems to have startled the law officers, because they finally turned around from the darkened road and took Marshall to Columbia.
>
> In Columbia, standing on a dark street across from the police station, Marshall was told to proceed to the station—alone. He knew better: a bullet to the back, a charge of trying to escape. "I told them that if we went over there we were all going over there together . . ." The magistrate administered a breath test and announced that Marshall was not drunk. He was released. (2016, 72–73)

After thirty-seven years of braving this kind of treatment, it must have been infuriating to be questioned by a small man like Strom Thurmond. And yet, like Robinson, Marshall felt as if the only way to reach the big dream was to retain an outward calm, a show of dignity. Nowhere in his responses did he voice his frustration or vent his anger, something that our students might find interesting when compared with the second possible approach: keeping it real.

This is the approach that eschews respectability politics, that calls bullies "bullies" with little care for how the words are being perceived. In its modern iteration, this approach is quick to call out microaggressions and is impatient with excuses. In the face of outright bigotry, this approach does not praise stillness, suppression of emotion, or silence. Had Marshall taken this approach, he would have pointed out to Thurmond how much his questions replicated Jim Crow foolishness. Had Robinson taken this approach, he would have walked over to Phillies manager Ben Chapman and told him to stop calling him a nigger. Had President Obama taken this approach, he would have publicly called Donald Trump's requests for his birth certificate racist. The consequences of all three of these responses would likely have been devastating; Marshall would not have been confirmed, Robinson would have been removed from major league baseball, and the media would apply Obama's declaration of racism to a broad swath of the electorate, turning it quickly into something the president would have had to apologize for before being able to move forward. But didn't Frederick Douglass follow this approach? Malcolm X? The Black Panthers? Black Lives Matter? Surely *someone* needs to ruffle feathers at whatever the cost.

Prompts such as these settle us in to the hard problem: What is the right approach? What makes it vary? Here, students can share what they have been taught about holding their tongues—and whether they plan to pass these values along to their children. A teacher can create endless thought experiments to be discussed—and so can students. Here's a sample student offering: *You are an ambitious minority lawyer at a law firm, and you are invited to a holiday party. Late in the evening, when everyone is a bit tipsy, your boss tells a joke that you consider racially insensitive. Everyone laughs. Noticing that you haven't joined them, the boss teases you, asking you to lighten up. If you check him publicly on his joke, he might be annoyed with you. And others might resent your changing the room's vibe. You don't feel like you have the relationship to talk to him privately. And if you say nothing, you feel like you condoned the behavior. What do you do?*

In another example, a teacher who works at an underfunded public school might want his ninth graders to consider the deleterious effect of inadequate school funding. When doing so in my school, I've shown my students interactive maps that show how much more neighboring school districts spend per student than Philadelphia's. Hooked, students might wonder who decided their education was worth thousands less. These questions give me an opportunity to explain how public school funding works—the collaboration between federal, state, and local governments that high school students are usually unaware of. Getting to what I consider the conversation's big moment, I've asked why Pennsylvania (as of this writing) ranks forty-fifth in the nation in the percentage of state funding spent on public education. I expect students to be outraged.

But what if they aren't?

Caught off guard, I might be tempted to add some racial and class dynamics. As of this writing, the website for the Philadelphia School District (https://www.philasd.org/) reports that in 2016, our public schools were 51 percent black, 19.5 percent Latino, 8 percent Asian, and only 13.78 percent white, whereas, during the same year, according to nearby Lower Merion's website (https://www.lmsd.org/), 9.8 percent of the students were Asian, 7.4 percent were black, 3.6 percent were Hispanic, and 73.6 percent were white. I might give them these statistics. In addition, I might say, the School District of Philadelphia has so many economically disadvantaged students that, as of 2014, it offered all of its students free lunch, as part of the Department of Agriculture's Community Eligibility Provision. According to Lower Merion's website, only 8.2 percent of students qualify for free lunch. Surely Philly kids deserve to have as much spent on their education, I pose.

The students would shrug. *Yes, that all seems unfair.*

I would become exasperated. In Hollywood, this moment would be climactic—swelling music, tears, urban students promising to start fighting for what they deserve. In my real-life classroom, kids are shrugging. To them, there aren't any surprises. In the best-case scenario, a few high-commitment students might engage with the idea. They might reflect on being asked each year to bring in a ream of copy paper as a "school supply" and how students in other districts probably aren't being asked to do the same. They might even ask me if there isn't a more equitable way than local property taxes to fund their education. But if my endgame is simply for my students to realize inequity, I am operating short of my students' potential. I have not presented the hard problem: Why should families with more money support the education of less-affluent strangers?

Years ago, colleague Pearl Jonas and I led this conversation with her ninth-grade African American History class. After the general facts were presented, we launched into an impromptu role-play where I portrayed an affluent parent from a suburban district. After hearing our students half-heartedly complain about the inequality, I stood up and said, "Hey look, I already pay thousands of dollars in property taxes to send my kid to the best schools in the state. Why should I have to pay for *your* education too?"

The students were shocked.

I doubled down. "Seriously, how is any of this my problem? If *your* schools suck, you all should get together and fix them."

As we had not properly oriented them to the role-play, I had to pause to make sure every student knew that I was playing a character in an academic thought experiment. This is important, because my statements could easily be read as ugly personal assessments of their worth. With this in mind, I admitted to our students that I didn't agree with what I was about to say. But we also reasoned that if they did not know how to articulate what they wanted, there was no way they would be able to fight for it when the time came. "So," I continued, sliding back into character, "how is your education my problem?"

More than a few students jumped enthusiastically to argue with my character. They started off by asserting that "poor minority kids need a good education too." I agreed, but countered that it wasn't my concern. A boy then asked, "How would you feel if you had to go to school with no supplies or no technology? At some of our schools they don't have toilet paper!" His classmates exploded, seconding his plea for empathy.

I shrugged. "But my kids do."

At this point one of them said, "Your character is a jerk." I challenged her to think about why I was a jerk. Was I racist? What if I were black? Black people live in Lower Merion, too. As far as this character was concerned, these Philadelphia students—regardless of their races—were trying to put their hands in my pockets. If they wanted me to ask my elected representative to push for a "fair funding formula," they owed me an explanation. At this point, I invited them to "pod up" and discuss strategies for winning me over. During the ensuing conversation, Pearl and I overheard kids taking on my antagonistic role, using it as a whetstone to sharpen each other's arguments. They came back at me with confidence.

"Mr. Kay, it's in your best interest to support us. When we grow up, we will be participating in the economy. You want us to have good jobs and pay more taxes to support society." Another pod added, "One of us could be the next president." Another, "Your children will have to interact with us eventually, and you don't want us to be stupid."

To honor their passion, I responded in kind. Pearl and I sensed that her students would feel disrespected if their antagonist offered an easy victory. "I'm going to be real with you," I said. "Lower Merion kids and Philly public school kids live in different worlds." Anticipating their responses, I added, "Not all Philly kids; I'm talking about your friends who attend comprehensive schools. Edison. Strawberry Mansion. Martin Luther King. Schools where 100 percent of the kids are economically disadvantaged. Do you really think that the average kid from Lower Merion will end up ever working alongside the average kid from Edison?" When they were silent, I added, "So that track will probably not work with me. Even if it did get you in the door, how long before I start looking at you all as *competition* for my kid?"

As the class period wound down, our ninth graders grew increasingly interested in learning how to effectively challenge my character. They were intrigued by the hard problem, the same one that their grown-up advocates are currently struggling with: *How can people be persuaded to invest in a stranger's children?* They asked us, "What do we need to say to you? What would convince you?" Leaving the character behind, I admitted that I didn't know. I told them that a lot of very smart people are just as stumped as they are—and that this conversation was essentially the current dispute in Pennsylvania's state assembly. Students would not be getting any easy solutions before the end of the class period, because frankly, they were too smart for easy answers. But the next few classes would provide the historical context, some more debate prep, and perhaps soon we could try it again.

When teachers move quickly to the hard problem, we don't just make it harder for our race conversations to be consigned to February Soup; we also mark certain race conversations as *worth remembering*. Think about it: Before reading this text, you have probably watched cable TV pundits debating race issues on a split screen. The host moderated the discourse with a signature level of either cynicism or stoicism. Both of the guests worked themselves into a fit of passion—it was *very* important that you, the audience, internalized what they said. Did you? How many of those conversations do you, an educator and lover of ideas, even remember? It is not as if they weren't discussing important things: Trayvon Martin, Sandra Bland, Eric Garner, the riots in Los Angeles or Baltimore, the protests in Ferguson. These discussions are about the intersection of race, power, life, death, and justice. And you might have watched for hours. What did they discuss? Some of your inability to recall particulars might have to do with natural inattention, but I would argue that most of it didn't stick because the conversation was predictable and rudimentary. Conservative and progressive lines were drawn; both sides launched familiar insubstantial bombs and went home. As fiery as the conversation grew, nobody expected the audience to remember it.

In contrast, Pearl's choice to discuss inequities in school funding was meant to be remembered. Her students must understand their own educations as a *political* issue, for to most adults, they are someone else's children and, as such, merely a political dilemma to be solved (or ignored). This particular race conversation was too important to be blended into February Soup.

THE PREACHER'S DILEMMA, PART 2

We dialogic teachers often assume that our students will internalize eureka realizations just because we have chosen to teach through discussion over lecture. We forget that even the most organically grown ideas want to be forgotten, that our students' minds have six more classes and a social life to contend with. The preacher's dilemma isn't just the struggle to make important issues feel relevant; it's the challenge to store the fruits of such conversations to last through a storm of distractions. I am reminded of an old minister who kept delivering similar sermons on gossip week after week until a brave congregant asked, "Why do you keep talking about gossip?" The minister responded, "I've been watching you. When you stop gossiping, I'll preach something else." The congregant smiled wryly and walked away, appreciating that his preacher did more than meditate on holy words. The old man apparently cared about securing their permanence.

Classrooms, like enthusiastic congregations, often show the *symptoms* of learning without much lasting absorption of ideas. Race conversations that teachers considered memorable may just have been energetic; what sounded like healthy disequilibrium may actually just have been confusion. We can't know the difference unless we are humble enough to check. Our dialogue often asks young people to explore, test, or even dismantle strongly held cultural values—a heavy lift for most students, a trauma for a few. A classroom culture of thoughtless or scant reflection disrespects this student commitment. They open up emotionally with the expectation that their stories will be appreciated. The more a dialogic teacher delays purposeful reflection, the more his or her planned conversational threads begin to fray. Students begin to see each conversation as its own self-contained story arc, which makes it easier for them to check out of Monday, knowing that Tuesday and Wednesday won't necessarily build on it.

Grant Wiggins and Jay McTighe offer a useful framework in *Understanding by Design* (2005) that they call the "Six Facets of Understanding." When we reflect on our discussion planning and execution, each of the facets can nudge us closer to consistent success:

Explanation:

Students should be able to articulate any theories that were discussed, any causalities that were proven, any systems that were deconstructed.

Interpretation:

Students should be able to engage in thoughtful exegesis of given quotes/ideas culled from a conversation. In doing so, they should be able to effectively create metaphors, stories, and analogies.

Application:

Students should be able to use whatever concepts were introduced during the conversation to create new artifacts of learning.

Perspective:

Students should be able to recognize multiple points of view in a conversation. They should understand how their perspective intersects with their teacher's, their classmates', or those present in the text.

Empathy:

Students should be able to project themselves into someone else's experience, ideally in an effort to understand their feelings and motivations.

Self-Knowledge:

Students should recognize their own biases, values, and thought processes.

Just as we should commit to varying conversational packages, we should also build a reliable and diverse collection of reflection activities to test Wiggin and McTighe's six facets. My undergrad professors were excited about "exit tickets," little pieces of writing that our students would submit on the way out of the room, explaining what they had learned from the lesson. We were also introduced to the "Do Now"/ "Warm-Up" exercises which, in addition to being an anticipatory set, could easily show what the students remember from the previous day. Both of these staples are easily applicable to a dialogic classroom. Yet we can do much more to see how much our students remember. The options, in fact, are limited only by our imaginations.

However, to make the most use of this freedom, I offer the following suggestions:

1. Every student should have a dedicated repository in which to gather their thoughts both during and after discussions. A notebook (separate from the personal journal) or a Google Doc will do just fine.

2. Students should show that they are listening actively by gathering key classmate quotes from conversations. I like to find an especially alert and quick note taker to jot their classmates' quotes on the board, just so that everyone has something to write down. These quotes, like minutes from a business meeting, can be shared, edited, and reflected on if need be.

3. We teachers should openly share some of our own discussion reflections. To model process thinking (and humility), we should tell our students how we think some conversations went, what we remember, what we would change, etc.

My conversational package is aided by all three of these suggestions. First, because I consider it critical that my students see conversational threads stretch from day to day, I often start discussions with a two-prompt warm-up. The first prompt is a written reflection on the previous day's conversation, and the next serves as orientation for today's. My students write silently on one discussion prompt at a time, normally not responding to the second until everyone seems to be wrapping up the first. These warm-ups are periodically collected and perused, the only grade being on completion and thoughtfulness. This allows me to assess the aforementioned application and self-knowledge facets. Second, at the end of a conversation, I ask students some version of *What do you think you will remember?* or *What questions do you still have?* or *Share something that a colleague said that impressed you.* This is normally done in whole-class format because I don't want students to feel like they missed something. There are many digital options here. Course management systems like Moodle, Blackboard, Schoology, and Canvas provide online discussion forums where students can reflect together. I like to post juicy (or overlooked) student quotes and ask the class community to reflect on them. Students can also be provided with a list of their colleagues' quotes and choose which to comment on.

Finally, as an English language arts teacher, I use projects themselves as reflective pieces. Students always create their own theses to prove, even first-semester ninth graders who have just learned what a thesis is. We track the main themes of every big conversation on the front board, and these stay up there until final essays are submitted. Students use this list to inspire their original theses. They have the aforementioned collection of colleague quotes to cite when proving their theses, and I teach them that conclusion paragraphs should explain a contribution that their thesis (and, by extension, the class dialogue) has made to scholarship on the issue. I openly tell them that this is how books end up being written. They, of course, like this a lot.

Discussion reflection also guides my students' creative writing. The rubric of every genre, from plays to memoirs to graphic novels, has a category that assesses the student's engagement of the particular unit's Essential Questions, which are *always* bound by a weekslong conversational thread. So, for example, I might ask Pearl's students to write memoir vignettes that try to expose how they've been impacted by inequitable school funding. Or they could write a play that replicates a passionate state assembly debate on the same topic. In either project students would have to not only cite the assigned text, but also reflect clearly on their class's wrestling with the hard problem.

When we ask students to engage hard problems, we respect them as scholars. Not only do we show them that youth have much to contribute, but we recognize that they will not be youth forever. Soon they will be our peers, and many will be fighting for justice in many of the same adult arenas. If, in our conversations, we are preoccupied with the shedding of predictable light, our students will be that much less equipped to handle fire when the moment comes.

Professional Practice

In closing Chapter 1, I mention that the safety of classroom spaces often directly mirrors the safety that teachers feel in their own meeting rooms and staff lounges. It is the same with conversational structures: The more static our professional development, the harder teachers have to work to find inspiration for diversifying conversational packages. If much of our PD time is spent in the adult version of whole class, as is usually the case, we are more likely to pick one structure (usually also whole class) and stick with it exclusively in our classrooms. And just like teachers, administrators often float new initiatives and conversational structures for a limited period of time before regressing to the mean.

Let's mix it up. For instance, some schools divide their teaching staffs into five- to six-person professional learning communities, which, if used imaginatively, could operate like Olympia Academies. Keep them small, informal, experiment oriented. Other schools create mentor-mentee pairings of veteran and rookie teachers. We benefit just as much from one-on-one conversation as our students do—veterans just as much as the new folks. Our conversations about school controversies should be deliberative, paired with consensus-driven decision making, if possible. Finally, just as threading conversations works to seal them into our students' minds, so too should teachers deeply explore one or two meaningful topics from multiple angles throughout the school year. It's even better if the consistent focus is one or two hard problems that impact the school community—such as reimagining the school's approach to discipline or encouraging more community involvement.

CHAPTER 4

ESTABLISHING YOUR PURPOSE

Like many teachers across America, I was nervous about opening the 2014–2015 school year. Over the previous summer, Black Lives Matter protests had erupted nationwide, images of which were still flooding my social media feed. I knew that many of my returning students would be coming into school hurt and confused. Some, as I'd seen on Facebook, were ready for a brawl—if they could only find someone with contrasting ideas to scrap with. Most were heavily anticipating a St. Louis County grand jury's decision of whether to indict Officer Darren Wilson for shooting an unarmed black eighteen-year-old, Michael Brown, in Ferguson, Missouri. Our school gathered for our first staff meeting with something less than our usual enthusiasm. We knew that Science Leadership Academy's ethic of care encouraged students to feel safe sharing their opinions. And we knew our students would have already aimed their dogged school-developed inquiry skills toward what was happening in Ferguson. Our routinized Getting-to-Know-You / How-Was-Your-Summer conversations were about to get a little trickier.

So, to set up our professional development, the staff watched a segment of Jon Stewart's *Daily Show*. This particular piece, entitled "Race/Off," had debuted to much acclaim on August 26, 2014. I love *The Daily Show's* genre-inspiring political faux-reporting, so I anticipated a terrific orientation for whatever was planned. The bit opened with Stewart making fun of the stern appearance of riot-gear-clad Ferguson police who "seem to be auditioning for *RoboCop*." He spent the next nine minutes panning his favorite foils, the commentators at the Fox News network. In response to a clip of Lou Dobbs asking a guest, "Why aren't we [the press] covering New York? Why aren't we covering black-on-black crime?" he quipped, "Yes! Why all the interest in holding *police officers* to a higher standard than *gangs*? They both flash colors . . . and yes, one of them has been sworn to protect and defend, but still . . ." Big laugh from the studio audience.

A few minutes later, Stewart narrowed his focus to attacking the Fox News hosts' incomprehension of America's racial inequities. He ran a clip of commentator Sean Hannity explaining what *he* does when he gets pulled over by the police. "I put my hands outside of the car. If I'm carrying a weapon, which I'm licensed to carry in New York, the first thing I tell the police officer is 'Officer, I want you to know I have a legal firearm in the car.'"

Stewart cut in, mocking Hannity's voice, "*Then* I brace myself for the Taser." Big laugh from the studio audience.

Hannity's clip continued, "I often would even . . . step out of the car, lift my shirt up so he can see where the gun is." Stewart's audience tittered with anticipation of the host's well-timed reply, which didn't disappoint.

"You really do have no f------ idea, do you?" As his audience exploded, Stewart rubbed his fingers into his temples in exasperation. "Basically you're saying that 'If only Michael Brown had, instead of holding his hands over his head, had reached down to his waist . . . and lifted up his shirt . . . to show the gun he did *not* actually have, this whole tragedy could have been avoided.'" Then Stewart proffered the segment's thesis: "Do you *not* understand that life in this country is inherently different for white people than black people?"

He continued by arguing that the real race conversation in this country should be "about how people of color, no matter their socioeconomic standing, face obstacles in this country with surprising grace." After a juxtaposition montage of Fox News's "War on Christmas" clips, Stewart challenged his studio audience with a thought experiment. "Now imagine that instead of having to suffer the indignity of a Festivus pole blocking [a Nativity scene] that you could have just set up in your own yard anyway . . . instead of that, on a pretty consistent basis, you can't get a f------ cab! . . . even though you're a neurosurgeon, 'cause you're *black*." Applause. "I guarantee you that every person of color in this country has faced an indignity, from the ridiculous, to the grotesque, to the sometimes fatal, at some point in the past couple of . . . *hours*."

After muted applause, Stewart ended the segment with a story. "We live in New York City, a liberal bastion. Recently we sent a correspondent and producer to a building in this liberal bastion where we were going to tape an interview. The producer—white—dressed in what could only be described as 'homeless elf attire,' strode confidently into the building, proceeding [sic] our humble correspondent—a gentleman of color—dressed resplendently in a tailored suit. Who do you think was stopped? Let me give you a hint: the black guy." Titters from the audience. Stewart finished the segment with a flourish. "And that s--- happens all the time. All of it. Race is there, and it is a constant. You're tired of *hearing* about it? Imagine how f------ exhausting it is *living* it."

As the lights in the room clicked back on, I was floored by an unexpected wave of annoyance. It was a specific pique, muted in nature, something that can be felt only by a minority person in a room of allies. As the staff was asked for our thoughts on the video, I fought a studentlike desire to leave the classroom, to take an extended bathroom break, to slip an earbud into my ear and play some music. I had never, in eight years at the school, wanted so much to escape a conversation. The *Daily Show* orientation had dredged up some visceral frustrations that I, frankly, had tamped down in order to stay "professional" alongside a staff of mostly white people. It wasn't just that, as a teen, I had been regularly stopped by the police. That particular indignity had long since passed into the realm of funny stories shared in the community of other black people—like tales about epic spankings from your momma. It wasn't just Stewart's unfortunate integration of respectability politics—as if neurosurgeons and people dressed "resplendently" in tailored suits were somehow less worthy of being harassed than teenagers wearing hoodies. It wasn't even the flippant assumption that every person of color had faced injustice in the past couple of *hours*.

My irritation had been triggered by Stewart's final challenge to "imagine" how exhausting it is to be black in America. To that, I'd mumbled under my breath, "You have no idea." Then, as our staff launched into reflections, I continued my snarky internal monologue. *Thank you, Mr. All-Seeing White Man, for reminding me that being black in America sucks. I just can't wait to have another conversation about it.* In retrospect, this was my impatience with Stewart's *light*, when everything in me wanted to start a *fire*. Specifically, I was annoyed by his ending the monologue about injustice with the conclusion that persecution is exhausting—without a transition to finding solutions. I wanted to flee the professional development meeting because watching *The Daily Show* had felt like participating in the previous chapter's Privilege Walk activity. I was the one continually stepping out, which was cool only if the endgame somehow involved showing me how to make things better. I did not respect Stewart's *purpose*—which I found inadequate—and as a result, I was hesitant to throw my full energy into the following race conversation about how our school would handle our students' reactions, feelings, and questions about the summer's events.

Chapter 1 focuses on building a classroom environment that is ready to engage in "house talk." Chapter 2 examines how we can develop the interpersonal skills necessary to have meaningful conversations about race. In Chapter 3, we looked at conversational structures, threaded curriculum design, and tips for avoiding February Soup. Now we have arrived at our most multifaceted challenge: working alongside our students to ensure that our race conversations always have clearly recognized—and respectable—*purposes*.

OWNING OUR PERSONAL CATALYSTS

While chaperoning a cross-country trip to the Grand Canyon, I met a wonderful history teacher named Cody Canning. During one of our conversations, he said, almost as an afterthought, "Teaching is a lifestyle, not a career." As I am a basketball coach, Sunday school teacher, and head of a youth-centered nonprofit, we chuckled at how much his comment seemed to validate my life's choices. After all, during the school year, I can be found teaching someone, somewhere, each of the seven days in a week. But Canning's statement subtly pointed out a clear spiritual benefit of our profession: that we, as teachers, know our sphere of influence. Our students. We read new books with them in mind. When our research hands us hard problems, we know that we don't have to wrestle with them by ourselves. Most importantly, we recognize our power and know where we can use it.

When teachers become aware of a particular social injustice, we might think, *I've got to do something about that!* Then, seconds later, *I'll teach my students about it!* From there, we launch right into designing a unit, a lesson, a threaded series of conversations. We never have to feel impotent—not when we remember our capacity to pull back life's curtains and inspire the next generation. In short, teachers can always plug into a greater mission. Not all careers offer this satisfaction.

However, this same privilege can make our students feel like repositories for their teachers' pain, confusion, or guilt. When hard problems are placed at their feet, they are often unsure where *they* can plug into a mission. A teenager who does not vote, has little money, and considers himself confined to the spaces that adult society has prepared for him might have much more trouble locating his sphere of influence. In such a situation, students are apt to question their teacher's *purpose* for even starting the race conversation.

Which seems like a good place to start.

It's important to acknowledge the baggage that we teachers bring to discussing race. There's our ethnicity, which either fits easily into our nation's questionable habit of categorizing people by color or doesn't. We were raised rich, middle class, or poor; conservative or liberal; secular or religious. We have our individual genders and sexualities. When asked what the universe needs to change, we can list our own hierarchy of concerns. We became teachers to either buck or continue a tradition. All of this (and so much more) colors our language, our responses to conflict, and our expectations for both individual and whole-class interactions. We can never be too aware of the things we carry, and we can never be too curious about our students' cargo. Teachers lug this baggage into race conversations that, in addition, are often inspired by unrealized or unexpressed goals. None of these personal catalysts are inherently harmful, and every race conversation is differently sparked. Yet, we might all recognize the following:

We Have the Race Conversation to Assuage Our Guilt.

A teacher's human empathy sometimes mixes with keen recognition of his privilege, which generates guilt. Whether it is the often-discussed white guilt or remorse over financial advantage, teachers can often lead race conversations in the heavy spirit of a mea culpa. A novel (like *Kindred*) about the antebellum South might trigger a teacher's regret for knowing little about modern-day slavery. A history of Gandhi's approach to nonviolence might trigger a teacher's shame for not sufficiently owning the benefits of colonialism. After a night of staring slack-jawed at the news, a teacher might feel the need to apologize for all the bad guys who look just like him.

We Have the Conversation to Be Cool.

A teacher recognizes that few of her colleagues are "talking race." In this, she sees an opportunity to forge a unique persona. She embraces the natural edginess of race conversations, the debates, the chances to dabble in the students' slang. She gets to finally use her knowledge of hip-hop. Race conversations let *cool teachers* orient with Chris Rock and Kevin Hart, with videos like the aforementioned *Daily Show* segment. Sometimes the students are entertained, sometimes they are moved to tears—regardless, they are in constant awe of the teacher's gutsy planning and iconoclastic delivery. Think Mr. Keating.

We Have the Conversation to Point Out the Elephant in the Room.

A teacher realizes that the classroom, at this particular moment, feels like an island. The real world is happening out there, with its passionate protests and magnetic rallies, while students are working through subject-verb agreement. The teacher can see students glancing at each other, restless and unsure whether *this* classroom is the place to share *that* emotion. Wanting their education to feel relevant, the teacher offers students the chance to discuss their feelings about whatever is happening Out There. The conversation is not necessarily related to the curriculum, but in this student-centered classroom, this seems unimportant. Connections can be made later, if at all.

We Have the Conversation for the Status That Comes with Raising an Army.

A teacher proudly identifies as an educator for social justice. He has read the right books and attends the right rallies. He teaches with a clearly identifiable hierarchy of concerns, the top of which might be racial inequity. When choosing his conversations' primary texts and supplementary sources, he leans as far from Eurocentrism as possible. By the end of each chat, students are closer to joining him in the movement.

We Have the Conversation Because We Just Like Talking to Them.

After hearing about the latest issue, or reading the latest book, blog, or article, a teacher can't wait to share it with her students. This teacher realizes that young people have a way of cutting quickly to the fairness of an issue, and that the energy and imagination of adolescence can lead to exceptional dialogue. Adults are jaded, overconfident in what they know; teens are pliant in the face of new ideas, unsurprised by their ignorance, and surprisingly trusting of teachers to remedy it. This all makes a classroom a wonderfully satisfying place for a teacher to unpack and process events.

None of these catalysts should cause shame. I have been, and will continue to be, moved by all five—especially the third (pointing at the elephant) and last (I just like chatting with students). All five have clear benefits and disadvantages. Guilt, when matured by reflection, can inspire a teacher to approach a sensitive subject with humility. However, we know that it also can lead to a destabilizing timidity in the face of kids' questions. There is nothing wrong with wanting to be cool. Contrary to the *Don't smile till December* orthodoxy, a teacher is allowed to value being liked by the kids. Charismatic leadership is no less legitimate than being autocratic or democratic. Yet, while it doesn't hurt to give students a flag to follow, the desire to be cool can easily trick teachers into forgetting (or willfully ignoring) where they are leading students. Kudos should be given to teachers who even *see* a racial elephant in the room, since most of us, most of the time, have little idea what is going on in our students' peer-to-peer conversations. Connecting meaningfully to a clear curriculum, however, is what grants lasting scholarly validity to our discussions. Those of us seeking to raise armies can proudly link ourselves to the heroes of the Mississippi Freedom Schools, or those who trained Student Nonviolent Coordinating Committee (SNCC) teen volunteers to sit bravely at segregated lunch counters. However, this focus can alienate students who do not share a teacher's political views or, worse, can lead to the oversimplified good/bad, win/lose dichotomies mentioned in previous chapters. And finally, nothing is wrong with loving to speak to the kids! When we stop valuing their opinions, we might be ready for a new profession. Yet, *they are not our racial therapists*, and they do not have to help us "unpack" anything. We must not forget who ultimately works for whom.

We must begin our discussion planning with honest reflection on our personal catalysts for two reasons. First, they are usually glaringly obvious to our students. Remember our teenage years, when we were well aware of the teacher who "thought he was cool," or the one who was clearly driven to touchiness by feelings of inadequacy? Those conclusions may have not much affected our willingness to participate in conversations, but they colored how we received the teacher's statements and practices. Second, and more important, our personal catalysts can push race conversations to the satisfaction of *our* needs, with less attention to showing kids the power of their voices.

PROPOSITIONS THAT ENSURE PURPOSE

We are at our dialogic best not only when most of our students are aware of *why* they are having a race conversation, but when they consider the conversation's purpose worthy of their committed energy and sacrifices. This starts with a reliable safe space, continues with a culture of threaded conversations, and is solidified by a teacher's careful attention to the following propositions:

Proposition 1: If the race conversation is about a hard problem, provide space and time for students to (1) locate their sphere of influence, and (2) explore personal pathways to solutions.

Proposition 2: Design race conversations that encourage students to follow *new* lines of inquiry.

Proposition 3: Students should be encouraged to "publish" whenever they feel ready. This opportunity must be built in to the culture of the classroom.

With each, I provide a sample discussion showing the proposition in action. Any of these sample discussions could branch into many reasonable directions, depending on students' comments and the activities that constitute a teacher's conversational package. Please read them with such flexibility in mind.

Help Students Locate Their Sphere of Influence and Find Solutions.

Proposition 1: If the race conversation is about a hard problem, encourage students to (1) locate their sphere of influence, and (2) explore personal pathways to solutions. If, as argued in the previous chapter, our students deserve to consider the hard problems, they must also be invited to solve them. This balance reminds them of their agency. Without it, the discussion of race controversies is likely to make students feel a bit like punching bags, peppered by jabbing misery narratives that set up a knockout conclusion. We teachers, with all of our culturally sanctioned agency, can be surprisingly blind to this barrage. Worse, our students often don't feel comfortable telling us when they feel beaten up. We might sometimes notice the symptoms: clandestine earbuds and extended bathroom breaks, unexplainable irritability and downed heads. Even if we, at our peril, undervalue our students' emotional safety, we must consider their academic satisfaction. Imagine the frustration of having various narrative bits dumped on a desk before you and being asked to contemplate them without the opportunity to put them together into a whole. Scholars hunger for a chance to imagine, test, and propose solutions to the problems that have been revealed by their studies.

For an example of this proposition in action, let's consider a hypothetical discussion that analyzes affirmative action. Honest discussions about racial preference in both college admissions and hiring can be particularly sensitive in a secondary classroom. Many students will soon be considering the weight of checked boxes on college and scholarship applications, and some are privy to their parents' strong opinions about perceived racial advantages in the labor market. Affirmative action also happens to be the sort of issue that, on its surface, seems far from students' locus of control. They do not set organizations' hiring or admissions policies, and they might never be in such a position. Whether it is to their perceived benefit or detriment, affirmative action is something that *happens to* them. The challenge in discussing it, therefore, is making sure students see where they can impact the practice, both now and in the future. Teachers might be tempted to give students a sense of control by challenging them to "win" a debate ("Stand on this side of the room if you think affirmative action is justified, this side if you disagree. Convince each other. Make sure you use facts to back up your opinion.") As with most controversies, students benefit from the chance to spar thoughtfully with opposing ideas. Yet we must not let the allure of passionate exchanges trick us into rushing the moment, especially if our students have not had ample opportunity to research the issue and prepare their language. A teacher's false sense of urgency might lead to a sloppiness that either threatens students' sense of safety or weakens bonds built by the work of Chapter 1. In addition, Chapter 3 reminded us to make space for students to change their minds when confronted by better logic, a point that should never be far from teachers' debate planning. On the whole, however, mere debating does not infuse a race discussion with lasting purpose. For this, students can be invited to explore how they can impact the issue itself, not just their classmates' opinions of it.

I might orient students toward this goal with something like the following two-part writing prompt: (1) *How important do you think it is for businesses to consider a candidate's race when hiring?* Then, (2) *How might such consideration help and/or harm a business?* Notice that neither question comes with an implied right, yes or no answer, as might be implied by questions like, "Is it important for businesses to desegregate?" and "What are the benefits of desegregation?" Experience has shown me the value of *scaling questions* (asking students to rank answers on a scale between two seemingly unacceptable extremes). The scale is often drawn on the board as a number line, with numbers ranging from one, "*never* consider race," to ten, designating race as "the *most* important qualification." This method implies that there are many legitimate opinions between the two poles. The second prompt provides two options and encourages students to consider both, a subtle push for the students to take a deliberative stance.

After this orientation, students would share their answers in a whole-class format, before which I would remind them that our goal was to gather students' ideas—not challenge them. This distinction is important; students are apt to feel more comfortable when they know each statement will not be followed by a classmate's quick or hasty refutation. It is important to practice this early in the school year, since many students are not used to teachers separating the collection of student ideas from the attempt to sharpen them. When students veer into challenging, as is natural when dealing with controversies, a teacher must nudge them to wait until all ideas are out there. In this discussion, first thoughts might be gathered on the whiteboard by a student. In the process, we'd collectively select any ideas rich enough to inspire further exploration.

For example, a student could offer, "A minority would feel uneasy working for a mostly white business." This might provide an invitation of personal sharing that helps students find their sphere of influence: I might ask students to remember a situation when they really *felt* their race. If they needed prompting, I might share my experience during multiple trips to Southeast Asia, where African Americans are ogled like purple antelopes. Students laugh when I recall a seven-year-old girl shouting to me in shock, "You are a *black* man!" They also love that, in Vietnam and China specifically, people ask to take pictures with my wife and me. I share that growing up in a black neighborhood and attending mostly integrated schools, I had never really felt "othered" by my blackness. And, I tell them, like many minorities, I am used to encountering lower proportions of people who look like me in my professional world. But being pointed at, that is jarring.

As students share their own experiences, I remind them to listen patiently to each narrative. No interruptions, no raised hands. Then students can show that they've been listening actively by pointing out interesting connections between their classmates' experiences. When facilitating, we should always keep a sharp eye out for such links, watching for any that could push us toward identifying students' locus of control. For example, a student might say, "Anyone who is thinking about their race during a job interview is going to be at a disadvantage. If you think you don't have a chance, you will do poorly."

To which a classmate might add, "Works the other way too. If you think you've got it in the bag, you'll do poorly."

In addition to whatever class text has inspired this appropriation conversation, it's good to have a few contemporary sources on hand, just in case students' connections speak to anything happening in the real world. This bridge linking our race conversation to those held outside our walls might help students to see where they might be able to influence it. This "thinking about race while interviewing" exchange would apply to most affirmative action sources, but here I'll connect it with an article from ESPN.com written by sports journalist Mike Sando, describing the NFL's Rooney Rule. The directive, adopted in 2003, requires teams to interview at least one minority candidate for each head coach opening. According to Sando's article (2016), the NFL hired twenty-one white first-time head coaches from 2012 to 2016, while hiring only one minority candidate. This is an identical ratio to one from twenty years earlier, when another five-year stretch produced only one minority hire. There has been no progress when it comes to hiring minorities for head coaching positions. This article piqued my interest because, in 2016, my hometown team Philadelphia Eagles had just completed a coaching search that involved one of my favorite players, Duce Staley. Staley, the only shining light on some horrible late-'90s teams, had started working for the Eagles as an assistant coach after his career ended in 2006. When, at the beginning of the most recent search for a head coach, he was the first person interviewed, I tried to fight my cynicism. I hoped that he wasn't being interviewed just to fulfill the Rooney Rule requirement. I thought, *Would I still interview for my dream job if there was a chance I was invited only to fulfill a diversity mandate? And if I did, how would the Rooney Rule affect my psyche and interview performance?* I would share these reflections with students.

After reading the article, students could break into pods or pairs to discuss how knowledge of Rooney Rule–esque policies might impact interview performance. As I wander around, I'd expect to hear students discussing the fear of playing into stereotypes, the frustration of knowing that numbers aren't on your side, and the overconfidence or complacency of knowing that they *are* on your side. On my tour, I'd sit in on each conversation for a few seconds, ask a pointed question or offer praise, then move on. I'd then ask the students, "Who are the key players in this?"

They'd say, with some variation, "White bosses. Minority bosses. Minority candidates. Interviewers." This might sound similar to the *Kindred* example in Chapter 3, where students were put into the positions of troubled protagonist Dana, her apathetic husband, Kevin, and the enslaved children. There, I described our challenge to invite students into available characters' shoes. I would take a similar approach here, knowing that it is hard to recognize one's agency in a situation without first understanding the social and emotional complexity. Buried in this complexity, students might find something, or *someone*, they have the power to impact.

I'd write the list of characters across the whiteboard. Then I would invite students to imagine a conversation with whichever figure from the whiteboard they'd like to engage. They would capture this conversation in the form of casual creative writing, what the teaching artists at the Wilma Theater call "disposable art": a script, some dialogue, a song, anything that can be either expanded into something powerful or thrown away without consequence. I'd make it clear that they are to speak *as themselves* to this figure. For example, a student might wish to encourage a minority peer who has an interview coming up at a mostly white university. What would she tell him before he interviews for his dream college? Why? Or perhaps a group of students might wish to collaboratively draft an interview policy that takes into account the unique pressures of interviewing as a minority candidate at a mostly white organization. If, after deliberation, they like this policy, they can move it from the realm of disposable art to something publishable, perhaps in a blog, or a letter to the editor.

Even though most of the power in the affirmative action issue is in adults' hands, many students will leave this particular conversation with something actionable. Some of this action might require patience, and we should be clear when actionable steps might require a longer view. Teens can volunteer for a campaign, but they must wait to vote. Teens can protest, but they might need to wait to invest significant money in causes. Eventually, they might find themselves drafting their own company's hiring policy—or they just might find themselves sitting across from a minority candidate who doubts that she's getting a fair shot. Students deserve to see a clear connection between their current race conversations and that moment.

Encourage New Lines of Inquiry.

Proposition 2: Design race conversations that encourage students to follow *new* lines of inquiry.

I tend to give *The Dead Poets Society,* and the entire genre of heroic teacher movies, a hard time. As argued in the introduction, the "Mr. Keating" archetype has more potential to discourage teachers than offer lasting inspiration. Yet, in fairness, I do appreciate the film's celebration of Walt Whitman's "O Me! O Life!" which Keating quotes in an abridged form for his students:

> O me! O life! of the questions of these recurring,
> Of the endless trains of the faithless, of cities fill'd with the foolish,
> —What good amid these, O me, O life?
> *Answer.*
> That you are here—that life exists and identity,
> That the powerful play goes on, and you may contribute a verse.

Then Keating famously adds a challenge: "What will your verse be?" He uses Whitman's elegy to invite his class of constrained students to express themselves, and to eventually consider their own words canon worthy. This approach is essential to any teacher who wants their classroom stance to encourage creativity.

However, Whitman's answer is even more useful as a tool to ensure that real-life students find purpose in a dialogue about race. As mentioned in the previous chapter, not all such conversations are about hard problems. Sometimes we are discussing race's role in arts and culture, history and science—and without the challenge of an immediate problem to solve, our students can rightly wonder why the conversation is worth significant investment. Yes, sometimes our students just need to know facts, roll them around on their tongues, test their merits. But ultimately, scholars are driven by the chance to say something new. Our discussion should offer students the invitation to see themselves as Washington, Du Bois, Gates, Morrison: people celebrated for generating fresh ideas about race. Students should recognize a canon not just of publications, but of philosophies—and they should own their ability to contribute fresh verses to it through rich conversation.

This mission requires dialogic teachers to nourish a pioneering attitude usually associated with universities, where scholars are expected to not dally on the often discussed, but to stretch the edges of scholarship. They are encouraged to search out new angles, make unexpected connections and discoveries, then test them through rigorous discourse with like-minded peers. There is no reason for secondary teachers to expect less from high school students. Their conversations can be driven by an effort to make meaningful contributions.

For example, let us consider a conversational thread examining the role of music in black history. Such a thread might launch from West Africa, with an examination of the role of griots, then move to the antebellum South and the spirituals of enslaved people. Then it might wrestle with the many controversies of jazz, the blues, and rock 'n' roll. All of these could have their own wonderful conversations. But to illustrate this second proposition, let's zoom in on a hypothetical discussion about the culture of hip-hop. This topic has its obvious benefits: The students are familiar with it, most enter the discussion with strong (and diverse) opinions to tap, and there is no shortage of contemporary outside sources. Such topics allow young people to interact with their teacher on something more like an even plane, with confidence that their expertise matters. Hip-hop's profanity, misogyny, and violence interact with uncommon truth, virtuosity, and delicacy to make it an intriguing beast to study. And, best of all, it is an emerging field that has only recently earned the right to be studied by serious scholars. A teacher can take students to the fringe of "what everyone else is talking about" pretty quickly. And from there, the students can launch forward into new territory.

In this hypothetical hip-hop conversation, a teacher might want to capitalize on the popularity of a current artist, Kendrick Lamar. As of this writing, Lamar has won seven Grammys, including Best Rap Album for *To Pimp a*

Butterfly and Best Rap Song for "Alright," and a Pulitzer Prize for *DAMN*. His genius has been widely recognized across the black cultural landscape. Pioneering hip-hop icons Snoop Dogg and Dr. Dre famously "passed the torch" to Lamar in 2011 at the Music Box Theater, while President Barack Obama proclaimed Lamar's "How Much a Dollar Cost" his favorite song of 2015. The teacher's orientation for Lamar should prepare students for his genre's coarse language, not because the students do not swear or because they have not heard such language before, but to acknowledge an aberration hiding in plain view. Profanity must be presented as a device whose merits can be discussed, not a cheap gimmick to grab the students' attention. I tell my ninth graders that when we study a source with mature language, I am trusting them to be their mature selves. I remind them that our study of such sources does *not* give them license to use profanity in our academic discourse.

This conversation might start with exegesis. A teacher could print out the lyrics of "Alright" and ask students to underline interesting lyrics and make annotations in the margins. This simple activity, when I have committed to it, has worked wonders to grow my students' confidence to make analytical leaps. Many of them are used to seeing texts only as wholes, and have rarely been asked to break texts into component parts. There are other ways in, too: Students can highlight lines and annotate them through different critical lenses. A teacher could prompt, *How might a feminist critic read this? A Marxist critic? Your parents? The people in your neighborhood?* This is an essential first step to seeing something new in the whole. A student's paper could look something like the one displayed in Figure 4.1.

This habit-forming activity takes a while to develop. Teachers must be patient, giving all students enough time to meaningfully interact with the text. The song would be played all the way through at least twice before moving on to a small learning community (SLC) share of individual analysis. Students could be prompted to note any interesting ideas that a peer has come up with. The teacher could move to whole class from this, asking students to share an interesting observation that they (or their partners) made. Unlike the more personal example used to illustrate the first proposition, the teacher wouldn't have to make a clear delineation between the uploading of ideas and debate. Students can respectfully debate analyses as they come. For example, if a student shares the note about Lamar's "Alls my life" line, also from the song

Alls my life I has to fight', Nigga! **Alls my life I . . .**	Why does K. say "alls," not "all"? Is he not educated? He is really angry or frustrated that he has to fight so hard all the time. The anger cuts him off.
Hard Times like yah, **Bad Trips like, "God!"**	Don't know what "yah" means. He was so high, he was calling out to God for help or for forgiveness. He was saying random things he remembered about God like the word "Nazareth." He's really ashamed.
Nazareth, I'm f---- up **Homie, you f---- up** **But if God got us, then we gon' be alright!"**	Wait, who is talking? Is K. talking to someone else who has drug prob? He says "if" God got us, like he is unsure. Why wouldn't God have us? Is this connected to "Alls my life" lines? He doubts God a little because he's had to fight all his life. But he has faith anyway that things will get better. The "we" is prob Black people.

FIGURE 4.1
This sort of line-by-line annotation and analysis encourages students to break texts into their component parts.

"Alright," a classmate might raise her hand to share that she recognizes the line as Sophia's from the movie *The Color Purple* (1985). There isn't much benefit to making this more-informed student wait until everyone has shared their observations. Some disagreements might not be as neatly settled, as one student might wonder why her classmate assumed that Lamar was singling out black people as the "we" of his chorus. She might think the class is drawing too many conclusions from Lamar's use of the N-word while ignoring his multiple allusions to the burden of fame and/or illicit riches. She points to lyrics like, "When I wake up / I recognize you looking at me for the pay cut" and "I can tell it, I know it's illegal / I don't think about it, I deposit every other zero." This could be one of many worthwhile student-inspired avenues this conversation could take.

As the sharing of initial observations slows, the teacher could nudge this conversation to the edge of the commonly discussed analyses of the song. Articles in Mic.com, *Vibe* magazine, and others have sought to explain "Alright"'s organic emergence as *the* anthem for the Black Lives Matter movement. Mic columnist Jamilah King explored this phenomenon in her February 2016 piece, "The Improbable Story of How Kendrick Lamar's 'Alright' Became a Protest Anthem." She recalls a story about a group of Cleveland activists witnessing the following altercation between a fourteen-year-old black boy and local police:

> We saw this encounter happening, saw this young man being arrested and so a number of folks went over to talk to the police

> to see what was happening," Treva Lindsey, an assistant professor at Ohio State University who witnessed the altercation, told *Mic*. "The situation escalated so quickly, so quickly."
>
> What happened over the next hour made headlines across the globe. According to several witnesses who spoke to *Mic* and news accounts from the time, scores of conference attendees gathered to confront the police about the boy's arrest. The police responded by pepper-spraying the crowd, causing a scene that drew even more protesters to the scene. Amid the chaos, someone asked the boy for his mother's phone number and called her. Soon, she was there talking to police, and the boy was released into her custody.
>
> Overjoyed, the crowd, which now numbered close to 200 people, began chanting the refrain from Kendrick Lamar's Grammy-nominated song "Alright." "We gon' be alright!" "We gon' be alright!" "We gon' be alright!"

The students could read King's full article, which juxtaposes the altercation with criticism that Lamar has received over his surprisingly conservative stance in the wake of Darren Wilson's nonindictment: He said to *Billboard* magazine, "What happened to Michael Brown should've never happened. Never. But when we don't have respect for ourselves, how do we expect them to respect us? It starts from within. Don't start with just a rally, don't start with looting—it starts from within." Another song from *To Pimp a Butterfly* ends with the line "Why did I weep when Trayvon Martin was in the street? / When gangbanging make me kill a n---- blacker than me? / Hypocrite!" This, to some, echoes the far Right's tactic of pointing to black-on-black crime as a more pressing conversation than police brutality. With this in mind, the Black Lives Matter movement's eagerness to adopt "Alright" as a rallying cry is fascinating. The students could wrestle with this. But there is a bigger prize. Jamilah King's article, and much of the current discourse, ends without actually answering some big questions: *How has this knotty song, rapped by this mercurial artist, become heir to Marvin Gaye's "What's Going On"? Will future generations look to "Alright" as Black Lives Matter's "We Shall Overcome"?*

From this prompt, this discussion could branch out in several directions. Students could look back at the analysis of their close readings to point out lines that target movement-minded people. They could debate the efficacy of using profanity or the N-word in an anthem, and whether such word choices limit who can find inspiration in it. They could examine "Alright"'s lyrics side by side with other anthems, looking for unexpected connective threads. They could propose other songs that would do a better job of capturing the spirit of the Black Lives Matter movement. They could discuss the merits of other songs for other movements. In all of these discussions, students are searching uncommon territory for unusual answers, pushing the edges of polite conversation, which is what drives us all to scholarship.

While every race conversation isn't going to push against the edges of what is commonly discussed, there is more potential to do so than we usually admit. Standing at the edge means we don't carry every conversation from the previous year. It requires a willingness to research the current conversations being held in both popular culture and the halls of academia. Too often, we approach the challenge of preparing students for higher education by frantically stuffing as many "prerequisite" race conversations as we can fit into our curriculum. We lead them through Du Bois versus Washington and Martin Luther King versus Malcolm X, hoping that college will push them to the edge of discourse. I'll always remember reading Jonathan C. Friedman's book *Speaking the Unspeakable: Essays on Sexuality, Gender, and Holocaust Survivor Memory* (2002), as a part of a Holocaust studies course at West Chester University. It blew my mind that people enduring such horrific brutality were able to engage in consensual sexual relationships with fellow victims in camps. Our class had incisive debates over whether this was evidence of the indomitable human spirit or something else. During these conversations, I couldn't stop thinking about how many times teachers had asked me to read *Anne Frank*. I'd felt cheated by the sameness; why had our high school classes spent so much time dissecting Anne's adolescent relationship with Peter, when we could have been dissecting the never-acknowledged sexual relationships among Jewish prisoners? Alumni of my African American Literature course have shared an inverse frustration. They enrolled in the same course in college, expecting to launch forward, only to sink back into the echo chamber.

The uncommon race conversation does not always have to wait for the prerequisite. In fact, if it does, we rarely get to the next level. Ultimately, the proposition to encourage new lines of thinking requires teachers to establish sufficient beachheads through careful orientation, then use controversial prompts and unique sourcing to launch students *forward*. If teachers need to go back to fill in a knowledge gap, so be it. But students of all ability levels, learning styles, and cultural backgrounds deserve to operate on the frontier of thought. There is no more effective form of intrinsic motivation than the opportunity to say something new.

Publish Whenever Students Feel Ready.

Proposition 3: Students should be encouraged to "publish" whenever they feel ready.

Once the second proposition is truly embraced, the final suggestion rolls forth naturally. The invitation to push the edges of race scholarship should come with legitimate opportunities for our students to have these ideas published. Some adults have always taken advantage of opportunities to publish. My father, Rosamond Kay, regularly writes well-received letters to the editor that end up published in the *Philadelphia Inquirer*. In more than a few of them, he has challenged a racial assertion that an article has made. In one 2017 piece by Alfred Lubrano, "The 'Imposter' Syndrome of First-Generation Penn Students: Uneasy Among Privileged, Distanced from Family," first-generation students at Penn shared how out of place, and ultimately disloyal, they felt at the Ivy League school. One woman said,

> "I'm from low economic status in a rural area. My father's incarcerated. And Penn kids are saying the best ways to stay warm in winter are $900 Canada Goose jackets! But I can't talk about things like that to my mom. I already feel disloyal to her," Duran said, crying. "I feel like I'm leaving her behind. My friends, too. We're in different worlds now."

Remembering his own college experience in the '60s at mostly white Lafayette College, my dad sent the letter shown in Figure 4.2. Contributors have the option of providing their email addresses, which, because he welcomes debate, my dad always provides. As wonderful as it is to publish and network in this more traditional manner, our students are coming up in an age of even greater opportunity. They no longer have to wait for someone else to disseminate their thoughts, and social media has nurtured their instinct to share their thoughts with the world. Think-pieces crowd their social media timelines every time a racial controversy appears, which encourages youth to cast themselves as critics in their retweets and shares. However, many of our students do not naturally connect rich classroom dialogue to the outside world's conversation. The main audience for their scholarly contributions remains the classroom community. Little happens to discourage this notion, since even the most progressive curricula rarely encourage publication.

Trailblazers can't be whiners

The first-generation college students interviewed in the Oct. 8 article "Crossing over to the Ivy League" come off as whiners.

Henry Ossian Flipper became the first African American cadet to graduate from the U.S. Military Academy in 1856. No white cadet spoke to him during his four years at West Point. Yet staff writer Alfred Lubrano fails to cite even one troublemaker at the University of Pennsylvania targeting these "crossovers" with disparagement.

It is a smear on the entire Penn community to imply that all of those there are materialistic $900 Canada Goose jacket-wearing people. There are friendly folks at Penn.

First-generation students did not get to Penn all by themselves. Someone in their blue-collar or poor or rural or nonwhite culture taught them academic discipline. Grateful youths never distance themselves from moms who sacrificed everything to get their child into a good school. Kids with healthy self-esteem go home and hug those who reared them, thus avoiding "Don't think you're better than us" admonishments.

My prescription for first-generation students to lose the "I don't belong here" syndrome is to read Langston Hughes' poem "I, Too": *I, too, sing America / I am the darker brother. / They send me to eat in the kitchen / When company comes, / But I laugh, / And eat well, / And grow strong. / Tomorrow, / I'll be at the table / When company comes. / Nobody'll dare / Say to me, / "Eat in the kitchen," / Then. / Besides, / They'll see how beautiful I am / And be ashamed — I, too, am America.*

FIGURE 4.2
For years, people have published letters to the editor like this one by my father. Now our students can do much more.

To be sure, there is much to discourage teachers from facilitating student publication. First, we might seek to protect our students from the world's perceived indifference to their opinions. We work hard to cultivate a sense of importance of students' ideas, and we do not want students to be disenchanted. Adults have a spectacular disinterest in youth opinions on social issues, evidenced most clearly closest to home by students' lack of input on the nation's conversation about education. Search opinion sections and news commentary for youth contributions, and find nothing. So when classroom dialogue produces great ideas, both students and teachers tacitly agree that nobody outside the room is likely to care. Furthermore, our students are often vulnerable, and criticism is often vicious. Our awareness of our students' ever-developing ideation and presentation skills might leave us wary of exposing them to possible embarrassment. Students' published opinions might seem myopic, silly, or offensive to more "mature" sensibilities.

Perhaps the biggest discouragement to publishing the fruits of our race conversations comes from uncertainty over whether we ever had permission to engage the topic. For generations now, teachers have hidden their most controversial discussions behind closed doors, sometimes in defiance of standardized curricula, sometimes to counter the ideology of the larger community, sometimes because we doubt our principal, department chair, or colleagues would approve. Should our students publish, we might face consequences—especially if we have made mistakes like the Think Like a Nazi prompt or the picking cotton activity from the introduction. There is little professional risk in keeping our classroom walls opaque.

Students do not often meditate on adults' indifference to their opinions about race issues. Most take the slight as a given—a temporary one, at that—as they plan to eventually grow up and inherit the right to contribute. Some even agree that their contributions might seem juvenile and embarrassing, and therefore sympathize with a teacher's reluctance to expose them to criticism. Many initially push back when a teacher encourages them to publish. They have been conditioned to see their secondary schools not as true academies, which, by definition, exist to further scholarship, but merely as mandatory conduits through which they pass from a mute childhood to an engaged adulthood. Yet, beneath all this doubt, our students have not lost their impatience with the kiddie table. Especially while pinned down within earshot of race conversations that impact them directly. And especially in instances where they know more about the topic than bloviating adults. This should sound familiar: It's the pinned-down itch we teachers feel during terrible professional development sessions run by facilitators who haven't had contact with real, living, children in a long time. We know what we know, and when we measure that knowledge against what is being taught, we invariably conclude that our seasoned opinions are much more useful than the facilitator's.

However, when students are encouraged to publish, they are challenged to repurpose this impatience. If the cyclical state of adult race conversations leaves them dissatisfied, they should nudge their voices into the fray, invited or not. They should be encouraged to refuse to wait for age or privilege to bestow its blessing. Such presumptiveness is risky, but teenagers have always had an interesting relationship with risky behavior. Healthy risk-taking offers them an opportunity to fail—and to do so while maintaining their self-worth. They also experience the thrill of having their ideas celebrated based on their own merit, not just because they might be precocious. I have seen this at work in my Slam Poetry League. I am the executive director of the Philly Slam League, a nonprofit organization that runs a season-long performance poetry competition for Philadelphia-area schools. Before finding the league, our young poets have often hidden their most vulnerable opinions in journals and cell phone notes, with little thought of ever letting anyone read them. When these teens join one of our league's poetry clubs, they are initially stunned at the prospect of "publishing" for teammates, let alone before an audience of three hundred at one of our citywide competitions. At their first competition, most perform with shaking hands, trembling voices, nervous eyes darting to their mentors offstage. They smile at the first affirming finger snaps from the audience, and the applause at their conclusion often seems to jolt them backward. While sitting in the audience, all of them have seen, at least once, a fellow poet succumb completely to nervousness and forget all of his lines. They have winced sympathetically as their peer runs crying from the stage, cursing under his breath, promising to be much better next time. They have seen people quit. The vulnerability of the moment is staggering, and yet, week after week, more students risk publishing in the same venue.

Many of these poems seek to extend the race conversations overheard in the adult world. In a performance at one competition, 2014's Brave New Voices International Competition, youth poets Veronica Nocella and Otter Jung-Allen wrote a poem titled "Letter to My Future White Son." It begins,

> Ten Lessons for the White Sons we Might have / Ten things we don't have to say, /
>
> but must teach you / because if we don't, every inch you grow
>
> could be another nightmare you'll give somebody . . .

When the performance is viewed on YouTube, one first notices the two poets on stage, both white, both wearing black T-shirts with "BLACK LIVES MATTER" emblazoned in a bold Kente pattern (see Figure 4.3). In the auditorium at Atlanta's Woodruff Symphony Hall, thousands of people fall silent at this startling juxtaposition. Everyone in the room immediately recognized the risk involved in such stark solidarity, knowing that each performance was being filmed and published online by YouthSpeaks, the organization that hosts the competition (youthspeaks.org/bravenewvoices/). These poets were speaking to the whole world. They would never again be able to retreat to total anonymity in the greater conversation on race. This was an abdication of their childlike *harmlessness*; from now on,

FIGURE 4.3
My students Otter (left) and Veronica (right) perform at Brave New Voices in 2016.

adults who didn't know them personally would be aware of their opinions. These children would now be the subject of conversations in rooms they weren't in, unable to step in and provide context, to offer rebuttals, to say, "Hey, I'm still learning, and so are you." Still, they stood.

Later on in the performance:

> When you fall off your razor scooter / You'll always have a band-aid the same color as you.
>
> Even as you get older / you'll be able to patch up any damage you make.
>
> Your band-aid boxes will teach you / that excuses aren't made for melanin . . .

Then later:

> The first time you are stopped by a cop
> He will see a rambunctious teen with too much time on his hands
> A good kid / Who made a mistake.
> He will not see / Thug.
> You will not think / Threat.
> You will think / Father.
> Think / Haven't I seen you around?
> Think / This shouldn't take long.
> The first time you are stopped by a cop / You get to come home.

And finally:

> I don't want you feeling guilty
> for an existence you simply can't help,
> But I don't want you to become another boy I'd cringe at.
> You'll be constantly reminded of how much you can conquer,
> of how much space has already been stolen for you.
> You'll never have to concern yourself
> with the aftermath of your leftovers . . .

You will be raised in a world where you don't have to look
at the kids who've fallen
if it makes you uncomfortable.
But in my house / you'll learn to help them up
and not expect thank yous,
to be an ally like your life depends on it,
because it doesn't / But it should.
To the white sons we might have—
you will not be silent in the face of destruction.
Not under my roof.

Published on YouTube, this championship-winning performance immediately took off in popularity. (Scan the QR code to see the full video.) Within days, the video had over a thousand views, in a month, tens of thousands. Multiple adults asked the teens for permission to use their piece to inspire conversations about white privilege in their classrooms, professional developments, and writing workshops. Otter remembered,

https://bit.ly/2Mkhi8D

> Strangers wanted to craft lessons around [our poem] . . . Someone asked if we could Skype-teach a lesson about white privilege to her class. And she lived very far from us. It was very impressive—intimidating, almost—to be barraged by all of this positive feedback, all of this affirmation. In a way the positive feedback was not about us . . . It was about what we were talking about. All these adults and teachers told us, "This is what your poem is going to *do*." They told us, "You are shifting something with this poem. You're going to change something with these words." For the first time, I was proud of my poetry not because of how it sounded, but what it could *do*.

The publication also attracted Internet trolls, a couple of whom made disgusting response videos that attacked the poets personally. As one of their mentors, I found that this stung deeply. When I encourage youth to publish, I do so trusting the adult world to be exacting, but civil. Occasionally this trust is broken. Reflecting on this painful betrayal, Otter warned me, "It's always important for the seasoned adults to let [students] know the risks, not first, but as a preliminary measure before they share their work, because publishing is the last, riskiest step in the artistic process. But at the end of the day, the most important thing is for youth artists to get their voices published. To be heard. Not only by other youth, but by adults especially . . . Even me publishing my voice in this interview is a way of correcting, or confirming, conceptions or misconceptions about me. On a larger scale, all of these adults are looking at youth with certain conceptions or misconceptions in mind. It's incredible how entitled adults can be toward youth voices and youth thoughts and youth emotions, and that's why it's important to disregard the risks." After a pause, Otter added, "Encourage your kids to jump in feet first. Because [your students] have, not a responsibility . . . but a *right* to correct people. They have a right to make sure that people understand where they're coming from, how they feel."

Earlier in this book, I recommend that teachers diversify their conversational structures; we shouldn't have our students prepare just for *the small-group unit* or *the few weeks we work in pairs*. The benefits of one major configuration (whole class, SLC, or one-on-one)—shouldn't work to the exclusion of others; all should blend together in a package of effective activities that serve all learning styles and create state changes. So it also goes with publication. We teachers can foster a *culture* of publication that doesn't just rush to display the dynamite project, but offers students the constant invitation to contribute one verse, then another, then another.

This process starts with the basics, an emphasis on developing community, the in-house celebration of ideas that comes from listening actively. Then, we can tell students that the ultimate publication of these ideas is a great opportunity, and that our discussion activities are meant to prepare them to do so, should they decide to take the plunge. Where students used to merely read and discuss a newspaper article, they now are invited to write letters to the editor in response. When our threaded lines of inquiry about hard problems produce nonconformist solutions, we no longer smile at the vague promise of the next generation. We invite students to blog about it. When the adult world asks what youth think about a race issue, we invite our students to curate a collection of journals or essays. But we don't wait for a publishing house to confer opportunity; instead we draw inspiration from the early pamphleting days of our republic, and encourage students to self-publish over a class website. My wife keeps a list of literary journals, such as *Teen Ink,* that publish teen authors, and after certain rich conversations inspire great pieces of writing, she requires her students to submit their work for review. (A website that provides a list of places to publish, NewPages Young Writers Guide, can be accessed here: https://www.newpages.com/writers-resources/young-authors-guide.) Upon seeing their work in print, her students are often overwhelmed by the response.

THE RISKY OUTLIER: THE POP-UP CONVERSATION

When establishing a *purpose* for a conversation, there is one outlier—the one-off, "pop-up" conversation. We have read an article, seen a movie, or watched a news report about a race issue and have decided that our students need to discuss it. This particular race issue has nothing to do with the conversational threads our students are currently following, but for whatever reason, we've decided that putting it in front of the kids *right now* is important. Perhaps we feel this urge after a Ferguson, a Baltimore, or a Charlottesville, or upon returning from any other long, hot summer. Perhaps an NFL player has decided to take a knee during the national anthem, and you are in a hurry to discuss it before the news media moves on.

This urge is often driven by one of the personal catalysts noted earlier—we *like* talking to the students, and we wish to help them process the news and vice versa. Conversations can also, when they involve pop culture, be driven by a teacher's urge to seem cool. Many first-time teachers, myself included, have brought hip-hop into the classroom when all else failed to keep the students' attention. During my first year at a struggling charter high school, I had so much trouble getting the students focused that I begged thirty old copies of *The Source* and *SLAM* magazines from my barbershop. My students and I discussed whatever kept them in their seats for twenty minutes; most of the topics, in retrospect, were explorations of black street culture. Was Meek Mill better than Jay-Z? Kobe or LeBron? Team Nike or Team Adidas? Maybe if I showed them

Dave Chappelle's satire or Chris Rock's N-word bit, they would like me. Maybe if they liked me, they would eventually do some work.

The motives are understandable, but pop-up race conversations are dangerous. Chapter 3 argues that we should not be haphazard when discussing race, for haphazard conversations can careen into unsafe conversations. Chapter 3 mentions the unreliable "breakthroughs" (kids crying and other bursts of emotion) that are more evidence of teacher-inflicted trauma than the onset of understanding. We must patiently apply our professional planning talents as often as possible. There is never a rush. If we take our time, we might remember a useful tidbit about our students (e.g., *Isn't one of Emma's parents a police officer?* or *Didn't Mateen spend time in a refugee camp?*). If we relax, we might be able to engage in a few thought experiments, asking ourselves questions like, "What if there's a kid who is offended by my connecting the journey toward marriage equality with the Civil Rights movement? How would I handle it?" or "What if a student has a parent who blames immigration for the loss of a job?" Taking our time allows us to chew on these possibilities and shrink the possibility of complete surprise. We might even anticipate where we'll be called to agility. Remember the young lady who didn't know that the Holocaust existed? Now, whenever planning that lesson, I think, *If there's a student who doesn't know about the Holocaust, we might have to pivot to the curriculum discussion. Be ready.*

None of this is to suggest that we submit to paralysis by analysis. It is to remind us that pop-up race conversations are risky, too often unnecessarily so. (Chapter 8 delves a bit deeper into an example of a risky pop-up conversation that occurred in my classroom.) It is okay to wait until we can incorporate the conversation into a planned thread, a focused line of inquiry. The topic is not going anywhere. But if we *must* dive straight in without much prep, there are a few guidelines to make sure that we ensure purpose:

1. We mustn't demand personal sharing without reestablishing clear discussion protocols. When we ask for vulnerability from our students, we communicate that the room is ready for their openness. We can't let their classmates' responses make us liars

in this regard. The vulnerability requested in our discussion prompts depends on our certainty that every student's voice will be respected and on our comfort level in reminding our students when they forget to do so.

2. In our discussion orientations, we must publicly own that it is a pop-up conversation. We have gone off-script, so our students should not spend the first twenty minutes trying to figure out how this source and these prompts relate to their normal classwork. Furthermore, they should know why we have brought this topic to them, why it is worth their time, energy, and vulnerability. I have discovered that students appreciate being let in on this usually hidden process. They are flattered that we want them to weigh in on race's role in politics, popular culture, sports, and that we cared enough to set the established curriculum aside for a day.

3. We need to give our students enough time to get to some conclusions. So often, the resources we bring in leave more questions than answers, which is a problem only if we do not give them enough time to at least work through their questions. It frustrates students when we refuse to allocate more than twenty minutes for a forty-five-minute discussion. If we prompt from an article about an NFL player's refusal to stand for the national anthem, for example, we cannot cut off a respectful but heated exchange between the child of a veteran and a strong supporter of the protest. Or, if we choose to discuss gentrification in a pop-up manner, we must not then rush students sharing their stories of displacement. If the bell ever cuts the conversation short, we must communicate a plan for continuance. If we do not, our students will, at very least, designate pop-up racial discussions as pointless distractions. At most, they will withhold their participation because the teacher seems to care more about the clock than their contributions. Both of these instinctive reactions hurt the teacher's *planned* conversations, which means it would have been better if the pop-up had never happened.

4. Finally, we should pay special attention to our summary and reflection. Because pop-up conversations are not linked to the rest of the dialogic curriculum, students might be tempted to casually

ignore what is being discussed, especially more grade-conscious students, who might sense a day off. If the pop-up topic was heavy, then our reflection should ascertain whether the students still feel safe. If we have dredged up raw emotions, we may even have to offer up a lunch period for one-on-one follow-up. If we have failed in our facilitation, apologies might be in order—which again should remind us of how important it is to develop house talk relationships. Finally, we should make it clear how much we appreciate the students joining our pop-up line of inquiry. This gratitude gives our students another chance to feel proud of themselves, for their teacher has valued their input enough to engage them in conversation that doesn't seem job related.

The more we want our students to buy in to our race conversations, the clearer we must make our purposes. Whether it is to celebrate the beauty of a culture, solve a hard problem, contribute to scholarship, or ultimately publish, our students must never be confused about *why* they are being asked to take such a demanding journey. In doing so, we should be constantly aware of our personal catalysts and how they interact with the purposes we share with students. For instance, if we are having a race conversation in order to raise up a student army, we've got to make sure that we agitate toward solutions. If we are pointing out an elephant, we should encourage our students to take outside ideas into the lab of our discussion protocols. If, through this exchange, students are pushed to the edge of scholarship, they should be invited to contribute by publishing.

Professional Practice

This chapter begins by reminding us to reflect on our personal catalysts for leading race conversations. These contemplations might be best written down in a personal journal (alongside other reflections about how one's teaching is going) and returned to when new ideas emerge. While many of these reflections should remain private, there are moments when it helps to share the journey with like-minded colleagues. If, for example, a teacher finds himself driven to a particular race conversation by the need to assuage guilt, or to be cool, this might signal that there is something wanting in his relationships with students. In this, it helps to not feel alone. If a teacher finds herself eager to point out a racial elephant in the room, it might help to see how that elephant manifests in other classrooms. Then teachers can coordinate an integrated curricular response that is less risky, and therefore less potentially haphazard. The same applies to teachers who want their students inspired to join social movement work. If such a conversation is sparked and maintained by one teacher, some students might attribute its urgency to their teacher's quirky passion. However, if the conversation is being held by a cohort of colleagues, students might more easily be attracted to the ideas, independent of their admiration for (or exasperation over) any particular "heroic" teacher.

A study of hard problems might push students to the edge of scholarship, at which point their teachers might encourage them to publish. The same holds true for teachers' professional development. We should, whenever opportunities present themselves, share our best practices not only with our colleagues, but with teachers outside our schools. This includes, but is not limited to, presenting at professional conferences and hosting a quarterly fellowship with colleagues from different schools. When our conversations produce especially good ideas, we should not be afraid to submit them to professional journals or send them to newspapers as editorials or letters. If you are fortunate enough to have the time to write, why not present an idea to a publisher, like Stenhouse, that is eager to present teachers' perspectives?

PART 2

A Study of Conversations

Throughout the first four chapters, I have attempted to weave in examples, both hypothetical and from my classroom. It is important that we see all the theories in practice, the rules enforced, the habits illustrated. The chapters in Part 2 fully describe four race conversations that have taken place in my classroom. Each of the first three have been attempted at least eight times in the past eleven years, with both ninth and tenth graders. They have succeeded and they have failed. The highs have been spectacular, and the lows have been humbling, occasionally forcing me to reexamine and tweak my processes. I describe not just the wins, but also the losses, the bad decisions, the unlucky variables. As you peer into my dialogic classroom, I hope that you will see how one teacher answers Douglass's challenge to push students' race conversations from light to fire. As you read through these examples, please take into account your own personal strengths and weaknesses, your own conversational package, and your students' cultural and academic backgrounds, and make any necessary adjustments.

CHAPTER 5

THE N-WORD: FACING IT HEAD-ON

As mentioned in Chapter 3, my freshmen students read Octavia Butler's *Kindred*. They also read August Wilson's *Fences*. My sophomores read Richard Wright's *Native Son*. My seniors have read *The Autobiography of Malcolm X*. When it comes to small-group free choice reading, freshmen might pick memoirs like Sanyika Shakur's *Monster: The Autobiography of an L.A. Gang Member*, or Alice Walker's *The Color Purple*, or Wright's *Black Boy*. All of these beautiful texts, and many more, have an added layer of difficulty when it comes to discussion, a crippling problem that stymies many meaningful race conversations before they even have a chance to bloom: their use of the word *nigger*.

It's really a mess of a word. More than a few modern school districts cite its prevalence to ban Mark Twain's *Adventures of Huckleberry Finn* from their classrooms. Frustrated by this, Alabama publisher NewSouth Books even created a version of the book that replaces *nigger* with *slave*, and *Injun* with *Indian*. The former epithet appears in Twain's book 219 times, which surprises me because it was one of the first "grown-up" books that my father read to me, uncensored, at my bedside. My seven-year-old self noticed the word, but it was always secondary to the image of a mischievous boy (like me) running barefoot through the woods, then floating down the Mississippi with an enslaved black man looking for freedom. I cared about the budding respect between Huck and Jim. I cared about the meanness of Huck's father as a greater symbol of the slaveholding culture's cruelty. Yet, for others, the N-word floats to the top of their consciousness. It causes teachers to cautiously navigate procedures, like reading aloud, that we usually spend little time worrying about. Students can offend peers by merely quoting a character's exact dialogue, which forces them into either a scared silence or the awkward verbal calisthenics of real-time NewSouth substitution.

THE N-WORD IN *KINDRED*

My first year teaching *Kindred* (Butler 2009), I anticipated the stiltedness that the N-word would bring to our conversations. In our racially diverse classroom environment, my students' interactions with the word would stress our three discussion rules (listen patiently, listen actively, and police your voice), inciting even more unpredictable conflict. When the students went to small groups, I would be nervous about being out of earshot. In whole-class conversations, my white students might decide that participation was not worth risking embarrassment or accusation. Thankfully, I realized that our sensitivity to the N-word (amid other abuses) was one of Octavia Butler's main themes in *Kindred*. Dana, the protagonist, is a modern black woman who has been transported to the antebellum South. Butler uses Dana as an avatar through which her readers can experience both the horrors and complexities of slavery. Dana brings her enlightened and empowered twentieth-century identity with her, with all of its sensitivity toward abuses. So, when crafting the unit's Essential Questions, I tried to get right to the heart of Dana's struggle: *What affects our sensitivity levels to abuses/words/ideas?* And we would initiate this thread by facing the N-word head-on.

Early in *Kindred*, Dana makes her second trip to the South. It is 1815. She meets a young white child named Rufus, who will grow up to become her master and complicated antagonist. During their first conversation, however, both are still trying to make sense of the time-travel predicament. The following passage shows up in my students' first homework reading:

> "Mama said she tried to stop you when she saw you doing that to me because you were just some nigger she had never seen before . . . "
>
> I sat down on the bed and looked over at him, but I could read nothing other than interest and remembered excitement in his eyes. "She said I was what?" I asked.
>
> "Just a strange nigger. She and Daddy both knew they hadn't seen you before."
>
> "That was a hell of a thing for her to say after she saw me save her son's life."
>
> Rufus frowned. "Why?"
>
> I stared at him.
>
> "What's wrong?" he asked. "Why are you mad?"
>
> "Your mother always calls people niggers, Rufe?"
>
> "Sure, except when she has company. Why not?"
>
> His air of innocent questioning confused me. Either he really didn't know what he was saying, or he had a career waiting in Hollywood. Whichever it was, he wasn't going to go on saying it to me. "I'm a Black woman, Rufe. If you have to call me something other than my name, that's it." (24)

The day after this first reading, I reminded my students that our *Kindred* conversations would be likely to push comfort zones. I then reminded them of a 2008 article from *Newsweek* titled "I'm Not Who You Think I Am" (Paik 2008), which we'd discussed at the beginning of the year. In it, an Asian American woman explores her sensitivity to perceived racial slights. At the beginning of this piece, she shares her frustration with being confused with other Asian women who "really, objectively, look nothing like" her. After sharing a few examples, she said,

> I have always felt justified in assuming that people who make these mistakes are, at some level, racist. Meaning that when they see me, their normal powers of observation switch off so that the only information their brains receive is: Asian.

Then, one time at a horse show, she mistook a stranger for her own ten-year-old daughter. This experience sparked a great deal of reflection:

> Even though I knew that this could not mean I was racist—racist towards my own daughter?—I was mortified nonetheless. "Oh I'm sorry! You all look the same from the top!" I said . . . By which I meant, all little girls with dark pigtails look similar to a taller person who is not really paying attention.

She ended the piece with this:

> A plea, then, for all of us to take the time to look more carefully. For those who see the race and not the individual: look harder. And for those who, like me, may be hypersensitive after years of not being properly seen, keep in mind that while there are people who are racist, many others are merely distracted, overeager, careless, tired, old. We, the thin-skinned, also need to stop applying the easy label.

Students have historically reacted well to this piece, which affirms the humanity of well-meaning people while also challenging everyone to reflect on their emotional reactions to perceived racial slights. Sometimes we *all* need to look harder, in our quest to both recognize and appreciate others' identity. And sometimes we *all* need to refuse the easy label.

After this orientation about hypersensitivity, I told the students that I "really needed their help with something," so that the class could actually discuss *Kindred* openly. I asked them to take out their notebooks (where they write their warm-ups) and prepare to respond to a particularly sensitive prompt. They would not be permitted to answer verbally, but there would be plenty of opportunity to do so later. When everyone was ready, I asked them to describe their relationship to "this word." Then, with a dry-erase marker, I scrawled N-I-G-G-E-R on the board. All caps, a large as possible, so that the epithet appeared to eat up the entire space. The kids giggled at first, some gasped, more than a few of them ignoring instructions to postpone any chatting with their classmates. I gently reminded them of these instructions, then added, "Everyone has *some* relationship with this word. Maybe you were told that you should never, under any circumstances, say it. Maybe you are new to this country, and are just now getting to know the word as other people use it around you. Maybe you say it often. This is private; nobody will see what you write. I just want you to reflect."

By this point, most students had started writing. After waiting a few seconds, I continued to ask probing questions. "How do you feel about this relationship? Does anything confuse you? Do you wish that you could change anything?" Throughout the warm-up period, I circulated, praising students for keeping their focus. I peered over their shoulders, pausing to further prompt students who hadn't found much yet to say. All the while, the word remained on the board—and students peered thoughtfully up at it over and over again.

After about five minutes, I offered the secondary prompt. "There are a lot of rules about this word. Who can't say it. Who can. When it can be said. What, if any rules have you heard?" There was much less hesitation on this question, probably because it seemed less personal. I continued to circle the room, offering encouragement and praise for the next three minutes.

THE IMPORTANCE OF OPTING OUT

Before moving to the rest of the discussion, let's pause for a quick warning: Even if we have created a familial, house talk environment, we must allow students to *opt out of* sharing intimate details that their classmates might find controversial. Let's say, for example, a white student has grown up in a household that uses the N-word regularly in its most pejorative sense. This student faces a choice when given the above *relationship* prompt: He could lie, say he has no relationship, pretend that his mother and father don't occasionally tell "nigger" jokes or complain about "niggers" moving into the neighborhood, or he could be honest. By denying a relationship to this word, he would incur no risk, as none of his classmates are expecting such ugly revelations. Or, he could choose to write the truth anyway and privately engage in uncomfortable reflection. Before this class, he might have pushed his parents' racist language to the back of his mind, but this prompt might lead him to contemplate reasons why they use it. From here, he might consider how these language choices impact his parents' politics. Then how their politics impact his. This arc of reflection, even if unshared with classmates, is well worth the prompt.

Knowing the social risks of going through the aforementioned process publicly, this student might decline an invitation to share his journal response. If we ignore this, and coax him to share anyway, he might—because he trusts us—admit, "My parents use this word all the time." His classmates, in even the best circumstances, are likely to buzz in response to this admission. Now facing rebuke, he might be convinced that his teacher had teased out a confession under false pretenses. That the class's "safe space" hadn't been quite sturdy enough for his truth, and now, thanks to his teacher's naiveté, he has to face far-reaching social consequences for choosing honesty.

I've unintentionally set kids up for failure like this. One year, I allowed confidence in my "safe space" to completely overrun my good sense. Expecting my students to separate raw emotions from intellectual N-word discourse, I declared that, as scholars in an academic space, we could *all* say the word. Yes. I actually gave *permission* to every student—then told them that such license was absolutely necessary in order to read the book smoothly. And because we all were a family (gasp!), we surely wouldn't hold our classmates accountable for simply reading what an author wrote. One of my favorite students that year, Freda, who is white (and now a remarkable teacher in Philadelphia), remembered that mistake. "I remember I *had* to read the N-word . . . And everyone was like, 'Oh, that came too easily out of her mouth, she must say that often, because she didn't hesitate!' And I was like, all right but he told us to just read it, so I just read it." At this point in our interview, the two of us laughed, remembering a moment four years later in my African American Lit course when the N-word popped up again for her. "Oh, and senior year when I saw it, I was like, 'I'm not making that mistake again. I'm not gonna have the kids call me racist again, I'm gonna stutter, and stop, and pretend I don't know how to pronounce it, how to say the word properly.'" We must not pretend that our decisions do not have social consequences for our students. With the most personal controversies, I allow students to choose whether to *opt in* to whole-class exchanges. They'll share when they are ready to share.

MOVING CLOSER TO THE EDGE OF SCHOLARSHIP: HIGHLIGHTING THE WORD'S COMPLEXITY

As expected, the first response to my N-word prompt questioned whether it was asking about the word *nigger* or its more socially dexterous cousin, *nigga*. My African American students made a lot of this distinction. The former, according to most, is what white racists say. The latter is a term that African Americans use "for affection." Which version was I talking about? There were many grave nods of assent. (Conversations like this one have been taking place in my classroom for over a decade, and the *nigger/nigga* distinction continues to be one of the first points that African American kids make.) I had anticipated this. And I wanted students to test their shaky *nigga* "affection" assertion. I answered, "I am not sure it is that simple."

They looked at me with reassuring eyes, as if it was a shame that I didn't know these sorts of things. Smiling, I said, "I've been on the basketball court when there's been nothing but black people. All is cool, people are using the word just like you say they do, until there's hard contact in the lane. Then one dude says to another, 'Ball' [Philly parlance for "you've just fouled me"]. Other dude responds with, 'Naw.' The aggrieved party waves him off dismissively and says, 'Check up.'" I looked around the room for confirmation, and a lot of the students seemed to already know where this example was going.

"Then the first guy says something like"—I paused for effect—"'*Nigga*, you know . . . ' And all of a sudden, an argument over a foul has turned into a fight. Right there at the top of the key. Dudes are in each other's faces, calling each other names. A whole fight. How many of you have seen a situation like this?" A few of the hands rose. "All I'm saying is that that word did *something* to the situation. Right? We weren't fighting before that—and there wasn't a white person around for *miles*." The kids chuckled. The students who brought up the issue nodded thoughtfully and looked back at their warm-up entries. I continued, "We've got to mean what we say. It's not as simple as 'black people replace the *-er* with an *-a*, and then use it for respect.' We've got a real complicated relationship with that word."

Nick, a black boy, raised his hand. "I think black people use the word to reclaim their power over it. When we use *nigga*, we are saying that racism didn't break us." He looked around the room for reassurance. "It actually feels good to say it. It's like being in a private club. I think other groups do the same thing, right? It's like the B-word with women. Nikki Minaj calls herself a bad bitch, and so does Rihanna, and I think Beyoncé too. It probably makes them feel like they are in control of the word for once."

A black girl, Sandra, raised her hand. "*I* don't use that word."

The boy asked, "Which one?"

"Neither. But especially the N-word. I was told that I shouldn't."

I asked, "By whom?

"My parents. They won't let me use it in the house at all. When I am around my friends and they say it . . . " This is a tenuous place in the conversation where the speaker tends to look around and identify friends. Again, it's important that the students have internalized the rule to listen patiently. "I don't say it. I don't get mad at them, but it just sounds *ugly* coming out my mouth." Thoughtful pause. "Ugly. Like people used to say that when people were lynched and slaves and stuff."

"Yup. Thanks for sharing. That last bit, about the lynching. That was powerful." I stopped to think. "Words are attached to images, right? For some people, the N-word is attached to images like lynchings and slavery. Your parents, when they say that you shouldn't use it, I bet they told you about bad guys using it while abusing and terrorizing black people, right?" She nodded. "Those images come from media, from books like *Kindred*, or maybe from life experiences." Here, I invited interested students to share words that describe images that seem attached to that word. They answered, and we compiled a list on the board.

During this process, a few black students shared anecdotes of being called *nigger* in the pejorative sense. This seemed to shock some of their classmates, who, I assumed, must have previously considered such usage more of a historical relic. Matching their vulnerability with my own, I shared a college memory: I'd caught a ride back from practice with a group of white rugby teammates. Just as we were about to pull into the cafeteria's parking lot, a car full of black students cut us off. Our driver yelled out of the car, "F------ niggers!" I'd gaped at him. Then, exasperated, down at my brown hands. Then back up to my teammates. None of them seemed to notice that anything had been said. Seconds later, we had parked and were out of the car—all going our separate ways. In my head, the scene repeated at full volume as I walked back to my dorm. I thought, *What just happened?* Then, after a second of painful reflection, *Why didn't I say anything?* I put that question to the students.

"Sometimes you get too stunned to speak."

"Maybe you were afraid to fight with them, because they were teammates."

I paused, smiling. "I should have *fought* them?" Some students nodded; a couple of them laughed. I followed up, "How many of you would have fought that boy?" Three hands shot up into the air. When asked why, they expressed shock over the disrespect of my antagonist. One asked if he apologized (he hadn't), and if I quit the team (I didn't). My student questioner appeared disappointed—shocked, even—as I imagine he had pegged me as more willing pugilist. I responded by admitting a tendency to put people in a box in my mind when managing uncomfortable social situations. In other words, I had been upset but not stunned, because I'd grown up assuming that people from the middle of Pennsylvania were inclined toward racism. Many Philadelphians carry derisive stereotypes about people who live in the swath of communities between Philly and Pittsburgh, and often share an apocryphal statistic that Pennsylvania has the highest concentration of KKK members in the North. These are hasty, mean generalizations, I know now—but my college-aged self didn't question them. As far as I was concerned, my teammate was acting to type. And as long as he didn't say it again within my hearing (he didn't), didn't attack me (he'd better not), and continued to pass me the ball when I was open, his N-word usage didn't seem worth the fight.

"How's *that* for complicated?" I asked my students. An easy joke came to mind. "It's like on Facebook when you have to label your relationship status. Sometimes you are *Single*, sometimes you are *In a Relationship*, sometimes *It's Complicated*." They laughed. Encouraged, I asked them to look back at their warm-ups. "After reading it, how many of you would tag your relationship with the N-word, *It's Complicated*?" About half of the kids raised their hands. I followed up, "What are some of the complications?"

Here, one of my black students—we'll call her Nia—shared a frustration. Apparently, in her recent past, some of Nia's white peers had seemed comfortable using the word in her presence. When pressed about it, these kids had argued that through some cultural combination of growing up in a black neighborhood and having friends of color, they were allowed to use it. Many of these offenders claimed to have received explicit permission to use *nigga* whenever they wanted to. This made Nia furious. She said, "*You* can't give somebody who *I* don't know permission to offend *me*!" A lot of her classmates seemed to agree, adding "Yes!" and "Right!" and "For real!" I teased this chorus for sounding like they were in church offering *Amens*—a jab that playfully reminded them not to interrupt. Nia continued, "I hear white people in the hallway sometimes, saying the word like it doesn't mean anything. And when I try to check them, they tell me to calm down, it's not that serious. Apparently the word's history doesn't mean anything, and as long as the intention is not 'racist,' it's okay to say it. And if I react to that nonsense, something is wrong with *me*!" She sat back in her chair, seemingly finished. Then, under her breath, "*You* just can't say it. It's simple. White people just can't stand somebody telling them '*No.*' Always got some excuse." This was probably meant to sound combative—both to her classmates and as a response to my rugby story.

I decided to ignore the tension and push directly to discussing her points. "I'm hearing several things. Tell me if I'm right." I turned to the board and was struck by the word still boldly scrawled up there. Finding some room beneath the earlier list, I started writing. "First, you argued that the difference between race and culture is important to the N-word's politics. Basically, brown skin is more important than a black-ish experience. At least when it comes to who can say the word." I waited for Nia to nod. "Second, you argued that black people shouldn't grant white people permission to use the word. Quick question before I write it on the board: Does that rule count for private conversations too? Or are you just saying that they can't give them a blanket license to say it in front of any black person they meet?"

Someone shouted out, "Don't do it! Friends don't let friends say . . . " The room cracked up at the student's reference to a classic Ad Council anti-drunk-driving slogan. Chuckling, I waited for Nia to weigh in. After a few seconds of contemplation, she clarified that her earlier argument was more about white people being granted blanket permission—although she agreed with our class comedian that it was dangerous to allow white friends to use it in some conditions while trusting them to not use it in others. I paraphrased this on the board. Then I continued, "Third, you disagree that intent is the point. People can't just detach the word from the images"—I pointed to our earlier list—"and experiences that other people associate with the word."

"It's like *redskins*!"

I beamed, as all dialogic teachers do when students unexpectedly connect to a previous conversation. In an earlier rhetoric unit, the class had analyzed the controversy surrounding the NFL team's nickname. After teaching the pejorative meaning of the term *redskin*—a Native American's scalp taken as either a souvenir or as evidence needed to collect on a bounty—we discussed whether team owner Daniel Snyder should have told his fans in a letter that the term now stood for "strength, courage, pride, and respect." I watched as the reference settled into the class, then said, "Yes, like *redskins*. And like other words, too, I'd imagine. According to Nia's logic—which I think is really sound, by the way—we should take into account our audience's perceptions before using a loaded term." I went back to the board. "Which connects to the fourth thing I heard Nia say: that people question her right to be offended by white people using the word. Then finally, she snuck one more comment in there that I don't want to overlook. Do you remember the last thing you said?"

"Yes. That white people don't like hearing minorities tell them '*No*.'"

"Mind if I push you a bit here?" She shrugged, seemingly pacified by the amount of attention that I was giving her original comment. Students almost always enjoy having their contributions dissected with the attention traditionally reserved for class texts. This modeling not only inspires students to listen actively to their classmates' contributions, but also sets them up for deliberative debates about the merits of ideas, facts, and interpretations—not conflicting student personalities. Already, I had filled up nearly all the free space left on the board with my analysis of Nia's comment. "So, first, you probably don't mean *all* white people." I threw out my hands in a wide, all-encompassing gesture. She smiled sheepishly. "No worries. I think you were getting to the heart of something bigger. You were questioning why nonracist white people have any desire to use the word in the first place." I felt this line of inquiry sniffing at the edges of a hard problem.

She was, and so were a few of her classmates. So I put the question out there: "Most of this conversation has leaned toward the politics of *using* the word. We've spoken a little about the complex emotions that the word stirs up, but then we got right back to legislating who can use it. That's okay for now, just as long as we realize that there is *so* much more to talk about." I let that sink in. "Nia argues that any white people who want to use the word do so as a reaction to being told that they can't. That makes it about defiance. Could there be other reasons besides defiance?"

"The word is everywhere." One of my white students, Cole, spoke up. "I don't use the word at all, that's what I wrote down, and I don't want to use it either. But that word is in our media, it's in the music and on TV and in the movies. I'd say that white people who *do* use it just want to be able to sing along."

"Do you?" another student asked, filling the silence while I wrote on the board.

"Do I what?"

"Sing along."

The air was sucked out of the room, followed by a wave of nervous laughter. I jumped in before Cole could answer. "Whoa! Good question, but let's keep it more general: A white person who likes hip-hop—we probably are talking about hip-hop, right?—a white person who likes hip-hop probably has some appreciation for black culture. And there are a lot of white people who like hip-hop. I don't have the stats in front of me, but I remember hearing that most rap music is consumed by white people. Can somebody look that up for me?" This sent a flurry of students to their cell phones. Without waiting for confirmation, I asked, "When these white people are in the car by themselves, in the shower, in their rooms with their headphones on, do they mouth the N-word? Do they sing along?" The class exploded into a chorus of "Yes!" and "No!" and "You know you do!" I laughed along, and Cole smiled, the pressure off of him to respond. If any moment showed the importance of family-building activities like Good News, High-Grade Compliments, and Burning Five Minutes, this was it. Cole was being playfully ribbed, but not attacked. Nobody, including the original questioner, had any interest in pushing him to actually answer the question. This wasn't an inquisition into whether Cole was a racist, and everyone seemed to realize that there was no point pushing him on it, especially as he had started off his comment by saying that he never said it.

Leaving it there, I added Cole's observation to the board. "One reason is to rebel against the restriction. Another is to be able to smoothly participate in popular culture. Any other reasons that nonracist white people would want to use the word?"

Jess, a white student, held up her copy of *Kindred*. "To be able to read this book aloud."

"Are you nervous that I'm going to ask you to read Rufus's part?" Like many English teachers, I often assign students roles and ask them to read the text aloud during reviews. I was intrigued that she had already anticipated a classroom complication of Rufus's N-word drop.

"I wouldn't do it."

"Fair enough." I then shared the earlier-mentioned Freda story, which brought a few giggles. "Rest easy. I will not be *making* any of you say it. But I like your point. How many of you, speaking mostly to students who identify as white here, have encountered this word in a classroom setting before?" It's important to note here: I've trained myself to use "identify as" as much as possible when referencing students' race. This acknowledges that race is a social construct, which we discuss early in the year, and allows students to make their own decisions about how and when to respond. Many hands went up. "Were there rules on who could read it aloud?" More nods. "Were these unwritten rules or openly stated?" Some of the hands went down as the students tried to remember. I called on Jess, who seemed eager to answer.

"Neither. We were reading *To Kill a Mockingbird* last year. And our teacher had this thing called round-robin, where the students had to read a few lines, then pass it off to the next person in the circle. So I am sitting there in class, kinda not paying attention, and then it's my turn. And when I look at the line, it's the little girl asking her dad what an 'N-lover'is. It's like your story, so I know how that girl felt. But my teacher didn't even seem to have a plan. She just kinda looked at me, like, *so what are you gonna do?* I didn't say it, but it felt bad, like I had been set up. And she kept doing it! I never liked round-robin anyway, but this made it even worse. I'm not allowed to say it, and the teacher is *making* me say it. It would be easier if we didn't read any books that had it."

"Thank you for sharing." I added, "Oh, man. That would make things simpler, wouldn't it? That's how some schools deal with it." I brought up the aforementioned bans on *Huckleberry Finn*. "Problem is, this word is so deeply interwoven in American history and black culture that it's hard to tell an honest story that doesn't reference it. In *Kindred*, Rufus was a seven-year-old Maryland white boy in 1815, so he probably called black people *niggers*. Let's look back at the text." I waited for everyone to open their books. "Look at Dana's reaction. She brings all of her 1976 indignation with her to 1815. She reacts like I imagine Nia would: 'I'm a Black woman, Rufe. If you have to call me something other than my name, that's it.' Octavia Butler is being super-honest about how this culture clash might have played out, no? There is absolutely no way that Rufus would have called Dana *black*. *Negro*, maybe, but not likely on this Southern plantation. So it comes down to whether schools should make kids read *honest* books about race, or books that avoid complications and awkward situations." I looked back at the multiple lists on the board. "We have a lot up here, and we just scratched the surface. There are the images that we have to contend with, the emotions that the word can stir up. There are the politics of who can say it, and when we scratch a little at that, there's the hard question of why different groups want to say it in the first place."

Inspired, a student named Ian blurted out, "I think that is Octavia Butler's point! You said that she wrote this book like it was an experiment to see how a modern woman would react to slave times. What if she is experimenting on us too? To see how we would react to the N-word?"

"You are reading my mind." I ran theatrically over to this student for a high five.

Pleased with himself, he continued. "If Dana stays longer in the South, she is probably going to hear that word more and more. And so will we. And we'll have to deal with it." His voice petered out as his classmates acknowledged his contribution.

I stepped in. "How many of you noticed the word when it first showed up? Like for some reason it rose up off the page?" Nearly all the hands went up. "Then how many of you stopped really noticing it a few pages after?" Most of the students nodded. "And the word is not likely to go away. We'll probably see it more and more if Dana keeps staying in the past longer and longer." I paused, pointing out Ian. "Ian's *thesis* is that Butler is experimenting with us. If she is, what do you think the results will be?" Students answered mostly by saying that they expected to eventually grow used to the word. I pushed, "To the point of not even noticing it?"

Ian checked in again. "Yes. I mean, most of us probably stopped looking up on the board. The N-word is *still* there!" His classmates gasped, some whispering "Yo!" at the realization. He continued, "Nobody asked Kay to erase it." He turned to me. "Would you have erased it if we had asked?"

"Yes."

"Were you waiting for someone to ask you to erase it?"

I smiled. "I'm not Milgram." Only a few weeks earlier, our class had been introduced to different social experiments, ending with a video of Stanley Milgram's infamous shock study. My students had been amazed that, under the right circumstances, a majority of people would kill someone with a deadly burst of electricity simply because they were told to. After the video and short history lesson, the students had been invited to design a social experiment that tried to answer one of society's hard questions. Many of them may have still thought Ian was on to something, so I wanted to set them straight. "Seriously, I wasn't trying to experiment on you. But

Butler might." I erased the word. "There. How's that feel?" A chorus of kids whispered, "Better" and "Whew."

SUMMARIZING AND PUSHING FORWARD

After noticing that the class period was nearly up, I started our summary process. This was tough; I mention in Chapter 2 how we can be tempted to milk the last drops from a controversial race conversation right up to the bell, and this N-word conversation was no different. My student-driven approach had frayed into so many loose threads: We had only scraped the edges of Nia's final comment about white privilege. We had not really dealt with Jess's curriculum proposal to teach only N-word-free books. We had not really tested Nick's assertion that black people enjoy our palliative, private, only-we-can-say-it club. Or his comparison to women's relationships to the B-word. And Sandra's N-word-free household was probably a gold mine of interesting related anecdotes. Pull on any one of these threads, and we could easily keep going past the end of the class period without providing the chance to reflect. However, this temptation to unravel even more hard problems can make the natural unpredictability of student-centered dialogic practice feel haphazard. And appearing haphazard, as explained earlier, is often the difference between students' experiencing a healthy disequilibrium and feeling unsafe.

So, with about ten minutes left, I started the summary segment by acknowledging our loose threads. While doing so, I complimented everyone, as I do often, on their focus and the active choice they made to listen to each other. I expressed gratitude for their openness, their willingness to disagree without being too combative, their interest in wrestling with ideas while respecting personalities. I reassured them that we would be spending the next few weeks exploring some of the arguments and observations that were offered up (a promise made much more believable by our constant note taking). But since class was about to end, we would need to figure out what *decisions*, *agreements*, and *action items* our conversation had led us to. Because we had spent the majority of the conversation in whole class, it made sense to pair up for reflection. The class had been dominated by some of my more verbose students, and many of the other students would benefit from reflecting verbally. I asked them to turn to a neighbor and discuss something that intrigued them from the conversation. They jotted these observations down in their notebooks. After a couple of minutes of reflection, I asked for volunteers to share these points with the larger community. By this time, I had erased the board, and now had space to list under a Stuff We Found Intriguing heading. After doing so, I asked everyone to get back into pairs one more time, preferably with someone else, and discuss whether our conversation had unearthed any observations that moved us forward.

During the sharing portion, they came back with a list that included the following statements:

1. We've decided that nobody can give anyone else permission to say the word.
2. We've decided that since people have a complex relationship to the word, we should spend more time trying to understand it.
3. Octavia Butler might be trying to experiment on us to see how sensitive we are to it, and if we change. This puts us in Dana's shoes.

With about two minutes left in the class period, one of my students asked me if the N-word was in my vocabulary, and how I'd felt about their conversation. I knew this was coming. As teachers, we should foster an environment safe enough for the exchange of conflicting ideas, which should make us wary about openly favoring one student's opinion over another. Yet, as I mention in Chapter 2, to completely ignore students' requests for our opinions is paradoxically dismissive of their voices. After choosing to make themselves vulnerable by investing in the conversation, it helps to know that their teacher's stake is not just in them, but in the ideas being bandied about. The trick, of course, is not to contribute in such a way that we discourage young people from sharing, either because they disagree with us or because they feel that we have offered *their* contribution more eloquently than they could hope to have done.

So when asked this direct question, I gave a direct answer. *Yes*. The word is a part of my vocabulary. I don't use it often, and after a few seconds of reflection, I shared two main instances that drag the word out of me: First, I say the N-word when using idioms common in black vernacular—phrases like *Nigga, please* or calling a bossy black person the *HNIC* (*Head Nigga In Charge*). Second, I grew up using the word to denote a more embarrassing subset of black people, the type comedian Chris Rock famously lambasted in his 1996 *Bring the Pain* show. More than a few of my students had seen it:

> There's a civil war going on with black people, and there's two sides. There's black people and there's niggas. The niggas have got to go. Can't do [nothing] without some ignorant nigga [messing] it up. Can't keep a disco open more than three weeks. Grand opening, grand closing! Can't go to a movie the first week it comes out, why? Cause niggas are shooting at the screen. What kind of ignorant [stuff] is that? "Hey, this is a good movie, this is so good I gotta bust a cap in here!" Hey, I love black people, but I hate niggas. You can't have [nothing] when you around niggas. You can't have no big-screen TV! You can have it, but you better move it in at three in the morning. Paint it white, hope niggas think it's a bassinet. Can't have [nothing] in your house! Why?! Because niggas will break into your house. Niggas that live next door to you break into your house, come over the next day and go, "I heard you got robbed." Nigga, you know you robbed me.

Knowing that I had only a few seconds left, I challenged them to reflect on how my answer fit in to their earlier conversation. My usage seemed to complicate not only the earlier assertion that black people use the word for respect, which Chris Rock clearly wasn't doing, but, more uncomfortably, Nick's thesis about the N-word symbolizing a reclamation of black power. If black people, like me, used the N-word to denote silly, dangerous, or stupid members of my own race, what was *that* all about? Self-hate? Identity politics? Or was it a kind of sibling teasing—like *I can insult my brother, but don't you dare*. Students nodded.

Inspired by the Chris Rock reference, I added on a supplementary homework assignment. I asked students to think of any media that purposely engages any of the points that were brought up during the discussion. I knew immediately which example I'd submit for discussion the next day: an episode of the television show *Black-ish*, where a black boy gets suspended for rapping the N-word during a talent show. (Kanye West's "Gold Digger": "I ain't sayin' she a gold digger / But she ain't messing with no broke niggas.") His nearly all-white school had a zero-tolerance policy on the N-word, which had been advocated for by the boy's mother. (The N-word is hilariously bleeped out in the show, with a pixelated blur covering the speaker's mouth.) The incident sparks many interesting family conversations, during one of which his father sheepishly admits that he sings unedited Kanye with his son in the car on the way to school. Sensing his wife's impending explosion, he preemptively pleads, "It's his birthright! Jewish kids get to go to Israel, black kids get to say this." His wife responds by explicitly banning the word in the house, which prompts a friend at work to shake his head and say, "They want you to live in a N-free zone."

To which the father responds, "I'm telling you, man, my house is not a home!"

In a debate with his father, he says, "That's exactly what the white man wants. He either wants nobody to say it because he can't, or he wants everyone to say it because he wants to."

The episode culminates with a school board meeting, where the father points out the frustrating complexities of the word. "Paula Deen says it and catches a little flak. But in turn gets $100 million in funding. Quentin Tarantino writes it more times than I can count in *Django* and he *wins an Oscar* for it." His son ends up not being expelled. I made a mental note to find these clips to mix in with whatever my students could find later that night. I thanked everyone again for their openness and dismissed them to their next class.

While many student comments like the ones mentioned here have been repeated in some form or another over the years, there is enough variety year to year to require a great deal of agility. Sometimes students are reluctant to share before I admit my personal experience with the word. And while I avoid this particular conversation if our classroom community has not built a solid foundation, sometimes we are torpedoed by student-to-student conversations that I was not privy to. Students like Nia, for example, sometimes express very specific "Stop saying it!" grievances against classmates who are present in the room. When this happens, I have to retreat immediately to a community-building stance: I express gratitude for the passion, but remind everyone that personal attacks are counterproductive. I remind them of our purposes, that the class is trying to tease out the word's complexities and make sense of the world of rules that we've attached to it. This is the space for analysis, not accusation. One might be surprised at how rarely conflict happens, however, given how prevalent the word is and how sensitive the students can be to its use. I attribute this relative peace to the community building—students don't seem to have much interest in "outing" each other as users of the word. And I try to be clear about my pedagogical intention: Most immediately, I want to help my students feel more comfortable when they encounter it in the text that we'll be spending the next few weeks discussing. If the N-word remains a conversational land mine, the class will miss out on some of the richest angles for analysis. More broadly, I want students to begin to understand the complexity of the N-word, so that they might be able to thoughtfully contribute to lifelong discussions about its appropriate use.

WHEN AN ADMINISTRATOR WALKS IN

One unique incident from early in my career stands out: Right after writing the N-word on the board, my principal walked into the classroom. My heart leapt into my throat. Remember, in the last chapter, I mentioned that many of us doubt whether we ever had permission to have meaningful race conversations in the first place? That's the feeling that hit me in the ribs as soon as I noticed him reading the whiteboard. My students' eyes darted back and forth from him to me; they gasped and giggled nervously. Caught in the middle of a sentence, I tried to interpret his face. He was clearly reading the situation, checking to see if my students were safe. An internal voice told me to keep moving, to trust the prompts and process. I cleared my throat and went right back to my questioning. He sat down on my desk, as was his habit, and smiled. Later, I asked him about his thoughts in that moment, and he said he was "watching to see where this would go." And as it moved along a similar path as just described, he started to participate. I was relieved.

I highlight this moment because it illustrates how important a savvy administrator can be to the process of having meaningful race conversations. Teachers are often annoyed by the tension that accompanies an administrator's visit to their classrooms. With the best intentions, principals and department chairs walk in with myriad checklists: Are the objectives and state standards written neatly on the board? Are the children sitting down, facing forward? Is student work posted on the walls? Has the teacher gotten to each of Madeline Hunter's seven planning steps? This nit-picking makes some teachers wary about encouraging the natural unpredictability of student-driven conversations. More so if the conversations are about race, because misinterpretations can put our schools in the news headlines. A natural reaction is to cloak these conversations in a veil of secrecy by closing the door so we can be "real" with our students. We can even be tempted to bask in our cool-teacher stance, positioning our honest curriculum as opposition to the "fake" policies of unfeeling administrators. Students notice this administrator-teacher tension, and with it, receive a message that good conversations are inherently subversive. Some might be. But when teachers teach students to automatically alienate those in power, our students miss a chance to discover new allies. And when administrators choose to hypercriticize the minutiae of a teacher's discussion, they risk having their values rightfully questioned. Do they really care more about seating arrangements than student engagement? Is their conception of "on-task" so myopic that it can't survive the occasional student looking up something on a cell phone? Administrators choosing to choke on gnats might not realize how much they make meaningful race conversations feel unworthy of the effort.

Instead, teachers and administrators should create systems that encourage trust in each other's professionalism. When my principal walked into my classroom, he'd already had full access to a unit plan that showed all the conversational threads—one of which would be Octavia Butler's use of the N-word. There were no surprises. And when he saw the word on the board, he scanned the room for signs that I had veered from the promise of my unit plan. I hadn't. He listened to students' comments to see if they were approaching the topic with scholarly discipline. They were, albeit with high passion. He looked to see if anyone had been alienated by the conversation. While some students were carrying the bulk of the talking load during whole class, their classmates were engaged in taking notes. These same kids spoke freely once the students shifted to small-group discussion, and when we went back to whole class, more of them decided to weigh in. Seeing that all was in order, my principal freed himself to participate in the conversation. This positioned him (to the students) not as an adversary, but as a scholar who recognized the value of race conversation. Of course, this did not preclude him from giving me critical feedback and advice. It only made me more likely to receive it in the right spirit.

If we are going to do this right, it must be with humility. Dialogic teachers need the counsel of administrators when planning thorny conversations. We need their backing when we mess up, their support when our students' vibrant conversations end up antagonizing the world's real bullies. Administrators, in turn, must recognize that any school that develops scholarly citizens employs teachers who are not only trusted to tackle hard problems, but are encouraged to do so. Top-down fear pushes teachers toward ordinary race conversations. Ordinary race conversations are stirred into February Soup. February Soup dishonors generations of educators, scholars, and freedom fighters; it allows our students to forget the slave, the abused, those who deserve to live again in our students' discourse, in their future votes, in their own families' house talk. This is too important. Teachers and administrators must not let our mutual high standards drive us to make enemies of each other. There are enemies aplenty.

PERMISSION

During the aforementioned conversation, Nia made the comment, "*You* can't give somebody who *I* don't know permission to offend *me*!" This admonition is not just for students. Regretfully, some white teachers might interpret this chapter as my giving them permission to use the word. Let me be clear. Doing so would callously dismiss centuries of explicit meaning making, would make light of our students' natural sensitivities, and would be ultimately both selfish and pointless. Our scholarship as teachers does not transcend firmly established rules of kindness and decency. No minority, myself included, can grant a white person permission to use a racial slur without consequence.

We always have to make adjustments. For example, as a man, I have to be especially careful with the ways I describe sexual assault. A student teacher once warned me, as I read and discussed certain violent passages of *Kindred*, that some of my girls were surreptitiously crossing their legs. She knew what I didn't—that this was a likely indicator that they were feeling unsafe. It would cost me nothing to adjust the way we reviewed those sections. A white teacher loses nothing if, instead of spelling out the slur, they write N - - - - - on the board. It even opens up a new prompt: *Why do you think I chose to write it like this?* A white teacher loses nothing if they eschew writing it on the board altogether: *I read this* Not Light, but Fire *book by a black guy and he wrote it on the board, but I didn't want to do that. What "rules" am I honoring?* The conversation can still flow, the thread can still be explored, the hard questions can still be asked. Let us all try not to focus on the wrong things—spelling the slur out on the board, or a teacher's speaking the word aloud, are the *least* important parts of this chapter's conversation. Don't let it be the decision that undermines everything.

Professional Practice: "Put This in Your Pocket"

Throughout this book, I have argued that our classroom approach to race should never be haphazard, that a threaded approach infuses each discussion with scholarly validity. There are no quick fixes to cross-cultural relationships, no surefire race curricula victories. Still, many of this book's strategies are useful in conversations that have little or nothing to do with race. When facilitating professional development sessions, I tend to highlight the following suggestions, welcoming colleagues to put these suggestions "in their pocket" where they can be quickly applied to any dialogic unit. Each of the remaining chapters in Part 2 will end by highlighting a few such ideas that influenced the preceding discussion.

1. I collected Carol Paik's 2008 *Newsweek* article about sensitivity to racial slurs before knowing how I would use it. Once we have decided that we're going to follow a discussion thread, *any* interesting article or video resource that is even tangentially related to that thread should be copied and stored in a computer folder. I've got a dedicated folder on my computer called "Race/Culture," and I might have used only 20 percent of it during discussions. But whenever I need an outside source, I know exactly where to find a smorgasbord of texts.

2. Earlier in this chapter, I mention that I've trained myself to use the phrase *identify as* as much as possible when referencing students' races. This habit allows students to make their own decisions about how and when to respond to prompts and acknowledges that a teacher's perception does not always match a student's reality. In recent years, I have had multiple students surprise me by identifying as a certain race during a discussion. Students from mixed-race ancestry have enlightened me and their classmates by sharing unpredictable perspectives. We have to be mindful of our power to shove students into undesired or incomplete categories. If we do so, they might, at worst, resent our overreach. This approach works for other social constructs as well. Consider the idea of family. We teach students who consider their grandparents, cousins, or siblings to be their parents. We teach students who have close "cousins" that they may only recently have discovered aren't blood relatives. Developing a house talk environment means both respecting and affirming students' power to name their cultural realities.

CHAPTER 6

"SAY IT RIGHT": UNPACKING THE CULTURAL SIGNIFICANCE OF NAMES

When leading professional development sessions, I know that I face the most critical professional audience in the world. Teachers are a tough crowd. We know what we know, and we know that the so-called expert sitting in front of us knows neither our students, our school, nor our situation. I retain a little clout when I mention that I'm still teaching, but the faces in the crowd nevertheless clearly say, "I still know more than you." So I lead off by acknowledging that I agree. When it comes to their particular experiences, I don't know much. In fact, before this idea became a book, it was a presentation called "Talking Race for Dummies," during which I'd introduce myself as a *Lead Dummy*. Beyond getting some ice-breaking laughter, I would establish that this would not be one of *those* PDs, but simply a fellow teacher sharing some mistakes and the strategies I'd learned from them. In doing so, I would try to reject the "They brought me here to fix your deficit" stance, ideally openly enough to inspire reflection on how we might do the same with students. I would tell my fellow teachers that we'd be starting from an individual position of strength. I'd ask them, "What is your best unit? The lesson that you knock out of the park just about every time. The one that, if someone walks into your class while you are teaching it, they are going to put you up for Teacher of the Year . . . Maybe you teach a fantastic *Lord of the Flies* unit. Or perhaps you get students fired up about dissecting frogs, or building toothpick bridges. Or you've figured out how to make the Pythagorean theorem sexy." The chill in the air disappears as teachers eagerly describe the unit that proves their awesomeness, then explain it to a neighbor. After an invitation to share with the whole group, I volunteer my own Teacher-of-the-Year staple, my Cultural Memoir unit. In it, this chapter's case study appears: an exploration of the significance of ethnic names.

No discussion in my curriculum produces as much participation; stories are shared by young voices that might have otherwise spent the year silent. Not once, in well over a decade, have I dismissed a class from an ethnic names conversation without students hanging back to share more about themselves. This conversation is so important that I've moved it to the winter months, after (forgive my corniness) noticing that it keeps the classroom atmosphere warm and welcoming.

DO WE SAY, "EWWW"?

To understand this conversation, one must understand its origins. My mother, Sherrill Kay, taught third and fourth graders at Loesche Elementary in Philadelphia for thirty-six years. I attended the same elementary school, so even as a youngster, I recognized units she loved enough to repeat. Among these, the one that stood out the most was her Cultural Food Festival. Loesche draws from a diverse neighborhood of cheaper housing in Northeast Philadelphia; in the early '90s, many of my classmates were the children of immigrants from Eastern Europe, Russia, and India. I was one of the last generations of desegregation students to be bused to a different neighborhood school, which made me one of the few black kids at Loesche. So when my mother asked students to bring in a dish that represented their cultural identity, it resulted in a feast of revelations. During this activity, I had my first potato latkes with applesauce, my first curries. I tried borscht and a few foods that my seven-year-old self could not identify. Each student who brought something had to stand before the class and teach their classmates how to pronounce the dish and explain how it represented their culture. My mother then encouraged every student to be brave enough to try everything, and reminded them to say, "No, thank you" if they were allergic. I distinctly remember her focusing on this point: "Do we say, 'ewww'?" She would pinch up her nose. The kids would giggle. "No, that would be rude. We say, 'No, thank you.' Somebody worked really hard to share something from their culture with you. And we want to show that we are grateful."

It was fascinating that my friends, when they went home to be with their own people, ate these different foods. Yes, as little kids, we all liked pizza—but I also liked corn bread, cabbage, and collard greens. Apparently it wasn't just me. Everyone lived in their own tasty universe, foreign from mine, and I thought, if they ate different things, what else did they do that was different? As I grew up, this perspective stuck with me: Somewhere, even close to my home, people are doing things differently from how I am doing them, and these things are as normal to them as my habits/values/routines are to me. This stance undergirds both the humility and the empathy needed to engage in meaningful conversations about race.

When Zac Chase started working at Science Leadership Academy, he brought Erin Gruwell's *The Freedom Writers Diary* (1999) to our ninth-grade curriculum. This text is a collection of students' journal entries that chronicle their mostly at-risk upbringings and their struggles to empathize with peers. Over the course of the years, Gruwell's students learn how to use writing for both catharsis and communication. This process guides them toward the empathy that had previously been so elusive. When teaching this text, teachers are meant to lead students through a similar progression. The Freedom Writers Foundation curriculum (www.freedomwritersfoundation.org) encourages teachers to use activities like the book's Privilege Walk (described in Chapter 3), to spark dialogue.

Conversations in my classroom followed a similar progression, and it quickly became clear that SLA's cultural diversity staggered our students. I'd asked freshmen to raise their hands if most of their classmates at former schools were of one race. Most of them did. Many were eager to share their first thoughts upon witnessing our school's racial diversity. They recalled fear: *What if these other kids were smarter, tougher, more "at home" at SLA than they were?* Moments like these flashed me back to my mother's food festival and the importance of making time to actually appreciate our differences.

Toward this end, my Cultural Memoir unit has moved away from *The Freedom Writers Diary* and become a three-week survey on cultural diversity. Every couple of days, we pick a different element of culture—names, languages, music, art, religion, and so on—and discuss the contributions made by these elements to our own cultural identities. My school's ninth-grade thread, Identity, is incredibly useful to these cultural discussions; it roots every conversation in our shared mission to figure ourselves out. At the outset of each discussion, students know that there is a possibility they will understand a cultural influence better than they did an hour before. If properly executed, these exchanges also encourage students to thoughtfully challenge any lingering fear of differences. Students would not only share, not only celebrate, but also try to ask hard questions about various cultural elements.

ETHNIC NAMES

The first target for exploration would be our names. As in the N-word conversation, I oriented students with a journal entry. I asked them to write about their relationship with their name. Did they like it? Not like it? Were they aware of its meaning? How had their name affected their movement through the world? Usually, students wanted to share right after such writing, but I wanted them instead to seek connections between their cultural experiences and others'. I again mined my experience with performance poetry for a good example, and I found an elegant one, a poem titled "My Namesake" by Hiwot Adilow. Adilow, a former mentee, was kind enough to share the draft version of the piece with my students, so that they could follow along with her viral 2012 YouTube video from the finals of the Brave New Voices Competition.

https://bit.ly/2JNVseY

I told my students I would be playing Adilow's three-minute video twice: the first time just to enjoy and absorb, the second time to highlight the parts of her story they related to. Here's the text of Adilow's poem (scan the QR code to see the video):

i am tired of people asking me to smooth my name out for them,
they want me to bury it in the english so they can understand.
i will not accommodate the word for mouth,
i will not break my name so your lazy english can sleep its tongue on top,
fix your lips around it.
no, you can't give me a stupid nickname to replace this gift of five letters.
try to pronounce it before you write me off as
lil one,
afro,
the ethiopian jawn,
or any other poor excuse of a name you've baptized me with in your weakness.
my name is insulted that you won't speak it.
my name is a jealous god—
i kneel my english down every day and offer my begging and broken amharic
to be accepted by this lord from my parents' country.
this is my religion.
you are tainting it.
every time you call me something else you break it and kick it—
you think you're being clever by turning my name into a cackle?
"hewhat?"
"hewhy?"
"he when how he what who?"
my name is not a joke!
this is more than wind and the clack of a consonant.

my father handed me this heavy burden of five letters decades before i was born.
with letters, he tried to snatch his ethiopia back from the middle of a red terror.
he tried to overthrow a fascist.
he was thrown into prison,
ran out of his home—
my name is a frantic attempt to save a country.
it is a preserved connection,
the only line i have leading me to a place i've never been.
it is a boat,
a plane,
a vessel carrying me to earth i've never felt.
i speak myself closer and closer to ethiopia by wrapping myself in this name.
this is my country in ink.
my name is the signature at the end of the last letter before the army comes,
it is the only music left in the midst of torture and fear,
it is the air that filled my father's lungs when he was released from prison,
the inhale that ushers in beginning.
my name is a poem,
my father wrote it over and over again.
it is the lullaby that sends his homesickness to bed—
i refuse to break myself into dust for people too weak to carry my name in their mouths.
take two syllables of your time to pronounce this song of mine,
it means life,
you shouldn't treat a breath as carelessly as this.
cradle my name between your lips as delicately as it deserves—
it's Hiwot,
say it right.

In the YouTube video, Adilow pulls the microphone to her lips with both hands to empathically deliver this last line, adding a quintessentially Philly eye-roll before exiting to thunderous applause. My students appreciated this. Some even shouted affirmations at the screen, stuff like, "You better tell 'em!" or "Yes, girl!" I repeated my instructions before returning to the beginning of the video. I noticed that more than a few of my students had already started to highlight sections of the writing. We watched the video again, and at the end, I asked them to explain their selected lines in one-on-one conversations. The hum of conversation was predictable, but after a few seconds, the volume rose exponentially. Not quite realizing what was going on because I had turned my back to cue up the next video source, I gently admonished them to keep it down. Then, after a minute, another burst of sound caught my attention. I turned to see my thirty students, every one, engrossed in fifteen of the most focused one-on-one conversations I'd ever seen.

I leaned close to the nearest pairing. A boy was explaining to another how strongly he related to the lines "hewhat? / hewhy? / he when how he what who? / My name is not a joke!" His name was BouBou, pronounced like Yogi's little friend from the Hanna-Barbera cartoons. BouBou's family is from Mali. A short freshman with an incandescent smile and chubby cheeks, he had a bubbly demeanor that seemed to have an onomatopoetic synergy with his name. Furthermore, BouBou's mind wandered often, which made him likely to either doze off in class or speak absently, to which his classmates would tease, "Oh, BouBou!"—invoking the homonym *booboo*, meaning "mistake." He acknowledged as much to his partner. He could understand the poet's eye-rolling frustration, but could not muster her anger. He had been teased, for sure, but had grown used to it. I tapped him on the shoulder and asked if he would mind bringing this up when we went whole class. He didn't mind.

A NOTE ON EXTENDING TIME

With similar comments popping up all over the room, I extended the normal three to four minutes of one-on-one conversation time to nearly seven minutes. On the surface, this is a small decision, but many potentially great conversations have been derailed by misapportioning time. Over the years, my personal conversational package has leaned toward limiting one-on-one conversations to under three minutes. Teaching a freshman drama course has taught me that student audiences start to fidget after about one and a half minutes. With my three listening rules in mind, it seems reasonable to ask students to hold it together for the same one and a half minutes before getting their turn to speak. Of course, this does not provide much time for thought gathering during the conversation, but I've found that wait time is best given during the prompting process, before they pair up. After repeating the prompt two or three times, I ask the students to think silently for a few seconds. During this time, students' hands go up and back down again, while others write or doodle in their notebooks. Most importantly, they get to gather their thoughts before turning to a partner. While I generally tell them how much time they'll have to discuss the prompt, it takes a few classes for them to understand just how quickly three minutes flies by. And I want it to fly—less time makes urgent conversations feel urgent. Yet, even with this urgency, students know that they do not need to get everything out in the moment, for more chances are coming. Within days, they grow used to me cutting one-on-one segments short, always claiming to have overheard some amazing ideas and expressing an eagerness for everyone to build on some of the genius being bandied about.

Normally, I fight the temptation to extend the time for small-group discussions. By definition, a dialogic classroom always has more time for dialogue, as student voice is a priority. The big enemy is stasis, the kind that lulls students into unfocused moments where the topic becomes secondary. I'd rather two groups feel rushed than seven feel tempted to play games on their phones as the conversation waits to move on. However, this name conversation presented a dilemma—*every* student was sharing a personal story, and nearly all of them involved some vulnerable personal revelation. They asked for more time, and they got it.

SHIFTING TO WHOLE-CLASS DISCUSSION

Eventually, we shifted to whole class. Here, the students were asked to read one of the lines that they identified with, followed by a brief explanation. Borrowing from spoken word poetry culture, I invited students to quietly snap their fingers to indicate that they too "felt" whatever line was being highlighted. Though I didn't require them to read the lines in order, the first student read Adilow's first lines: *i am tired of people asking me to smooth my name out for them / they want me to bury it in the english so they can understand*. Many snaps. One student, named Amani, told her classmates that she is Palestinian and Austrian, which most of them did not know. She followed up by telling us that everyone pronounced her name incorrectly. I had expected this revelation from students with more culturally obscure names, but her case caught me off guard. I had taught many Amanis, with no problems ever being pointed out.

Stunned, I asked her how we had been messing it up. Her response was, "You all say Ah-*mahn*-ee. That's not it." Her classmates gasped. "It's pronounced Ah-*man*-eee. Like you are saying Amanda, and replacing the *da* with an *i*." Immediately, her classmates started trying out the correct pronunciation, until the room sounded like a bunch of toddlers sticking their tongues out at a doctor's office. Amani blushed at this, smiling at her classmates' silliness. Those nearest to her asked her to say it again and again, until I interrupted. Deciding to prod her a bit, I teased, "Now, why did you let me call you the wrong name for an entire semester? 'A-*man*-eee.' I could have gotten that one right!" I feigned disappointment.

Enjoying herself, she responded, "I really don't care. It doesn't matter if you call me A-*mahn*-ee; I'm used to it." Her classmates were still rolling her name around their tongues, and I shushed them. She continued, "It doesn't bother me. I don't feel like correcting people all the time."

One of her classmates said, "Your name's not that hard."

Amani shook her head. "People are used to the other way to say it. It's like she [pointing at the poet, whose image was still projected on the board] said; people want to 'bury my name' in their English. If they don't know how to say it, they don't try very hard. And there are only so many times that you can correct someone before they start acting like you're some kind of inconvenience." This statement brought up many hands, eager to share what I assumed would be corroborating stories, but I sensed that Amani wasn't finished. She added, "Siri cannot pronounce it even when I put the phonetic spelling of my name in." Smiling at this addition, she reiterated that this whole thing wasn't, in her words, a big deal. This was the second time in ten minutes that I'd heard a student claim that getting their name wrong wasn't a big deal. I wanted to push on this, then realized that we'd analyzed only one line of the poem. I pocketed this line of inquiry, confident it would come up again.

One of Amani's classmates shared two lines that followed the thread: (1) *i will not break my name so your lazy english can sleep its tongue on top*, and (2) *no, you can't give me a stupid nickname to replace this gift of five letters.* While he didn't have a revelation as stunning as Amani's, this nickname point had the potential to spark controversy. I, for one, use nicknames to build community with my students. Nicknames are not related to any perceived difficulty pronouncing names: Mike might become "Mikey," and the verbose Zoey from Chapter 3 is usually "Zo." (I am often "Shmay" to her.) While always affectionate, sometimes my nicknaming solves a problem—I once coached two Sams, a difficulty that I solved by pointing out their obvious physical differences. My wiry shooting guard was "Skinny" Sam, while my center was "Big White" Sam. This latter nickname is problematic—I own that—but it was given by his teammates, and he took pride in being one of the only two white players on the team. The other, his good friend, was comically smaller than he was. Also, it made him sound like a shark. All this to say that playful nicknames are a big part of my classroom culture—and I was curious where this line would lead.

A student named Georjelis raised her hand. Inside, I leapt for joy, thinking that a good story might be coming. Georjelis is an effervescent young lady with deep reservoirs of hope, the sort where teachers feel an acute responsibility not to plant any cynicism. Listening actively comes naturally to her; she looks at her classmates with so much empathy that it can be overwhelming. At the beginning of the year, when I stumbled over her name while taking attendance, she gently invited everyone to call her "Jelly." I assured her that I try to get everyone's name right, and that if she pronounced it again for me, I'd surely get it. She'd shook her head, as if I somehow couldn't comprehend my tongue's limitations and reiterated, "You can call me 'Jelly.'"

And now Georjelis told us where she got her nickname. After moving to Philadelphia from Venezuela in elementary school, she did not speak English. Her teacher at the time asked her how to pronounce her name. After trying to say *Gee-hor-ell-ees* multiple times, he said, "I'm going to call you 'Jelly.'" Her classmates started calling her "Jelly," and voila! New name.

I asked her, "Do you realize how interesting that is? You actually got named by your teacher. Your third-grade classroom was like Ellis Island." I explained the reference, about people having their names shortened and Anglicized upon entering the country. She nodded as I continued, "It wasn't really a nickname either. A nickname is something that is mutually agreed on, right? This guy decided to call you 'Jelly' out of his own . . . weakness." I paused. "Isn't that the line Hiwot uses?"

Her classmates scanned their papers, until someone raised his hand to quote, "*or any other poor excuse of a name you've baptized me with in your weakness*. I like how she used the term *baptized*. The religious metaphor is great." Upon being asked to explain baptism to people who might not understand, the same student said, "You go into the water as one person and come out as someone else."

Impressed, I added, "There's a before and after with baptism. Hiwot seems to feel threatened by the attempt to change her into 'lil one,' 'afro,' or 'Ethiopian jawn.' Those are 'poor excuses' for names. And . . . " I heard the same student gasp, as if just realizing something. I stopped talking and told him to go ahead.

"Sorry, but I think I got something. When I think of baptism, something made me think of colonialism. Back when Europeans went around 'discovering' the world, they made the people they found become Christian. And I think sometimes they forced people to be baptized." He was clearly proud of this point, but unsure of the veracity of this last part. I told him to keep going. "It's like she [Hiwot] is saying that people are trying to colonize her by changing her name." The class snapped their fingers in appreciation of this leap.

I turned back to Georjelis. "You don't seem to mind being called 'Jelly.' It's not like 'Venezuelan jawn.'" She, and most of her classmates laughed. "And thanks for sharing your story, by the way. It's fascinating." Though she seemed happy to be the center of this analysis, I felt the need to clarify, "The name 'Jelly' is awesome because you are awesome. I think what your classmates are saying is that your old teacher may have been out of line. He had a lot of power over you—especially in elementary school. Did you feel like you could have said, *No, that's not my name, and I'd appreciate it if you could try again*"?

"No."

"That's the colonization point then. Your given name is beautiful, and it means something, I am sure."

She nodded. "Jelis was going to be my name, after my grandfather, but my mom wanted a longer name like hers. She's Yoluybeth. So she added *Geor-*, but I'm not sure what that means." Knowing that the last source for the conversation would spark a thread about the sound of names, I asked her to keep what she just said in mind.

Another young lady named Oluwatobiloba raised her hand. She went by "Tobi." She asked if she could discuss more lines from the poem that related to where the class seemed headed. She read the following section:

> it is a preserved connection,
> the only line i have leading me to a place i've never been.
> it is a boat,
> a plane,
> a vessel carrying me to earth i've never felt.
> i speak myself closer and closer to ethiopia by wrapping myself in this name.
> this is my country in ink.

Tobi had been back to her birthplace in Nigeria only once. Adilow's allusion to a pilgrimage home resonated strongly with her own desire to return. She spoke with a *double*-consciousness that brought Du Bois to mind: a black girl conscious of white people's assessments of her and an African conscious of how other black people measured her. Her name, which means "God Is a Great King," had been shortened in her younger years, when black classmates could not pronounce it. During her one trip back to Nigeria, her grandmother—who had given Tobi the name—had asked why she had shortened it. She'd sheepishly replied that she did not know, but had returned to the United States determined to demand the full pronunciation. True to her word, when she returned for third grade, she introduced herself to her teacher as Oluwatobiloba. It worked for a few minutes, until she was asked to draft a name tag. She told our class, "I knew my name had thirteen letters, but I didn't know what letters it included. I wanted to crawl under a rock and never come out." She went back to Tobi, and never went back.

ESTABLISHING PURPOSE: USING A MENTOR TEXT TO SPARK THE CONVERSATION

This level of vulnerability brings to mind the importance of making my purpose for having the conversation clear, described in Chapter 4. Toward this end, I peppered this name conversation with reminders about its attendant writing project, a memoir vignette that explores the relationship between students' cultures and their identities. Every line from an outside source was meant to inspire the students' own stories, and they were encouraged to listen actively to each other's comments because they might find inspiration for their project there. I followed Adilow's poem with an example vignette from Firoozeh Dumas's *Funny in Farsi: A Memoir of Growing Up Iranian in America* (2004). In the vignette, titled "The 'F Word,'" Dumas shares her own experience with her name:

> My cousin's name, Farbod, means "Greatness." When he moved to America, all the kids called him "Farthead." My brother Farshid ("He Who Enlightens") became "Farts--t." The name of my friend Neggar means "Beloved," although it can be more accurately translated as "She Whose Name Almost Incites Riots." Her brother Arash ("Giver") initially couldn't understand why every time he'd say his name, people would laugh and ask him if it itched. (62)

Dumas continues by poking fun at our American desire to shorten names, then teases us for being unable to do the "tongue aerobics" required to "pronounce *kh*, a sound more commonly associated in this culture with phlegm, or *gh*, the sound normally made by actors in the closing moments of a choking scene." She completes the teasing with a metaphor that brings my mom's classroom food festival to mind: "It's like adding a few new spices to the kitchen pantry. Move over, cinnamon and nutmeg, make room for cardamom and sumac" (63).

Here I paused to tell a quick story. On a vacation to Laos with my wife, we encountered a group of apprentice monks while touring one of their temples. A particularly friendly apprentice, around sixteen years old, told us that the group's English classes would be starting soon, and if we wanted to hang around, we could surely participate in their lesson. Excited, we did just that. The monks' teacher was excited that we'd be able to model English in an American accent, so he brought us to the front of the room to sound out a few words. My key word was *the*. The apprentices, all of whom were teenagers, kept replacing the *th* sound with an *f*. No problem, I thought. I'll just teach them how to gently lay the tip of their tongues between their teeth. I opened my mouth to model it. Hilarity ensued, as the class erupted into a vibrating chorus of *tbbbt* sounds, the sort that little children make when they stick out their tongues to tease each other. When our young friend who had invited us saw me chuckle, he challenged me to say a few words in Lao. I could not. The point, of course, is that we should have empathy when it comes to pronouncing names. "Other" languages aren't the only ones to require "tongue aerobics."

I asked the students to share any experiences with learning new sounds, and some did. We continued Dumas's vignette:

> My name, Firoozeh, chosen by my mother, means "Turquoise" in Persian. In America, it means "Unpronounceable" or "I'm Not Going to Talk to You Because I Cannot Possibly Learn Your Name and I Just Don't Want to Have to Ask You Again and Again Because You'll Think I'm Dumb or You Might Get Upset or Something." (63)

Fed up with this and all of her classmates calling her "Ferocious," twelve-year-old Dumas decided to add an "American" middle name. She chose

Julie for its simple sound. At the beginning of sixth grade, she noticed that people could now remember her name—until an unexpected problem arose:

> All was well until the Iranian Revolution, when I found myself with a new set of problems. Because I spoke English without an accent, and was known as Julie, people assumed that I was American. This meant that I was often privy to their real feelings about those "damn I-raynians." It was like having those X-ray glasses that let you see people naked, except what I was seeing was far worse than people's underwear. It dawned on me that these people would have probably never invited me to their house had they known me as Firoozeh. I felt like a fake. (65)

I took this opportunity to point out that Dumas's dilemma sounds similar to that of people who have had experience "passing." I explained the term for students who might be unfamiliar: Members of a minority cultural group/race might "pass" when, for whatever reason, they can present themselves as majority. In the African American community, the term generally refers to light-skinned black people who have entered the workforce as white. My grandmother recalled a time in the 1930s when her younger brothers walked into Cleveland's Halle's department store and, seeing their aunt working behind the counter, shouted, "Hi, Aunt Martha!" She immediately leaned down and told them, "Y'all have to get out of here. You're going to make me lose my job." They scurried away and got spanked when they got home. A less lighthearted example occurred when our family was planning a family reunion in Columbus, Ohio. One of my cousins tried to contact a local cousin who had lost touch with the family. They had been childhood friends. When finally tracked down over the phone, she told us in no uncertain terms that she wanted nothing to do with our family. She had grown up, started passing, gotten married, and had children and now grandchildren, all of whom thought she was white. We were to never call her again.

One of the unforeseen consequences of February Soup is that we are led to think that conflicts like these are only historical. However, many students, when given this "passing" lens through which to view Dumas's dilemma, see immediate connections in their own families. Middle Eastern students have "passed" as Latino to avoid being viciously stereotyped as terrorists. Biracial students have chosen to disown whatever side of the family causes the most complications. And in recent iterations of this conversation, students have brought up the Rachel Dolezal fiasco.

Dolezal was the president of the Spokane, Washington, chapter of the NAACP until she resigned following allegations that she was only "passing" as black. Her estranged parents outed her in an ABC News interview, producing childhood pictures of a younger, blond, blue-eyed version of their daughter. The situation grew into something of a national joke. On social media, the hashtag #AskRachel ridiculed her situation with mock black culture quizzes. There was a particularly biting caricature by Maya Rudolph on *Late Night with Seth Myers,* where she answered the question "Are either of your parents black?" by pointing to her bird's nest of a wig with an indignant sniff. When students brought up Dolezal in our discussion of Dumas, I invited them to ponder the conversations about white people that Dolezal would have been privy to as she played this role. How much did it compare to what Dumas might have experienced when she was known as Julie?

The Dumas memoir continues:

> When I went to college, I eventually went back to using my real name. All was well until I started looking for a job. Even though I had graduated with honors from UC-Berkeley, I couldn't get a single job interview. I was guilty of being a humanities major, but I began to suspect that there was more to my problems. After three months of rejections, I added "Julie" to my resume. (65)

I asked my students, "What do you think happened?" They were able to anticipate Dumas's following words:

> Call it a coincidence, but the job offers started coming in. Perhaps it's the same kind of "coincidence" that keeps African Americans from getting cabs in New York. (65)

We finished the vignette quickly, because I wanted to keep Dumas's employment dilemma at the top of the students' minds. Our final source would be from the documentary *Freakonomics* (2010), based on the best-selling book of the same name by Steven Levitt and Steven Dubner. The movie has a section titled "A Roshanda by Any Other Name," which takes students from a challenge to respect and appreciate the cultural complexity of names to the hard questions I want them to wrestle with. After a lighthearted anecdote about a mother who mistakenly named her daughter Temptress, trying to honor *Cosby Show* actress *Tempest* Bledsoe, the film introduces the work of Harvard economics professor Dr. Roland Fryer. Fryer studies what he calls Cultural Segregation, which he defines as the gap between white and black cultures. In an interview, Fryer says, "One embodiment . . . is what you name your kid. It's one of the few cultural items that we can really measure precisely." He described a 2003 study where he and *Freakonomics* coauthor Levitt compared children's first names to their eventual life outcomes. They analyzed the naming records of every baby born in California over four decades. Among other things, they noticed that African American parents were more likely than any other ethnic group to give their children unique names. In the interview, he tracked the naming patterns of African Americans over the decades: "In the fifties we saw huge overlaps in the naming patterns of blacks and whites, people naming their kids John, Michael. Names like that. And around 1968 or so—in the Black Power movement, actually—you saw distinct bifurcation, with black names getting more distinctively black, and a lot of them were Islamic names. Because the Black Power movement was about identity—*Who are we? Who are you? Are you part of us?*" He paused. "It wasn't until the late '80s and '90s that we started to get the *made-up*, concatenated names that you see now."

The movie cut quickly to a series of street interviews about *made-up* names. One black man said, "This generation today, they sort of changed the whole name concept. They have names that are thirty letters long!" Another said, "Everybody's trying to do something unique. They're trying to name their kid something different, you know?"

On cue, it cut back to Fryer. "We had 228 unique versions of the name *Unique*! My favorite was . . . " The movie cut to a series of caricatured black women, gesticulating as their names were scrawled across their bodies. "U-N-E-Q-Q-E-E, and another of my favorites was U-N-E-E-K. There are a lot of people trying to be unique." One girl in the movie, who looks to be around my students' age, looked at her name's spelling (U-N-E-Q-U-E) and shook her head. (See Figure 6.1 for a still shot of these four women with their names.) I paused *Freakonomics*.

Leaving the image shown in Figure 6.1 up on the board, I asked if anyone had any observations. The students started sharing made-up names they'd encountered, while some shared that their parents had created theirs. The latter sounded vaguely like a series of confessions. Sensing their embarrassment and recalling some of their comments during the viewing, I asked, "What is a *ghetto* name?"

My students laughed. I assured them that I was serious. "When we were watching, I overheard some of you saying that those spellings were *ghetto*. We know this word. We say it. What do you say now? *Ratchet*?" This caused more laughter, but this time more tension-deflating than nervous. "*Ratchet*. *Hood*. *Ghetto*. What makes a name any of these things?"

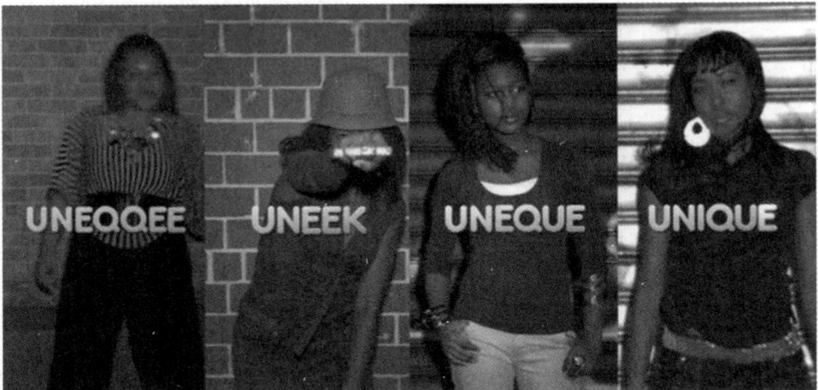

FIGURE 6.1
Here, *Freakonomics* seems to make a troubling assertion about names. I try to pause the video at this very moment, so my students can notice and analyze it.

"My name is ghetto." One of the class's most dependable voices, Mia, spoke up. A spectacular student who would go on to attend Yale, Mia rarely spoke without considerable reflection. Her classmates seemed confused as she gathered her thoughts. Finally, she said, "My name isn't Mia."

Gasps all around, including from me. Normally, my attendance sheet has captured every freshman's given name. I asked her dumbly, "What is your name?"

"Ja'mia." She weathered another wave of astonishment, then continued, "Yes, it's even got an apostrophe. I don't know what my mom was thinking!"

"What if she was just thinking that she liked the sounds?" I threw my hands out in mock exasperation. "Dr. Fryer used the word *concatenated*. Do you know what that means? No? To concatenate means to link something together." I encouraged them to copy the definition in their notebooks. "Can we agree that Dr. Fryer uses the word with a snide tone? Like he's making fun of people?" Most nodded. "He seems to have an issue with parents linking sounds together to make *unique* names. And"—indicating Mia—"we seem to have an issue with it too. It's *ghetto*. And if it is *ghetto*, it is ugly. So why, then, are these names not appreciated as compositions, like a string of notes in music, or an abstract art piece that hangs in a museum?"

A NOTE ON "GHETTO"

This question drew on an earlier classroom activity that bears mentioning. While introducing the *Native Son* unit (a conversation highlighted in the next chapter), I'd asked the students to reflect on the word *ghetto*. As in the N-word activity previously discussed, I wrote the word on the board. I asked students to respond in their notebooks, in three-minute intervals, to the following prompts: *Who*, *What*, *Where*, *When*, *Why*, and *How*? They were encouraged to see each prompt in all its complexity; for example, they could answer the first as "*Who* is ghetto?" or "*Who* uses the word *ghetto*?" or "*Who* is offended more by it?" After all the prompts were addressed in writing, students shared in pods, with the goal of better understanding the term's complexity. We then transitioned to whole class and collected the conversation on the board. With Chapter 2's variation on Ecclesiastes in mind, I told everyone, "There's a time for debate and a time for gathering thought" and reminded students that this was not the time for debate, that two opposing points could live side by side on the board. For example, under *What*, one student might focus on behaviors like excessive profanity in public spaces. Another might describe black vernacular or African American Vernacular English (AAVE). Under *When*, my Philly students tend to giggle and say "now," although someone is always eager to educate classmates on the term's Holocaust usage. Nobody is wrong. We are not debating the merits of each usage, just collecting and verifying our experiences with the term.

This activity is followed by a slide show that describes the Great Migration of African Americans from the rural South to other parts of the country between 1910 and 1970. The first slide is a census map from 1910, showing that most African Americans lived in the South. I asked students to describe what they knew about African Americans' lives in that part of the country at that time. After they shared various February Soup observations about oppression and racism, I told them that we'd focus on Jim Crow laws. Students were shown examples of laws such as the following, which did truly exist in the twentieth century:

> **Georgia**
>
> All persons licensed to conduct the business of selling beer or wine shall serve either White people exclusively or Colored people exclusively and shall not sell to the two races within the same room at any time.
>
> **Virginia**
>
> The conductors or managers on all such railroads shall have power, and are hereby required, to assign to each white or colored passenger his or her respective car, coach, or compartment. If the passenger fails to disclose his race, the conductor and managers, acting in good faith, shall be the sole judges of his race.

Students examined each law in pairs. Why didn't Georgia want "White" and "Colored" people to drink beer in the same room? Why would a train passenger in Virginia risk not disclosing his or her race? And if a passenger risked passing for white, what criteria might a conductor use to sniff them out? Nose width? Hair texture? Do you think they noticed the irony of such Naziesque techniques—when their country was at war with Nazism? While most students were familiar with bus segregation, few had understood the pervasiveness of Jim Crow.

From this, the discussion turned to the terrorism that supplanted rule of law in the Jim Crow South. I didn't linger here, only asking students to share what they had been taught about lynchings. We cobbled together stories about Emmett Till and church bombings. Knowing that *Native Son* discussions were coming up, I promised that we would be exploring mob violence deeply soon. We discussed the sparse economic opportunities with similar brevity. Students didn't know much about sharecropping, so I filled them in. After all of this, I asked how they would react to living in such an environment. Most replied, predictably, that they would try to move. The slide show then showed census maps from the Great Migration. Since many of my students are African American, I asked if any knew if/when their family moved north. More than a few of my students did, and shared stories that they'd heard. Finally, I asked what kind of environments many of these African American families encountered when they reached Philadelphia, Chicago, New York, Detroit, or any of the other cities from the census map. More specifically, how did so many of them end up concentrated in North Philly, Harlem, and the South Side of Chicago? This led to the introduction of redlining and other malicious policies that formed the modern-day *ghetto* that most of my students had described.

In her oft-cited TED Talk "The Danger of a Single Story" author Chimamanda Ngozi Adichie (2009) says, "Start the story with the arrows of the Native Americans, and not with the arrival of the British, and you have an entirely different story. Start the story with the failure of the African state, and not the colonial creation of the African state, and you have an entirely different story." When students start their examinations of the ghetto with its failing schools, high crime rate, and dilapidated housing instead of with people of color's endurance through Jim Crow laws, sharecropping, and mob violence, students are denied the opportunity to understand the ghetto's complexity. When denied such an opportunity, it is easier to be repulsed by ugliness, where students might otherwise celebrate resilience.

From this stance, classroom conversations can explore how African Americans drew spirituals from slavery, the blues from sharecropping, jazz and hip-hop from the "hood." Beauty, then, is to be measured not only through Eurocentric ideals, but in divergence from these ideals—sometimes because of oppression, sometimes just because, as Gwendolyn Brooks (1960) puts it, "We Real Cool."

HARD PROBLEM NO. 1

So, I asked my students, why are uniquely black names not more appreciated as compositions? Why should prospective parents choose from a pot of acceptable names in order for their child's name to not be *ghetto*? The answers, received in a whole-class format, started with, "Because if they don't, the name will be *different*, and people assume that things that are different are ugly." And "It will look like your parents can't spell." These and other comments were followed by real-time rebuttals, like, "That's not true, though!" and "But that's stereotyping!" At each, I reminded students that their classmates were merely answering my prompt, not expressing their own opinions. Still, the temperature of the room had risen. A student expressed, defensively, that she didn't want a "basic" name anyway. Some of her classmates agreed. Eventually, someone said, "People assume that if you have a distinctively black name, that you are from a ghetto family, and you might be from a ghetto neighborhood, and you might have some ghetto tendencies. Like you might be loud or disrespectful."

I asked, "How might that perception—even if it isn't true—hurt you?"

"You might not get a job."

I had been waiting for this. Telling them to keep this answer to my prompt in mind, I continued the video. Soon after the four unfortunate *UNIQUE* caricatures, the narrator introduces Dr. Sendhil Mullainathan, another professor of economics at Harvard. Mullainathan was interested in finding out how much the pay gap between whites and blacks was affected by the latter's not being hired in the first place. He designed a resume study to test this, which he described:

> What we did was make up 5,000 resumes. Half of them we put an African American name [Tyrone], half of them we put

> a white name [Greg]. Otherwise, the resumes were the same. And we sent them out. And then we said, "Which will get called back more?"

Here, I paused the video to ask, "What do you think happened? Who got more calls, Greg or Tyrone?" The students answered "Greg!" in near-unison, as if it was a silly question. When I asked them why, a student cited the previous comment, that bosses assume that Tyrone is more likely to be disrespectful, loud, and unmanageable. He might need more time catching up to the skill level of his colleagues because of his inexperience. I followed up with, "So in bosses' eyes, Greg is easier to work with than Tyrone. It's not that Tyrone is *bad*, it's just that it's a little more likely that the process will be smoother with Greg."

An African American student chimed in, "It also depends on the kind of business. If I am selling things, for example, my customers might trust Greg more than Tyrone. They might even be afraid of Tyrone. So, even if I am not racist, if I am selling to racist people, I might not want to hire Tyrone." When a classmate asked if that was itself a racist stance, he said, "Yes, in a way, I guess. But I'm in business to make money, not save the world." Though the language was combative, the tone was playful, and the honesty of the point seemed to resonate. I asked for a simple up-and-down vote on whether Greg got more calls, and it was unanimous. When the video replayed, Mullainathan resumed his explanation:

> What we found was that, the same resume, when it had an African American name, was about 33 percent less likely to get an interview than when it had a white name. It means that if a white person is looking for a job for ten weeks, an equivalently skilled African American person would be searching for fifteen weeks. And those are five long weeks if you are unemployed.

Then, considering the results, Dr. Mullainathan provided our conversation's hard problem:

> The names we used in our study were names like *Lakisha*, *Jamal*, *Tyrone*. Based on our results, it raises a question. I'm an African American parent; I'm thinking about naming my child. Tyrone sounds like a very good name. I might have had a grandfather named Tyrone . . . Should I name my child Tyrone? Yes, if you name your child Tyrone, you have made it harder for them in the labor market. On the other hand, should you give in to that? Should I give in to the prevailing norms, or should I express my individuality? It's a bit of an ethical quandary . . . You might choose a distinctly black name as a way to signal something about yourself, and about your commitment to the black community. And that's a way to show other African Americans, *look: I am really black*.

I stopped the video; the rest of the documentary goes on to make some interesting, yet slightly classroom-inappropriate, social-class observations about names. Asking students to answer in their notebooks, I rephrased Mullainathan's question. "Considering the findings of both studies, would you give your child a name that was distinctively black?" At a student's request, I expanded the question to include all names that were distinctively *not white*. They wrote for three minutes, silently. Then I asked them to share in pairs. While roaming around the room, I overheard many citing their own parents' decision making. When I brought them back to whole class, I mentioned this observation. Then, to match their openness, I shared my own parents' dilemma. Both had distinctive names. My father, Rosamond, inherited his name from his father, who, in turn, inherited it from *his* father. He loved his name, but like Dumas, found himself ceaselessly frustrated by white people's need to shorten it to "Rosey" after Rosey Grier, the NFL star. A self-described Sydney Poitier moderate (who didn't even *like* sports), my father let white strangers truncate his name. In his thirties, however, he demanded to be called Rosamond. My mother's experience wasn't as dramatic—people just never spelled her name correctly. She would introduce herself, "I'm Sherrill with two *R*s and two *L*s." When it came their turn to face Dr.

Mullainathan's question, it was a no-brainer. They went as commonplace as possible with *Matthew*. Then, to leave no doubt, they flipped through a name book to pair it with a perfectly "nice" middle name: *Evan*. There was a brief discussion about adding the *Rosamond* that I use now, but, in my dad's words, they "chickened out." Students asked what my name would have been if I'd been born a girl. *Emily*. They found this hilarious.

Similar alternate realities and Mullainathanian dilemmas were shared. When it came to their own future choices, students generally expressed disappointment at the 33 percent statistic, but were at near consensus that they felt free to pass on their culture's naming conventions. In most shared opinions, the *concatenated* names of the 1980s and 1990s had softened the ground for more unique-sounding names. My students found themselves agreeing with Dumas's assertion at the end of her vignette:

> Despite a few exceptions, I have found that Americans are now far more willing to learn new names, just as they're far more willing to try new ethnic foods. (2004, 67)

Yet, even as she uplifts, Dumas hedged with the following story:

> Of course, some people *just don't like to learn*. One mom at my children's school adamantly refused to learn my "impossible name" and instead settled on calling me "F-Word." She was recently transferred to New York where, from what I've heard, she might meet an immigrant or two and, who knows, she just might have to make some room in her spice cabinet. (2004, 67)

HARD PROBLEM NO. 2

The hard problem presented by scholars Fryer and Mullainathan, then brilliantly illustrated by artists Dumas and Adilow, was this: How should BouBou, Georjelis, Oluwatobiloba, Amani, and Ja'mia interact with people who *just don't like to learn*? And names were just the beginning. Over the next few weeks, we tackled the same hard problem regarding other cultural elements. Language was next, where, among other prompts, we analyzed the statements of South Philly's Joey Vento, an Italian American pizza shop owner whose sign, which read, "*This is AMERICA—WHEN ORDERING SPEAK ENGLISH,*" attracted national attention many years ago. We pause a news interview with Fox News's Glenn Beck long enough to copy a quote from Vento on the board:

> I don't understand. You don't want to assimilate into this country and learn our language, well, then you shouldn't have came here then. Stay where you was. (2007)

From here, students did the exegesis activity first discussed in Chapter 4, where students "broke down" Kendrick Lamar's "Alright," only this time they were doing it in one-on-one conversations. I asked them to circle a word in Vento's quote, then explain to their partner how this observation might reveal Vento's true reasoning. As with "Alright," students enjoyed hunting for uniquely "deep" observations. An example: One student pointed out the irony of Vento's vernacular grammatical slip-up at the end, arguing that his "stay where you was" showed that he himself had not fully mastered the English language. Another pushed back that Vento was merely appropriating South Philly slang, that most people on East Passyunk Avenue spoke like that. If so, Vento might be showing that he had assimilated at a street level *past* the King's English, something that the son of immigrants might have been proud of. We continued in that fashion until nearly every word was circled, before giving the same attention to the patriotic iconography on the sign: American flag, bald eagle, bold letters, italics, caps—all above a strikingly spare black-and-white reminder: "Management Reserves The Right To Refuse Service."

This was a man, a *type*, really, who was spectacularly disinterested in adding more room to his spice cabinet. And, just like the teacher who renamed Georjelis, the students who made fun of BouBou, and the people who insist, despite constant correction, that Amani pronounces her own name wrong, his type cannot be entirely avoided. Not only do they make our cheesesteaks and share our lunchrooms, but they also vote in our elections, draft and enforce our laws, write our histories. In this series of conversations, students disassemble the Joey Ventoian instinct to say *ewww*, articulate its many weaknesses, and challenge any who still hold it to try gratitude instead.

PURPOSE, REVISITED

I would not hold these name conversations without giving students the opportunity to write memoir vignettes. There are multiple reasons. First, even with a varying conversational package, students will be eager to share more stories than classroom time allows. They must always know that there is another depository for their anecdotes. Second, memoirs are perhaps the easiest way to contribute to scholarship. Nobody is an expert on their lives but themselves, and nobody has more power to clear up cultural misconceptions. In order to conceptualize the life of the enslaved, the world needed Olaudah Equiano and Harriet Ann Jacobs just as much as it needed Harriet Beecher Stowe. And now, we need *A Long Way Gone* and *I Am Malala*, *Angela's Ashes* and *Girl, Interrupted*.

Finally, holding these conversations without allowing students to celebrate themselves in ink risks their leaving each conversation remembering only the sting of their "othering." We want to make doubly sure that this does not happen. I pair the memoir with an analytical essay where, if they wish, students may engage the Joey Ventos of the world in debate. Without an endgame writing opportunity, these conversations might cause hurt instead of building confidence. The last step is to make sure that, if students are interested, there is a way they can publish their memoir vignettes on our class blog or submit them to our school's literary magazine.

Professional Practice: "Put This in Your Pocket"

1. In this chapter's "Note on Extending Time" section, I describe the prompting process before a one-on-one discussion. The note focused on the timing of prompts, trying to find the balance between encouraging a sense of urgency and giving students enough time to express

themselves. This has a companion reminder, one that I've consistently offered to student teachers and people transitioning to a more dialogic approach: *While repeating prompts during wait time, avoid subtly changing them or asking too many follow-ups.* Often, we will over-talk when offering ideas for students to respond to. This might be because we are unnerved by their silence, thinking they need us to offer a slightly more digestible interpretation of the prompt. Other times, we give voice to more complex ideas as soon as they enter our minds, which leads us to unintentionally overwhelm students. I've caught myself doing this frequently, sounding like this: *Turn to a buddy and talk about the significance of your name . . . Where did it come from? Why did their parents give you that name? . . . Are you named after someone? . . . What do you feel about it? Why? Has that feeling changed?* And the more they look at me, the more I keep going. Finally, when I shut up, a student might raise her hand and earnestly ask, "What do you want us to talk about?" Some of her classmates, who have been able to sift through my wordiness to find my point, might giggle at this. I just overloaded her working memory. Her classmates were able to select *one* of my questions as a jumping-off point, and deftly ignore the rest. She could not, and I've unintentionally set her up for embarrassment. Ask one prompt at a time.

2. One of the mentor texts from this chapter was Firoozeh Dumas's memoir, *Funny in Farsi.* When reading the text many years ago, a former colleague, Alexa Dunn, reached out to Dumas to speak to her students. She accepted, much to the students' delight. My ninth graders have had similar success getting Jean Kwok, the author of *Girl in Translation* (2010), to respond to their questions via email. I am always honored when authors take the time to join our conversations, and after these (and other) successes, I've encouraged students to invite them to do so. Some authors, knowing that my students were using their texts to spark conversations, offered even more effusive encouragement, going as far as asking my students to send them their final projects. There are a lot of kind professionals out there who are eager to help us encourage our students' voices. Give them a chance to do so.

3. A last point on the relationship between mentor texts, conversational packages, and publishing: I've always tried to maintain the following bedrock understanding: If students are reading and discussing memoirs, they must write memoirs. If they are reading and discussing poems, they must write poems. Whatever I am asking them to analyze, they must be encouraged to create. This, as argued in Chapter 4, allows students to see themselves as a fresh generation of artists, thinkers, and doers—not just passive consumers of other people's ideas. My experience working with teaching artists as part of the Wilma Theater's Wilmagination residency program has further pushed my thinking on this. Through Wilmagination, which "provides fully subsidized, project based theater residencies in Philadelphia high schools" (https://www.wilmatheater.org/education/wilmagination), my drama classes are generously treated to a matinee play. They then spend four to six weeks discussing, writing, and creating an original theatrical performance inspired by the play's themes, which they perform before their friends, their families, and their classmates. During this process, students who rarely speak during whole-class discussion often reveal incredible analytical prowess while "speaking back" to our mentor text through dance, song, or art. Some students reveal incredible flashes of humor that, in my classroom discussions, had gone unnoticed. This continually humbles me, and reminds me how little I actually know about my students despite

our house talk activities. I remember to not only keep my conversational package as diversified as possible, but to be as imaginative and expansive as possible when defining what it means for them to "publish" their responses to our conversations.

CHAPTER 7

PLAYING THE OTHER: THOUGHTFULLY TACKLING CULTURAL APPROPRIATION

In 2015, *Hunger Games* actress Amandla Stenberg, then sixteen years old, posted a school project to Tumblr that quickly went viral. In the project, a video podcast titled "Don't Cash Crop on My Cornrows," she and a classmate entered the thorny debate around cultural appropriation. On camera, Stenberg opened by teaching her audience that "Black hair has always been an essential component of black culture. Black hair requires upkeep in order for it to grow and remain healthy, so black women

have always 'done' their hair; it's just a part of our identity. Braids, locs, twists, and cornrows, etc. Cornrows are a really functional way of keeping black-textured hair unknotted and neat, but, like, with style." She paused before continuing with, "Hair is such a big part of hip-hop and rap culture. These are styles of music which African American communities created in order to affirm our identities and our voices."

Stenberg noted that "As the early 2000s turned into the 2010s, white people began to wear clothing and accessories associated with hip-hop. More and more celebrities could be seen wearing cornrows and braids . . . By 2013, the fashion world had adopted cornrows as well. Cornrows were seen on high-fashion runways for brands like Marchesa and Alexander McQueen, and magazines had editorial campaigns featuring cornrows as a *new* 'urban hairstyle.'" She went on to describe non-hair-based examples of cultural appropriation, including Miley Cyrus's twerking, and Katie Perry's use of AAVE, and watermelon eating in her 2014 music video *This Is How We Do*. She then mentioned Iggy Azalea, the Australian-born blond rapper whose song "Fancy" reached No. 1 on *Billboard* magazine's charts in 2014.

The podcast then took a bitter turn, as Stenberg recapped the racial unrest following the Trayvon Martin decision, in which Florida native George Zimmerman was found not guilty after shooting and killing a seventeen-year-old black youth. She noted that while many celebrities "spread awareness and shared condolences," others remained silent. Stenberg paraphrased tweets from black rapper Azealia Banks, "White musicians who partook in Hip-Hop Culture and adopted *Blackness*, Iggy Azalea in particular, failed to speak on the racism that comes along with Black identity" (@azealiabanks, December 3, 2014). This issue demonstrated, for Stenberg, one of the many complexities of cultural appropriation. However, Stenberg chose to sidestep the Azalea/Banks dispute and instead offered a series of declarations, starting with, "The line between appropriation and cultural exchange is always going to be blurred, but here's the thing: Appropriation occurs when a style leads to racist generalizations or stereotypes, but is deemed as high fashion, cool, or funny when the privileged take it for themselves. Appropriation occurs when the appropriator is not aware of the deep significance of the culture that they are partaking in. Hip-hop stems from a black struggle, it stems from jazz and blues, styles of music that African Americans created to retain humanity in the face of adversity." She then brings the topic full circle. "Braids and cornrows are not merely stylistic, they are necessary to keep black hair neat." Then finally, Stenberg offers a question: "What would America be like if we loved black people as much as we love black culture?"

In Chapter 4, I offered three propositions that ensure that our conversations have a clear purpose. The last of these was that we should encourage our students to publish whenever prudent and possible. Stenberg's podcast is a lovely example of the kind of thoughtful, passionate, well-researched contribution that our students can offer to the greater world. It is limited, sure, as are most opinion pieces, regardless of the author's age. Stenberg dodges a hard problem that she'd carefully set up: *Must people who appropriate black culture always stand up for issues that concern the black community?* It would be impossible for her to answer this definitively in the last two minutes spent on her group's project—and doing so would have led her away from her potent "What would America be like . . ." rhetorical flourish. If anything, Stenberg's project shows how slippery a hard problem can be, and how easily our students can unintentionally disengage it before all the meat is off the bone.

Her rush to offer a final definition for cultural appropriation is understandable, given the high emotions that accompany this topic. My students, anecdotally, spend more time arguing about cultural appropriation than other contemporary racial issues. This makes sense. Other contemporary hot-button conversations tend to be mostly adult business (the role of race in the 2016 election), or involve remote, easily *othered* bad guys (police brutality against black men and women). Cultural appropriation, on the other hand, is intimate. For students of color, the debate is about the proprietary nature of their style, their music, their speech patterns, any and all cultural elements that are the source of pride. From here, it's hard to approach phenomena like Rachel Dolezal, the white woman who passed for black, with objectivity. Furthermore, in a diverse classroom, the offending act might be happening two desks over: a white girl wearing cornrows, a black boy who loves anime, an ill-conceived Halloween costume, the wrong music blasting from a wealthy classmate's car stereo. This proximity means that offended students can actually confront perceived violators in ways that they can't engage, say, Darren Wilson, the former Ferguson, Missouri, police officer who shot and killed Michael Brown. These confrontations are made more contentious when the accused consider themselves the victims of hypersensitivity and ignorance: Isn't it a compliment to copy someone's style? What made it yours to begin with? Did you know that dreadlocks were worn by Celtic cultures too? This *purposes* conflict (see Chapter 2) pits others' perceptions of a person's actions against that person's actual intent. Stenberg's piece urgently tries to provide clarity for both sides—*this* counts as cultural appropriation, *this* does not.

Definitions are important. But in this case, the effort to define *cultural appropriation* is the *least* interesting part of any powerful class conversation. For our reference in this chapter, the *Cambridge Dictionary* defines cultural appropriation as "the act of taking or using things from a culture that is not your own, especially without showing that you understand or respect this culture." A teacher could set out to teach students that styles that lead to racist generalizations or stereotypes are unacceptable, and that privileged cultures should have enough empathy to not find humor in taking on racial stereotypes. But, as argued in Chapter 3, we should not tarry long on the simple stuff on the way to the hard problem, especially one as juicy as Stenberg's battle of the Azaleas. Why quibble over whether Elvis, Iggy, Macklemore, or Eminem had the right to take up a traditionally black music genre? They already have, and many more will, regardless of whether we have defined such behavior as *cultural appropriation*. Instead, dialogic teachers should encourage their students to explore why we appropriate, why it can be so viscerally offensive, and most importantly, what responsibility—if any—people owe the cultures they copy. Following are two cultural appropriation conversations from my unit on Richard Wright's *Native Son*. The first asks students to understand the influence of stereotypes on cultural appropriation, while the second challenges them to articulate why people are so passionate on both sides.

It is important to note that early versions of my *Native Son* unit did not engage cultural appropriation. Only after two years of dissecting the text did I notice this particular gem tucked between larger themes of individual agency, racialized violence, and prejudice in our justice system. I say this to remind us how important it is for administrators to give teachers the time to "get good" at teaching a text. Too often teachers, especially those working with at-risk students, are forced to adopt every new initiative that rolls down the pike. This disincentivizes the reflection that unearths some of our best conversational prompts.

"LET'S PLAY WHITE": CULTURAL APPROPRIATION IN *NATIVE SON*, PART 1

If the name conversations discussed in Chapter 6 encourage my students' most passionate responses, Richard Wright's *Native Son* inspires their longest and most ardent commitment. The classic text, with its gritty naturalism and page-turning suspense, is written at a sixth-grade Lexile level, which helps struggling readers spend more energy analyzing than deciphering. The protagonist, a young black man named Bigger Thomas, is magnetic. The setting, the Black Belt of 1930s Chicago, resembles the urban Philadelphia neighborhoods that so many of my students recognize. The plot features at least two murders, a lynch mob, crass sexual deviancy, a thrilling manhunt—and ends with a dialogic teacher's best friend, a trial. Wright's language mixes the edginess of street lit with the poetry of Ellison's *Invisible Man*. His themes both evoke the Du Bois versus Washington debate and portend Tim Wise's writings about white privilege. Most important, students walk into class excited to discuss the book. The teacher, for once, has to match the text's energy and keep up with its momentum.

The first major conversation of the unit asks students to dissect and analyze the term *ghetto*. This conversation, described fully in Chapter 6, encourages students to reflect on any preconceived notions they may have about Bigger Thomas's neighborhood. It also introduces the lenses of Jim Crow, racialized violence, and the Great Migration, all of which are necessary for students to fully understand *Native Son*. When the reading starts, the students meet Bigger at his family's one-room, rat-infested apartment. After cornering and violently killing a rat with a cast-iron skillet, Bigger is driven from the apartment by his mother's nagging accusations: "We wouldn't have to live in this garbage dump if you had any manhood in you . . . Suppose those rats cut our veins at night when we sleep? Naw! Nothing like that ever bothers you! . . . Bigger, honest, you the most no-countest man I ever seen in all my life!" (1999, 9).

Bigger meets up with his friend Gus, and they idle around the streets. A plane flies overhead, which sparks a friendly debate over whether or not Bigger could ever be a pilot. Gus wins with, "If you wasn't black and if you had some money and if they'd let you go to aviation school, you *could* fly a plane." Both men laugh at the absurdity of Gus's *ifs* before Bigger says, "It's funny how the White folks treat us, isn't it?" (17).

They smoke cigarettes and lean against a wall until Bigger, clearly more bothered by the earlier exchange than he'd let on, turns to his friend and says, "Let's play 'White'" (17). Over the next two pages, the two friends take turns mimicking conversations between important white people. First up is a generic general being ordered by his superior to "Send your men over the river at dawn and attack the enemy's left flank . . . Send the Fifth, Sixth, and Seventh regiments . . . and attack with tanks, gas, planes, and infantry" (18). They break character to laugh at the idea that neither knows what "left flank" means. The next white caricature is Gus's J. P. Morgan, who wants to "sell twenty thousand shares of U.S. Steel in the market this morning . . . just dump 'em at any price, we're holding too much" (18–19). Bigger apparently likes this impression, for he compliments Gus with "I bet that's *just* the way they talk" (19). Seeking to one-up his friend, Bigger pretends to be President Roosevelt, calling for an emergency cabinet meeting. When Gus asks why it's so important that they meet, Bigger responds, through laughter, "Well, you see, the niggers is raising sand all over the country . . . we gotta do something about these black folks . . ." (19). Gus responds, "Oh, if it's about the niggers, I'll be right there, Mr. President" (19).

Here, I ask students my first question: *What do Bigger and Gus's caricatures reveal about their idea of whiteness?* This prompt is inspired by Wright's constant contrasting of a mystical "white world" with the reality of Bigger's Black Belt:

> They had the feeling that the robbing of Blum's would be a violation of ultimate taboo; it would be a trespassing into territory where the full wrath of an alien white world would be turned

> loose upon them; in short, it would be a symbolic challenge of the white world's rule over them; a challenge which they yearned to make, but were afraid to. (14)
>
> Then they guffawed, partly at themselves and partly at the vast white world that sprawled and towered in the sun before them. (18)
>
> It was a shadowy region, a No Man's Land, the ground that separated the white world from the black that he stood upon. (67)
>
> And now, here it was. He had always felt outside of this white world, and now it was true. (221)
>
> Why should not this cold white world rise up as a beautiful dream in which he could walk and be at home, in which it would be easy to tell what to do and what not to do? (241)

It seems important to Wright to prove how alien the white world was to Bigger and his ilk, so it makes sense for students to consider whiteness's perceived attributes. When first asked, students usually focus on *power*. In a recent discussion around this point, a student cleverly phrased it, "Bigger and Gus talk about white people like they are monsters. Or gods. They have so much power over things, like moving armies and making money. But Bigger doesn't have any power. His mom was just cursing him out for not having the power to move his family out the 'hood.'"

The choice to make discussions student-centered means that we, as teachers, must discern which student comments are rich enough to be redirected to the rest of the class and built on. We fail at this nearly as often as we succeed. But years of scrutinizing texts has revealed a cheat code: breaking student comments into key words and phrases that can be analyzed individually. This is tricky to pull off in real time—we may have to buy a few more seconds, ask students to repeat themselves if we need more time to dissect. Doing so encourages them to be clear, and most important, models that listening actively demands that one take the time to *hear* a comment before responding. Upon hearing the clever student's quote, my brain highlighted the words *monster*, *god*, *power*, and the phrase *move his family out the 'hood.* Of these, I was most intrigued by the supernatural comparisons. I wrote *Monsters?* and *Gods?* on the board, complimented the comment, then said, "Let's stick there for a second. Why would Bigger and Gus see white people as *monsters*?"

With the last chapter's *ghetto* conversation still fresh, the answers were predictable. Students described the Jim Crow and Klan terrorism that Bigger had likely witnessed. After turning the focus to *gods,* I was amused by one student's slightly irreverent connection. Alicia said, "*Gods* are powerful beyond all of our understanding. They control everything. And they do it without any rules. They just do whatever they want, really. And we spend all our energy trying to understand and . . ." She searched for the right word. "*Justify* their behavior. Like black people trying to *get* white people."

The class really seemed eager to respond, but I challenged her to root her point in the text. She had no problem. "We got a general, a rich guy, and the president. All three aren't seen by the people they impact. All three can ruin someone's entire life without ever really knowing them. And look at what Bigger says . . ." She opened the book and checked something. "Yeah. He orders the general to send in 'tanks, gas, planes, and infantry.' He is about to kill a lot of people on both sides. And he says it so . . ." She stopped again, looking again for the perfect word, as was her habit.

"Cavalierly?"

"What's that mean?"

"Like he doesn't care that much whether his soldiers live or die." I repeated the word a few times, asking them to get it down in their notebooks. I motioned for Alicia to continue.

"He does the same thing with the rich guy. He moves money all recklessly. 'Just dump them at any price,' he says. If it hurts poor people, it doesn't really matter."

Ty, a classmate, chipped in. "Building off Alicia . . ." This phrase, more than any other, evidences the health of a classroom community. With it, Ty is saying, *I acknowledge that I would not have had this idea without Alicia laying a foundation. Her idea is a tangible thing that I am grateful for the chance to build on.* His citation doesn't just mean he was listening actively to Alicia; it also makes the thread clear and traceable. Students have surprised me by remembering which of their classmates was responsible for an idea days after it was first uttered. Ty continued, "The president caricature is godlike too, but different. He's not . . . cavalier. He's just straight-up dangerous. And he's focused on black people in a way we think God is focused on us. You can tell because he's ready to drop everything to meet about 'the niggers.'" Ty, African American, blanketed the N-word with air quotes.

I saw a chance to push a little harder. "So Bigger and Gus think that white people are all-powerful, reckless with that power, and yet still oddly obsessed with black people. This last part—I wonder what would make Bigger feel that way. I mean, he has next to no contact with them, right? Is it wishful thinking? That he hopes that people in the white world are busy thinking about people in the Black Belt?"

A few hands shot up, and I called on Erica, who didn't tend to speak much. "It's like celebrities. We like to pretend that they know who we are and care about us, but they don't." I overheard some gentle teasing of students who were well-known fans of Beyoncé and LeBron James. *They don't care about you!* answered by, *She loves me, she just doesn't know it yet.*

Another voice, Donovan, edged in, "Or, maybe it's like Mr. Kay said. Bigger and Gus have lived through oppression. You don't randomly lynch people or make Jim Crow laws. That stuff was on purpose. Someone *is* having meetings about how to hurt black people. Their game is not ridiculous."

"No, it's not." I smiled. I had been waiting for someone to make some version of Donovan's point. Now that he had, I could finally transition to the meat of this cultural appropriation conversation. "Not ridiculous at all. In fact, how many of you have played this game?" They were not expecting this, and there were a lot of giggles. Raising my own hand, I asked again, "How many of you have *played white*?" Nearly every student of color in the classroom raised their hand. One asked if it applied only to playing white, to which I answered, "Good question. Let's keep this to just playing white. For now." Students noted that some of their white classmates had raised their hands, which they found hilarious. Motioning for hands to go down, I asked, "What does it look like when you do it? Any volunteers?"

The class *oohed*, and a few of my goofier personalities kept their hands up. Curious, I picked one of my white volunteers. She prefaced with, "We don't call it 'playing white.' But we still do the same thing, like making fun of Starbucks girls." Her classmates loved this—some called out "Oh, does that count? I do that!"—before I shushed them. I asked her to do the voice, and she responded by ordering a fancy latte in what my generation would call a Valley Girl affect, broken up by red-faced fits of laughter. Classmates of all racial backgrounds agreed that she had given us a solid impression.

After giving the room a chance to settle, I said, "So the same question applies to you then. What do these caricatures reveal about *your* idea of whiteness? What is similar to Bigger and Gus in 1930s Chicago? What is different?" I asked them to turn to a neighbor for this one, and said we would be back together in three minutes. As usual, I walked around. After less time than I'd promised, I brought them back to whole class. They shared observations about how different their modern impressions were from Bigger and Gus's—there was no awe, no godlike power. No fear.

However, one student added, "The tone is the same." Indicating the Starbucks girl actress, she continued, "Indifferent. Really casual, like whatever happens in the world is cool, because you run it."

"That's so interesting, because it's a stereotype, right? I mean *all* white people do not run the world. Many of them have very real problems. How come your white impressions don't reflect that? Do you see impressions of poor white people?"

Most of them shook their heads. One said, "We don't see them. And if we did, we wouldn't make fun of them." My brain spun out clips of *The Beverly Hillbillies*, *Deliverance*, and *Honey BooBoo*. I wondered why none of my students could recollect lower-class whiteness being exploited for comedy. I made a mental note to enter this conversation next time with media examples like these—perhaps even the eleventh chapter of Nancy Isenberg's 2016 book *White Trash: The 400-Year Untold History of Class in America*, in which Isenberg describes the popularity of *Deliverance* and the odd journey of Tammy Faye. Still, I could neither ignore nor dismiss the similarities between Bigger's urban perspective and that of my students. Nor could I dismiss what was now a startling connection—one I *had* prepared for.

"How many of you have heard of minstrel shows?" A few hands rose. I asked for a volunteer to explain the term for classmates who might be unfamiliar. This approach requires patience, for while I am no historian, I'd spent hours the previous night boning up on minstrelsy. Any information offered by students was sure to be at best incomplete, and at worst misleading or inaccurate. We face this decision more often than we realize: It is more expedient for teachers to prime the conversational pump by providing our own background information. Still, doing so positions the teacher as expert, which, true as it may be, dismisses an easy opportunity for kids to practice an often underassessed facet of understanding: the ability to teach each other. Plus, we don't realize how often our students consider us showoffs. And how rarely they find it endearing.

A student turned to her classmates and said, "I think I saw a movie about this. People used to go to shows in blackface and make fun of black people."

"Why did they do that?"

She chuckled. "Because they were racist? I don't know, Kay."

A few more student contributions built on this foundation. I then offered a barebones history of minstrel shows, culled mostly from Chapter 6 of Jabari Asim's book *The N Word* (2008). Together, the class read sections that explained the following: From the early nineteenth century to the early twentieth, one of America's most popular forms of entertainment cast troupes of mostly white musicians, actors, and (most interestingly to my students) the precursors of modern-day spoken-word poets, as cartoonish black caricatures. These shows advertised themselves as "innovative performances derived from 'fieldwork' conducted on the plantations of the South. Blackface comedy, according to such claims, was a faithful introduction to the 'sports and pastimes of the Negro race'" (75). Here I stopped briefly to check if students understood what this meant—mainly that these shows considered themselves displays of *scientific research.* It wasn't, as Bigger and Gus said after their game:

> "I bet that's *just* the way they talk," Gus said.
>
> "I wouldn't be surprised," Bigger said. (Wright 1999, 19)

It was more like *We have studied this and can speak with absolute certainty that this is "how they talk."* It is, essentially, the difference between getting your laughs from the class clown and taking in a funny lecture from your eccentric science teacher. With this clear, we got down to specifics, working through the structure of the shows before settling on the shows' common language. Dan Emmett, a nineteenth-century entertainer whose troupe is generally considered the first to blacken the faces of an entire band, saw an opportunity to build on the minstrel trend of using "gibberish as a reasonable parody of black speech." He published a series of *Negro Sermons* containing lines like, "Den yoa see de meanin of de 'postle when he say: de 'archiloozikus winky-wamity, an reelderackus weltigooberous am too flamity bango, for de crackaboolity ob its own watchafalarity" (Asim 2008, 76).

I asked for a few volunteers to attempt to read the above gibberish from Asim's book. They had trouble doing so, and most seemed to find its awkward racism unnerving. Finally, we reviewed Asim's description of minstrelsy's most famous artifact, Jim Crow. The character began as a dance, performed by enslaved children in the Sea Islands of Georgia to accompanying lyrics such as these:

> Where you going, buzzard?
> Where you going, crow?
> I'm going down to new ground
> To knock Jim Crow. (77)

T. D. Rice, a traveling white performer, claimed to have witnessed a black laborer named "Cuff" doing the routine. Rice, sensing an opportunity, persuaded Cuff to teach him the step and song, which he then performed for various audiences to much acclaim before getting a gig in New York City. At each show, Rice "accented his lines with gestures and movements allegedly taken from his direct observations of blacks." For this, he was "frequently praised by whites for the accuracy of his performances" (Asim 2008, 78). Rice gradually modified the Jim Crow ditty with "a liberal distribution of [the word] *Nigger*, presumably in keeping with the tone and style of typical minstrel patter" (78–79). Here, Asim makes a connection that astounded my students:

> "Delineators," as minstrels were sometimes called, often declared their fitness to perform their material by asserting their authenticity as "niggers" in the same manner that modern

> rappers proudly (and loudly) lay claim to their status as "real niggas." For example, a minstrel might proclaim: "I'm a full-blooded niggar, / Ob de real ole stock, / And wid my head and shoulder, / I can split a horse block" (79)

I asked students for any examples that backed up Asim's comparison. They provided these:

The Notorious B.I.G.'s "Real Niggaz"
On the road to riches and diamond rings
Real niggaz do real things
Hangin wit the b------ is the song I sing
Real niggaz do real things.

Meek Mill's "Real Niggas Come First"
Niggas claiming they real
they wrist and neck ain't official
They got me out in the field
a nigga back on his gristle.

Jay Z's "Moment of Clarity"
I gave you volume after volume of my work
so you can feel my truths
I built the Dynasty by being one of the realest niggas out
Way beyond a Reasonable Doubt.

The listing went on for nearly a minute. With each example, students showed various levels of both connection and consternation, until one student, Tim, whined playfully, "You always ruin things."

"I do?"

To ironic applause, he cited a moment from his freshman year, when a lesson on the Marxist literary lens ruined Disney's *Aladdin* movie. "We don't want to think that deep about it all the time, Kay. You always make everything out to be so bad."

"No I don't!" I shouted, mockingly defensive. "Wait, do I?" Most of his classmates, some of whom I hadn't even taught in ninth grade, agreed. This ruining was not a new accusation, and I took it more seriously than I let on. "You ruin things" can be a compliment as long as students are pointing out disequilibrium—that they never feel quite settled, that no idea is safe from rich analysis. It is a problem, however, if they are trying to communicate that my curriculum seems determined to sap their joy. In Chapter 3, I recommended that we avoid a Jeffersonian dismissal of minorities' joy. Remember his foolish, myopic, and unmistakably sinister statement, "Among the Blacks is Miser enough, God knows, but no Poetry." I should never be eager to frame my students' world as a gauntlet of oppression, aided by their own deleterious cultural elements. Scholarship is not the cultivation of paranoia. I shouldn't want to ruin hip-hop lyrics any more than I want to ruin kids' memories of watching cartoons on the couch on Saturday morning.

Here, however, I took comfort in the specificity of Asim's assertion. He wasn't disparaging hip-hop as a genre, only pointing out a queer correlation between nineteenth-century minstrels and Jay-Z. And if students held the correlation under the right light, they might discover what such gamesmanship reveals about our racial perceptions. With this in mind, I asked Tim to share what he'd found so unsettling about Asim's observation. He responded with, "It's just that rappers say it all the time. Like *all* the time. And finding out that it comes from this . . ."

"I don't think he said that, though." I asked everyone to look back at the quote. "He didn't say that minstrel shows *caused* rappers' obsession with 'real niggas.' He just noticed a similarity."

Another student added, "I want to help Timmy out. It's upsetting because rappers are dead serious about being real. Realness means everything to them—you hear it in the beefs they get into: 'I'm realer than you! You're a fraud, blah blah blah.' It's like the preacher in the thing we just read. He thinks he's saying everything right, keeping it real. But it turns out people outside his community think he's a joke. Nobody likes people making fun of you behind your back."

Tim was grateful for this explanation. "This movie I saw, *Dear White People* [2014], had a scene at the end . . ." He was interrupted by the exhortations of classmates who, I assumed, had seen the movie. I hushed them, and he continued with, "These white college kids threw a party at the end where they dressed up like black stereotypes. They had braids and Afro wigs and they wore gold chains and bandanas like gang members. They had fake guns that they waved around. There's this black kid there who is uncomfortable being laughed at, and he ends up calling his friends to bust up the party." Tim's friend, sitting in front of him, turned to him to whisper something. Reminded of a detail, he added, "Before he busted up the party, the kids were having a fake rap show, and he went up and did a rap where he explained why he was mad."

This brought up the need for a snap decision: Do we take a couple of minutes to watch Tim's scene? We've all had to adjust to our students' thirst for immediate gratification; when a source like this is described, some students constantly ask, *Can we watch it now?* while their classmates don't wait for permission and pull out their phones. I had a vague memory of this movie, and considered it relevant enough. Yet, I'd already planned to use a video source, and I am generally wary of having so many outside sources that they distract from our thread. Here, though, I figured that Tim should be rewarded for both his sincere investment and mindful connection. I cued up the scene on YouTube.

Dear White People's party scene starts with a white boy, wearing the red handkerchief and sunglasses of a caricatured Bloods gang member, performing a misogynistic rap verse to applause. The aforementioned black student then snatches the microphone for his own verse:

> My name is Lionel / Some call me Ly
> Most people think / I talk kinda white
> But that's all right / that's all cool
> I'd rather be white than *tap dance* with you.

After this, he throws the microphone to the floor, smashes the DJ equipment, and topples the floor-to-ceiling speakers. Pandemonium ensues as black students rampage through the party, ripping the minstrel costumes off of the partiers. I stopped the video, intrigued by Lionel's verse. Turning to the class, I added, "When he says *tap dance*, he is talking about minstrel shows. It's an allusion!" (My students had only recently learned that device.) When it was clear that they understood, I asked a familiar question. "What's the point of his allusion?"

Various students answered with statements that I paraphrased on the board, like, *It's better to speak "properly" and be judged fraudulent by fellow minorities than be a minstrel.* And, *When minorities play into stereotypes, they are doing the minstrel's job for them.* I asked students to turn to a neighbor and share opinions about *Dear White People*'s apparent thesis. I strolled around, taking in the emerging debates: Some students thought the film's point pretentious and judgmental, that it seemed to lock minorities into an unrelenting fear of stereotypes. Students raised points like these: *So what if black people like soul food? So what if their music celebrates the most taboo aspects of ghetto life? Why should minorities waste their time worrying about whether white people were laughing about them behind their backs?* These sentiments were countered with, *How can minorities expect respect if they confirm the lowest expectations? It's one thing if the stereotype is harmless—like liking fried chicken—but another thing entirely if the stereotype is that minorities are all violent, or drug addicts, or anything else that is a lie. Or worse, stereotypes that are the white power structure's fault, like how minorities are poor, or they have worse educations that come from worse schools. And if white people are laughing at minorities behind their backs, they surely won't treat them better.*

I was pleased enough with Tim's thread to keep following it, but before doing so, I wanted to root this sprawling conversation back into *Native Son*. "So on one hand, we have Bigger and Gus—and most of you—*playing white*. On the other, we have this minstrel culture of *playing black*. Both groups, if you ask them, would claim that their impressions are based on reality. Yet both groups depend on stereotypes to make their impressions land. You all are presenting two different arguments about how the cultures being copied should engage these stereotypes." I paused to see if everyone was with me, then continued, "You're not the first people to have this debate. People write *a lot* about it. I'm going to show you an example, and you tell me what you think."

Spike Lee, in his 2000 movie *Bamboozled,* had offered up a heavy-handed satire of both white and black America's embrace of what was, to him, minstrelsy. I'd come ready with two clips, the first of which shows a black screenwriter named Pierre Delacroix (performed by Damon Wayans) pitching a new variety show to a white network executive, Thomas Dunwitty (performed by Michael Rapaport). Pierre, speaking with a wonky inflection that nears some of my students' "white" impressions, laments that his art has "never dug deep into [his] pain as a Negro." To change this, he has created *Mantan: The New Millennium Minstrel Show*, which he is certain will "promote racial healing." He warns Dunwitty that "it's going to take a lot of courage and backbone" on the part of their network to go through with the project. Two young black actors then enter, the first of whom is introduced as Mantan, the second as Sleep 'n Eat. This meeting seems to be the first time that the latter actor has heard his character's name, and his smile fades. Delacroix ends his introductions by testing out language for his show: "Mantan. Sleep 'n Eat. Two *real* coons!" At this, the other actor turns discreetly to his partner and mouths the slur as if to ask, *Did I hear that right?*

A giddy Dunwitty can't get enough of this pitch. He encourages Delacroix to "swing for the bleachers." Encouraged, Delacroix lists his "dusty duo's" character traits: "Ignorant! Dull-witted! Lazy! Unlucky!" Delacroix describes Mantan as an "uneducated Negro, but with educated feets! Who by some stroke of unbelievable stupidity always makes his best-laid plans go haywire!"

Dunwitty exclaims, "This could be bigger than *Friends*, *Ally McBeal*, even my boys *Amos and Andy*!" This prompts Delacroix's business partner, who had entered with the two actors and had been sharing their puzzled expressions, to complain that black people will certainly be outraged by the show. Dunwitty brushes this concern away with, "So what? We'll just give the NAACP a little donation. I've dealt with those guys before." He asks Delacroix for the character list, which he finds out includes Topsy (from *Uncle Tom's Cabin*), Sambo, and Aunt Jemima, whom Delacroix assures will still "rock the doo-rag." They haggle over the setting, moving from the projects to a plantation before settling on a watermelon patch. Finally, Dunwitty asks the actors directly if they would mind performing in "just a little" blackface. Mantan doesn't mind, but Sleep 'n Eat resents the suggestion. Dunwitty waves off the concern by saying, "We're just keepin' it real." Before the actor can respond, Dunwitty sweeps everything off the boardroom table and asks if Mantan would mind showing him some moves. Excited, the actor changes into tap shoes and hops up onto the table. He dances vigorously as Dunwitty nods his head and sways delightedly to the rhythm. At the end of the dance, Dunwitty shouts, "Yo, yo, yo! This kid is off the hook! This kid is off the hinges! That is what I'm talking about! *Mantan*! We're gonna get paid!" He runs upstairs to tell his colleagues, leaving Delacroix and his team at the table.

His skeptical partner delivers the scene's last words. "This . . . is some bulls--t."

I paused the movie to ask for my students' observations. Remember, it is best to tackle one task at a time. Again, with heavy sources like *Bamboozled*, it makes sense not to rush into analysis—and hasty argument—without first gathering students' observations. We must, essentially, set the table before we eat. The first comments connected Mantan's actual tap dancing to Lionel's promise not to do so. The *tap dance* allusion was now apparently clear to my students. Then they mentioned Dunwitty's office decor, which featured striking portraits of sports heroes Kareem Abdul-Jabbar, Muhammad Ali, Michael Jordan, Willie Mays, and Hank Aaron. African-seeming wooden statues were displayed around the room. This was connected to his speech, which was littered with black-sounding slang and excessive profanity. Students contrasted this with Delacroix's nasal "white" voice. This, students said, was consistent with how they'd imagined Bigger and Gus's white impressions.

Tim chipped in, "Delacroix said 'real' a couple times."

"Yep, that's the same claim that Asim talked about." I paused, thinking that some students might not understand the more dated racial slur. "Just to be clear, *coon* is a slur. Did you know that?" Surprisingly few students raised their hands. I smiled. "Okay, yeah, don't say it."

Another student, Taniya, said, "I noticed that line about the NAACP." Her classmates nodded, and she continued, "The white guy isn't worried about getting in trouble because he can pay them off."

Transitioning gingerly to analysis, I asked her why she thought Dunwitty felt so sure of this.

Taniya looked up at the board, eventually finding the answer in her classmates' observations. "Because he thinks he knows black people so well. You know how people think they know everything about something because they saw a movie about it?" There was a chorus of agreement from her classmates. She continued, "He thinks because he watches black people play sports and collects African souvenirs and knows some of the slang that he . . . *knows* us."

Taniya's neighbor, Kim, raised her hand. "Did Spike Lee read the book you just had us read?"

"Asim's book came out after *Bamboozled*. But he might have researched the same stuff. Why?"

"The book says that minstrel shows claimed to be based on research. So people who went and saw the show probably left feeling that they were experts on 'blackness.' What Taniya just said made me think of that. This guy"—she indicated Dunwitty—"is probably rich, so he probably got those things in Africa, like on a safari. And since he makes TV shows, he probably knows black celebrities and goes to parties. So he feels authentic."

I smiled. "*Authentic*. I like your word choice! Authentic enough to argue that he's just 'keepin' it real' by running with this minstrel idea?"

Hands shot up, eager to contribute to Taniya and Kim's thread. Many expressed frustration about people with minimal, or superficial, experience in a culture claiming the authority to represent it. I leaned into this, asking just how much experience an outsider needed to avoid such rebuke. This split the Kim/Taniya crowd into two factions: those who thought that, through a deep study of real issues, outsiders could gain an authentic voice, and those who thought that no amount of research could lend authenticity to an outsider's take on minority culture. This dispute over the worth of lived experience seemed to fascinate both sides, especially when the latter faction was challenged to decide which lived experience counted as authentic. Were a middle-class half-black person's opinions on African American issues more or less authentic than a poor Afro Latina's? Why?

I encouraged both sides to watch a recurring *Saturday Night Live* sketch called "Black Jeopardy," which features contestants answering trivia questions about black culture. The joke of the sketch is threefold: First, the black contestants are stereotypicaly loud, flamboyant, low-income ghetto dwellers (the sort that Spike Lee might deride as minstrels). Second, the "black culture" prompts are caricatured "ghetto" expressions. (*She do hair. Raheem wants to borrow your bike to go to the store right quick.*) Third, one contestant is usually white. In one such sketch, comedian Louis C. K. plays Mark, a professor of African American Studies at Brigham Young University. The professor spends much of the sketch finding his research not very useful when answering prompts like, *She think she cute.* (Answer: comedian and actress Mo'Nique.) Eventually, he chooses the category White People, and is prompted, *White people are always lying about this.* His answer: *We don't have any money.* His answer is correct, but then the host adds, "The truth is, we would have accepted any answer." This particular sketch ends seconds later with a Final Jeopardy prompt: *Rap songs that begin with the letter* N. The host ends with, "I'd watch myself, Mark."

After hearing me describe this sketch, a student named Oliver said that he'd seen it. A few others had, as well. Oliver pointed out that he hadn't found it very funny, and he'd been surprised that *Saturday Night Live* had felt so comfortable running it. Spike Lee's *Bamboozled* scene had given him a new perspective: "If the people who write these sketches feel like they understand black people, like Dunwitty does, then they can write almost whatever they want. Plus, the actors are black, and I guess they feel that it's okay because none of them is complaining. It gives them permission. Like in the *Bamboozled* video. One actor is uncomfortable, but he probably doesn't say anything because his buddy seems cool with the idea."

I was lucky with the next comment. Sara, who seemed to be one of the few students in the room who knew anything about Spike Lee before this conversation, told her classmates that *Bamboozled* was probably Lee "trolling" Tyler Perry, the creator of television shows like *Meet the Browns* and *House of Pain*, as well as both the wildly successful Madea movie franchise and the plays that inspired them. Sara had seen Spike Lee's interviews where he labeled Perry's work "coonery buffoonery." After a heated debate emerged within certain circles of the black community, Perry had invited Lee and other critics to "go straight to hell." Trying her best to extrapolate Lee's point for her classmates, Sara argued that Spike

Lee sees a cycle. People like Delacroix and Dunwitty glorify minstrel-ish stereotypes, which gives people like the *Saturday Night Live* writers cover for "Black Jeopardy," which gives college students the idea that blackface parties like the one portrayed in *Dear White People* are okay.

I made a big deal of this, running over to the board to diagram Sara's reasoning. Then, unexpectedly, one of her classmates said, "But if people do not find stereotypes offensive, what is the big deal? It's just fun. If you don't like Madea, don't watch it. If you don't want to go to the blackface party, don't go." He paused, sensing his classmates' impending outburst. "I mean, I wouldn't go, but they wouldn't invite me anyway."

I hushed an immediate rumble of dissent. "Wait. Wait. Before anyone responds, I think Spike Lee put a scene into *Bamboozled* to test whether we actually still find minstrelsy offensive. We have heard a lot about minstrel shows, but we haven't actually seen one. I'm going to show it to you—but I need to let you know—it's pretty heavy. But I also think it's about as accurate a representation as you'll ever see." Moving back to the projector, I oriented the next clip. Delacroix's show had been accepted—however, a new, all-white writing team had muted his intended satirical tone. (Oliver wondered aloud if this is what happened to dilute the satire of the aforementioned "Black Jeopardy" sketch, asking, "What were they even making fun of?") We fast-forwarded to the filming of Mantan's pilot episode. The show opens with Mantan and Sleep 'n Eat introducing themselves to their studio audience as "two *real* coons." Right then, and often throughout the clip, Lee's camera cuts to the audience to catch their reactions. In each cutaway, white patrons seem both uncomfortable and confused. On a stage constructed to look like an antebellum plantation, Sleep 'n Eat explains that the two characters had "left the hustle and bustle of uptown Harlem to return to our roots." A stream of jokes follows as Mantan tees off on black people's penchant for being incarcerated, their magical regard for watermelons, their poverty, and their drug addictions. The routine is peppered with '90s-era black culture references: Kirk Franklin, the rapper Juvenile, the "running man" dance. Eventually, an APPLAUSE sign lights up. The black patrons laugh as the white patrons study them, searching for permission to do the same. After everyone seems to feel free from judgment, the whole studio explodes into cheers. I stopped the film.

The room was dead silent. I looked around patiently until Oliver, seeming to speak for everyone, said, "What *was* that?"

"A minstrel show."

"Why did anyone ever think that was funny?"

I sent that back to his classmates. Some explained that the blatant racism had made them feel awkward, which made them laugh. A black student said that he'd laughed because of how "over the top" the stereotypes were. Another laughed because she "got" Lee's satire, and mentioned comedian Dave Chappelle, who had allegedly quit his own Comedy Central variety show after deciding that it closely resembled a minstrel show. Thanks to YouTube, many of her classmates were familiar with some of the show's sketches, many of which had last aired nearly a decade earlier. Chappelle had described the incident to *Time* magazine in 2005:

> The third season hit a big speed bump in November 2004. He was taping a sketch about magic pixies that embody stereotypes about the races. The black pixie—played by Chappelle—wears blackface and tries to convince blacks to act in stereotypical ways. Chappelle thought the sketch was funny, the kind of thing his friends would laugh at. But at the taping, one spectator, a white man, laughed particularly loud and long. His laughter struck Chappelle as wrong, and he wondered if the new season of his show had gone from sending up stereotypes to merely reinforcing them. "When he laughed, it made me uncomfortable," says Chappelle. "As a matter of fact, that was the last thing I shot before I told myself I gotta take f—ing time out after this. Because my head almost exploded." (Farley 2005)

This, I told the students, brought the conversation back to *Native Son*'s white world/black world dichotomy. The citizens of both worlds apparently rely on stereotypes to understand, criticize, and entertain the "other." Historically, people of color seem to face an added problem: How should we engage destructive stereotypes that are rooted in white supremacy? As entertainers? As consumers? It's one of the hard problems that I'd wanted to put before the class. Especially as they got to know Bigger Thomas better. In Thomas, Richard Wright had created a stark manifestation of all that 1930s white America feared: a violent, unhinged, ignorant black man roaming a ghetto with too much time on his hands. Replace the first letter of "Bigger" with an *N*, and you get what Wright was aiming at.

Wright's brilliant design didn't end here. Within a few pages of *playing white*, Bigger Thomas, in all his ugliness, collides violently with the real thing: a young, delicate, upper-class white woman named Mary Dalton. When they meet, each is certain that they understand the other, both having been steeped in stereotypes about the other's world. Bigger's belief that whites are—in my students' words—godlike, generally cavalier, yet strangely focused on harming black folks leads him to preemptively hate Mary. Mary's belief that Bigger's ghetto is a fascinating hellscape whose inhabitants deserve pity above all else triggers a series of bad decisions that eventually end her life. Neither character can authentically *see* the other, a prospect whose implications Wright clearly wants his readers to wrestle with. But while doing so, our classroom conversations unearthed an interesting phenomenon: Most of the students hate Mary nearly as much as Bigger does. And here, organically, a second powerful cultural appropriation discussion emerged.

THERE'S SOMETHING ABOUT MARY: CULTURAL APPROPRIATION IN *NATIVE SON*, PART 2

Mary Dalton is alive for only about twenty pages of *Native Son* before being brutally murdered (after allegedly being raped) by Bigger Thomas. In death, she is the Scottsboro Boys' Ruby Bates and Victoria Price, or Emmett Till's Carolyn Bryant—a symbol of violated Southern white womanhood in need of avenging. The lynch mobs come, the show trial follows, and neither the verdict nor the punishment surprises. It ends the way all such stories end, with a dead black man and the perceived trespass over racial lines thwarted. However, before her posthumous plea for vigilante justice, Mary shows herself to be different from Bates, Price, and Bryant in one key aspect: She *really* likes black people, is fascinated by their culture, and is committed to fighting for a postracial world.

My students meet her only a couple days after first discussing cultural appropriation. Bigger has gotten a job working as a chauffeur for Mary's father, Henry Dalton, a millionaire Chicago businessman. He didn't want the job, a fact that Richard Wright used his white world motif to express:

> Suppose police saw him wandering in a white neighborhood like this? It would be thought that he was trying to rob or rape somebody. He grew angry. Why had he come to take this goddamn job? He could have stayed among his own people and escaped this feeling of fear and hate. This was not his world; he had been foolish in thinking that he would have liked it. (44)

The Dalton family exacerbates Bigger's anxiety by treating him more or less like a human being. After hiring him for $25 a week, Mr. Dalton brags that he supports the NAACP, which Bigger has never heard of. Bigger is given a room and some new clothes, and told about their former "colored" chauffeur, a man named Green who'd stayed ten years before "taking a job with the government." Another servant hints that the Daltons had paid for Green's night schooling, and that since "Mrs. Dalton's always trying to help somebody" (55), Bigger might have hit the jackpot.

Enter Mary. From the moment she is introduced to Bigger, she complicates his potentially lucrative situation. First, she asks him, in front of a clearly disapproving father, if he belongs to a union. When Mr. Dalton chides her, she turns to Bigger to tease, "Isn't he a capitalist, Bigger?" (52). Bigger hangs his head, embarrassed that he doesn't know what a capitalist is. Then, a few pages after persuading her father to let Bigger take her to the university, she asks her chauffeur to drive her to meet her radical boyfriend instead. Bigger does so, but is so visibly uncomfortable that Mary tells him, "'Take it easy' . . . 'You'll understand it better bye and bye'" (65).

My students usually review this section dramatically, with a student reading Mary and another reading Bigger. (I can be a bit selfish with the Bigger role, taking it myself in the absence of a sufficiently charismatic reader. I do the same with *Fences*' Troy Maxon.) I normally have to pause here to ask which students recognize the "bye and bye" reference. Few do. It means "at a future time," but for most of us it is from a traditional hymn, "When the Morning Comes," that I grew up with in church. The song has the following refrain:

> By and by, when the morning comes,
> all the saints of God are gathered home,
> we'll tell the story of how we've overcome,
> and we'll understand it better by and by.

It's an allusion that Mary makes clear with her next line: "Isn't there a song like that, a song your people sing?" (65). I ask them to analyze the refrain, which essentially is an expression of faith that all life's hardships will eventually be understood. Its composer, Charles Albert Tindley, was the son of a former slave. Upon learning this, my students read his lyrics as a direct commentary on racialized hardships: Eventually people of color will understand *why* they have been so oppressed. Some students dig a bit deeper, realizing that Tindley's "saints gathered" probably refers to an afterlife—implying that people of color won't understand oppression until they die.

When students had read the passage for homework, some had been instinctively put off by Mary's "your people" comment. Now that they understood her reference, a few raised their hands to protest her flippant use of the lyric. *By and by* is not a call to, as Mary says, "take it easy," when someone asks one to lie to their boss. Students point out that the lyric is, at best, a promise that God helps the oppressed know why bad things happen to good people. At worst, it is a lament that the downtrodden will be confused until their oppressors send them to the afterlife. Mary isn't even close to understanding the reference.

This tension between Mary's character and my students continues a few pages later, when she makes a similar statement. They have since picked up her boyfriend, Jan, a communist activist. Jan insists that he drive the car, making Bigger slide over and sit wedged awkwardly in the middle. The text here reads, "There were two white people to either side of him; he was sitting between two vast white looming walls. Never in his life had he ever been so close to a white woman" (67). Jan asks Bigger where the three could get a meal on Chicago's South Side. Feeling that her boyfriend hadn't been clear, Mary added, "We want to go to a *real* place. Look, Bigger. We want one of those places where colored people eat, not one of those show places" (69).

Here, I pause our performance to ask what Mary means by a *real* place. Many students say that she wants to be wherever the black people are. When I press, the answers are interesting: "She wants to feel cool," and "They probably have the best music." The more mischievous students offer edgier contributions like, "Black people season their food better." (I try my best to read the spirit of comments like these, which, if meant to demean, have little place in academic discourse. I have to be careful, though, because although Mary's comment deals in stereotypes, any thoughtful analysis must at least acknowledge them. If I overreact to comments like these, my more gregarious students might stop participating. In this particular case, I contextualize such statements with something like, "Mary might think that, yes . . ." and move on.) Occasionally, a student will add a nonracial analysis: "It's like when someone visits Philly and wants to get a cheesesteak. People hear that you should go to Pat's or Geno's [nationally famous spots in South Philadelphia—recall the latter once displayed Joey Vento's infamous "Speak English" sign noted in Chapter 6] but anyone from Philly knows that you can get a good steak at most corner stores. When my cousins come to town, they want to go to the stand [mobile food cart] up the street from my house. They want to eat what I eat, not what tourists eat." At this, most students nod and share their own examples. Still, many seem to sense something untoward in Mary's request for a *real* place.

So, apparently, does Bigger, who after telling her about a spot called Ernie's Kitchen Shack, is floored by Jan and Mary's request that he join them inside for a meal. He refuses, which makes Mary cry. Embarrassed by her outburst, Bigger relents, taking the couple inside, hoping not to run into anyone he knows. As soon as he sits, however, his shoulder is grabbed by his girlfriend, Bessie, who is clearly angered by the clash of worlds her boyfriend has ushered in. As she stalks away, Jan looks at Bigger and says, "You got something there," then adds, "Did I say that right, Bigger?" (73). Context clues show my students that Jan is attempting some dated ghetto slang that he thinks Bigger would know. Mary interrupts to scold Bigger for not eating the plate of fried chicken that has just been brought to the table.

"'It's good!" she exclaims (74).

At this point, more than a few of my students usually interrupt our live performance to grumble beneath their breath. This provides a natural opportunity to ask how they feel about Mary. I take a straw poll of first impressions, asking students to raise their hands if they (1) like Mary, (2) are indifferent about Mary, or (3) can't stand Mary. The majority vote in the last category, and I tell them to get ready to tell me why. But I suggest that we finish reading the scene out loud so more evidence is on the table.

After dinner, the three characters return to the car, this time with Bigger driving and Mary and Jan in the backseat. The following conversation ensues, which seals the deal for Mary's detractors:

> "No, I want to work among Negroes. That's where people are needed. It seems as though they've been pushed out of everything."
>
> "That's true."
>
> "When I see what they've done to those people, it makes me *so* mad . . ."
>
> "Yes; it's awful."
>
> "And I feel so helpless and useless. I want to *do* something."
>
> "I knew all along you'd come through."
>
> "Say, Jan, do you know many Negroes? I want to meet some."
>
> "I don't know any very well. But you'll meet them when you're in the [Communist] Party."
>
> "They have so much *emotion*! What a people! If we could ever get them going . . ."
>
> "We can't have a revolution without 'em," Jan said. "They've got to be organized. They've got spirit. They'll give the Party something it needs."

> "And their songs—the spirituals! Aren't they marvelous?" Bigger saw her turn to him. "Say, Bigger, can you sing?"
>
> "I can't sing," he said.
>
> "Aw, Bigger," she said, pouting. She tilted her head, closed her eyes and opened her mouth. "Swing low, sweet chariot, Coming fer to carry me home . . ."
>
> Jan joined in and Bigger smiled derisively. Hell, that ain't the tune, he thought.
>
> "Come on, Bigger, and help us sing it," Jan said.
>
> "I can't sing," he said again. (77)

Years of February Soup have familiarized most students with "Swing Low, Sweet Chariot" and the history of Negro spirituals. Mary's singing, which my student actors generally infuse with an over-the-top Valley Girl inflection, often causes a swell of derisive laughter that takes a while to die down. After it does, I return to my poll and ask for explanations. A recent exchange started with the most common complaint:

"She's so annoying!"

No doubt about that. The natural follow-up was to ask what about Mary is so annoying, and for respondents to cite the text, not their classmates' acting choices. They returned invariably to her *your people* comment. I asked what's wrong with saying *your people,* since Bigger is, indeed, a member of a black community. After all, Mary couldn't rightly claim "Negroes" as *her people*. A couple of students stumbled trying to explain their irritation, and settled instead on mock-shivering with disgust. One said, "You just don't say that." When I pressed, she added, "It sounds like she's saying that Bigger knows all of the black people in Chicago just because he's black."

Another student added, "She's pointing out how different blacks are."

I pushed further, feigning skepticism. "Are either of those things untrue? I doubt that Bigger knows everyone in Chicago, but we have no evidence that he's unpopular. And doesn't everyone in the 'hood know each other?" Some chuckled at this. "And plus, you've just learned how packed-in everyone was in these tenements. Families are literally sitting on top of each other. Bigger probably knows his neighbors better than Mary knows hers. And the other thing—that black people are different—didn't they at least live differently?"

Some students nodded. I immediately made it clear with the class that I was sparring with them, intentionally probing their assertions for defect. In Chapter 2, I noted the importance of expressing yourself clearly so as to avoid unproductive tension with/between students. This emphasis on clarity has, in recent years, led me to openly label any deliberate stance changes. Most of the time I'm just facilitating: operating as the conversation's traffic cop, offering orientation before, summary after, inserting clarification when needed. This is the default—what students expect. However, certain conversations call for deliberate antagonism. Perhaps students have too much confidence in a half-examined idea, and they need the shock of debate to shake off the cobwebs. When this is the case, it helps them to know that a teacher is no longer facilitating, but actively engaging in a deliberate practice meant to sharpen their ideas. This clarity is important for two reasons: First, if students think I am still playing traffic cop, any probing might seem like an effort to ticket a violation. This gets the students' blood up, and they start remembering any classmates' opinions that did not earn a similar ticket. From here, they surmise that their teacher is, at best, playing favorites. At worst, the teacher is using their facilitation platform to proselytize. Second, we must remember that students' own shift from fixed to growth mind-set might be more violent than teachers anticipate. We don't know how deeply rooted their opinions are, especially about race. If we start probing a half-formed opinion, we might unearth some "my grandmom always said" generational axioms that students aren't prepared to handle. A light debate for a teacher might feel, to them, like a barrage.

Still, we must spar. Not because every half-formed idea is worth twelve rounds, but because students need to learn how to articulate their opinions amid direct scrutiny. They must not wilt at the slightest pressure from a perceived authority. Also, we hope to inspire a generation of students who realize that most ideas improve through pruning. When I am most effective at building a sparring-friendly community, I've found that students ask classmates to poke around in their ideas for flaws. When I am less effective, they merely seem to tolerate my intrusion. In the former situations, there are two things (besides openly acknowledging any shift in approach) that I've had to keep in mind:

1. I must remember to deal in probing questions, not declarative statements. That way the exchange doesn't seem to have been initiated only to highlight how much more I know about any topic.
2. I've got to remember that good sparring partners know when to ease up. They are getting paid to test the actual fighter's skills, to help prepare them for a contest—not to knock them out in the practice ring. I must not, in my challenging of students' ideas, seek to actually beat them. Only to jolt them into deeper reflection.

I got the sense that my students' instinctive aversion to Mary was worthy of a good sparring session. So, when nobody had a clear answer to my *your people* challenge, I asked for anyone to provide a more reasonable excuse to hate her. A student, Leah, raised her hand. "She makes those songs sound fun, when they are all about struggle."

"Did that make you cringe?"

"Yeah. She don't know anything about the pain in those songs. She's sitting up there in her mansion, she don't know anything about slave songs. She's laughing like they funny. And you got the nerve to ask him to sing too, like it's his job to entertain you. Please!" This last phrase, spat at the fictional character herself, sent the class into titters.

Another student, Demi, added, "Mary acts like those songs are hers. But she doesn't know anything about them."

I took a few more comments, most of which parroted Leah and Demi. When it seemed that the class was near consensus around these reasons, I threw out my jab again. "Doesn't Mary know how ignorant she is? Isn't she out here with Bigger trying to fix that?" I had them turn back a few pages in the text, and had a volunteer read a section where Mary regards the Black Belt through the car window:

> "You know, Bigger, I've long wanted to go into these houses," she said, pointing to the tall, dark apartment buildings looming

> to either side of them, "and just *see* how your people live. You know what I mean? I've been to England, France and Mexico, but I don't know how people live ten blocks from me. We know so *little* about each other. I just want to *see*. I want to *know* these people. Never in my life have I been inside of a Negro home. Yet they *must* live like we live. They're *human* . . . There are twelve million of them . . . They live in our country . . . In the same city with us . . ." her voice trailed off wistfully. (69–70)

After the reading, I added, "Mary admits that she doesn't know anything. But she claims that she wants to learn. And that she wants to learn by *doing*. Getting up in a black person's home, seeing how they live. Even when she sings, "Swing low . . ." she asks Bigger to *help* them sing it. And, come to think of it, when Jan tries out some black slang, he asks Bigger if he used it right. Is Mary really acting like the culture is hers?"

Demi was undeterred. "She doesn't get points for that. She's driving by the ghetto talking about black people like they're zoo animals. Like she's on a safari. But . . ."

I interrupted her, apologizing hurriedly for breaking my own listen patiently rule. "I want you to finish—please don't forget your point—but if I don't say it, I'll forget it. You mentioned a safari, which reminded me of . . ."

She interrupted me right back. "I was going to get to that, Kay. Chill out." The class *oohed*, and I shut up. "The guy in *Bamboozled* with all the trophies and posters on the wall. Mary is just like him. But a young him before he got all cocky . . . Now back to what I was saying." I put my hands up to signal that I'd learned my lesson about interrupting her. "Mary is *still* acting like she owns black culture, just like she would own some zoo tickets. She gets to step in and eat some Negro food, sing some Negro songs, use some Negro slang or whatever, not care about how uncomfortable it makes a legit Negro, like Bigger, feel."

"That much is true," I allowed. "But my question is, why do any of those things make Bigger, or any of you, feel any type of way? Mary likes the culture! It's cool to her! It's fun!"

"Like I said," Leah stepped in to say, "it ain't fun . . . She don't get to have fun with it."

"Only black people do?"

"Yes."

There was a murmur as students considered the implications of this declaration. I pressed a bit more. "If Mary can't sing spirituals, can Macklemore rap? Your thesis seems to be—and correct me if I am wrong—that people shouldn't enjoy a culture's good stuff unless they've lived through the struggles that created it." Leah nodded, though she was clearly still reflecting. Seeing this, I disengaged and turned to her classmates. "What do you think?" When no hands shot up, I asked students to discuss it with their neighbors. The buzz on this one was low, but steady. I noticed a few things: (1) More students than usual seemed discomfited by the idea that there were things they were not allowed to enjoy. (2) Students asked each other more questions than usual—*But what if I like this? Does this count?* (3) A prompt that, on the surface, would not seem designed to elicit strong emotions stirred more than a few students like Leah to an intensity bordering on agitation.

After a few minutes, I brought the class back together. Rather than repeating the prompt, I shared my observations and asked them to weigh in. Before calling on the raised hands, which now were abundant, I complimented them on their listening, which was always tougher when emotions started to run high. I told them that I was proud of them.

The first comment was from Taylor, a good friend of Leah's. She was upset because she felt that Leah's point had been oversimplified. "I don't think she's trying to say that only black people get to appreciate black culture. White people get to listen to black music if they want to." She paused, and I apologized for misinterpreting Leah's point. I was fairly certain that I hadn't gotten anything wrong, but, as I just mentioned, the goal of sparring isn't to bury a student. Kids should never be denied an opportunity to retreat from a stance with dignity. Taylor continued, "It's about paying your dues. It doesn't matter if Mary is sincere. It's that she benefits from something she didn't create."

I was confused. "Benefits? Nobody's paying her."

"I bet she gets recognition for knowing black stuff with her communist friends. That's what's so wrong. Black people had been singing those songs for years and nobody in the white world gave them anything. Slaves died singing those songs. How many jazz artists died broke? We got people like Elvis Presley singing black music and getting movie deals out of it—and today kids know who he was and not the black people who did it first." Taylor, who clearly cared deeply about music, turned to her classmates. "How many of y'all know anything about Chuck Berry?" Nobody. "Little Richard?" Nobody. She turned back to me. "That's why we don't like Mary. She shouldn't get to benefit from something she didn't create."

Another student, Ross, stepped in. "I'm okay with her singing those songs and eating the food. I think people should be able to like what they like. My problem is that she doesn't respect the culture. She just thinks it's cute." When an interested classmate asked what he meant, he explained, "It's just the feeling I get from reading it. You know when your little brother does something like draw a picture on his sneakers? When you see it, you're all like, 'Awww, look what he did. It's so cute. You're such a good artist!' But for real, you don't think they're good. It's just *cute* because he don't know you're not supposed to draw on sneakers. That's what Mary's like." He looked down at this book and quoted, "'They have so much emotion! What a people! . . . And their songs—the spirituals! Aren't they marvelous?' C'mon. Of course black people have emotions. She's acting like she didn't *expect* them to have any feelings. She has no respect for the culture."

THE HARD PROBLEMS

Demi, Leah, Taylor, and now Ross had built their responses on an underlying assumption. I'd been waiting for one of their classmates to bring it up—but nobody had. So, after passively taking in a few more responses, I said, "I think we are skipping something." I walked over to the board and wrote, in oversized letters,

Can a race "own" a cultural element?

As they read, I added, "You know what I mean? We're calling it *black* music, *black* style, and *black* food. Ross claimed that Mary didn't show respect for the culture. Know what that sounds like to me? Like—and don't laugh—it sounds like gangs on the corner selling dope. You know hustlers don't let just anyone work on their block without paying respect." They started to laugh, tipped off by my warning that this analogy was tongue-in-cheek. I had been impressed with Ross's analogy because we had worked hard to develop that specific interpretation skill, and he'd created his on the spot. Mine, less impressively, had come with me to class. I continued, "And that respect is money. 'You want to work my block, you have to pay me a cut.' But it's not *his* block. It's nobody's block." Then I cut the analogy short, thinking for the first time that certain students may have lost family to street violence. Retreating hastily, I asked, "Y'all were laying out rules for how outsiders like Mary should engage stuff that another race owns. But we didn't talk about whether a race actually *owns* anything."

After a few comments, a girl named Ariana contributed her own analogy. "I think different races can own things. It's like having a patent. If they created it, they have the right to benefit from it. And that race gets to make the rules for everyone else who uses it."

"What if there is a dispute over who created it?"

"There's no dispute over spirituals. Or rap music."

"No argument there. But there are other music disputes." I turned over to Taylor, our established music nerd, who nodded wearily. Looking back at Ariana, I said, "But if we talk about style . . . how about dreadlocks?" There had been a recent uptick in social media disputes over who should be able to lock their hair. I took my next few lines directly from the reply threads of memes (see Figure 7.1) that students had circulated. "After you get a few comments down the list, there's always someone who challenges the assertion that black people were the first to lock their hair. They say something about the Celts in Europe, or the aboriginal people in Australia, or sometimes they go all the way back to prehistoric times when nobody had a brush or comb—everyone's hair must have been locked. That's just what hair does when you leave it alone. Then someone comes back with, 'Yeah, but when people lock their hair now, it's to appropriate Rastafarian culture.' And the other person, if they haven't been blocked yet, says, 'How you gonna tell me what I'm trying to do.' Then they throw down and start name-calling and it all unravels." The students seemed to immediately recognize the exchange. Versions of this dispute had popped up all year. Some had ended friendships.

Ariana held firm. "I get your point. But it's like what Ross said. It's about respecting what other people feel. I think that when some white people wear dreadlocks, or other things that people consider nonwhite, they think that buys them a ticket into spaces that aren't for them. Black people want to be left alone sometimes; they don't want a white person in their face pretending to be just as *with it* as they are. Know what I mean? That's annoying."

"Like Mary."

"Like Mary. She's not about that life. She thinks she gets to go to Bigger's restaurant just because she and her boyfriend know a little slang and can sing a little song. That's a restaurant where black people go to get away from white people. She's not welcome. And she doesn't get it."

Reggie, who seemingly had been lying in wait for this moment, addressed Ariana directly. "But *why* though? Why do black people feel the need to own something that white people can't touch? I get that you want whites to show respect. I get that blacks want to benefit, as long as anyone is benefiting. But I don't get the need to mark territory. It's like a . . . fix-

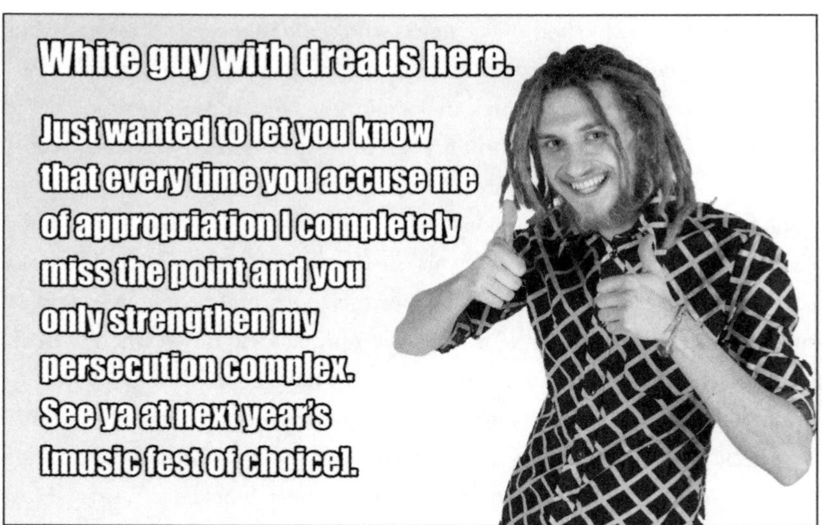

FIGURE 7.1
There is no shortage of memes making this sort of "point" about appropriation.

ation." He motioned with parallel palms in front of his eyes, mimicking a horse's blinders.

Leah answered forcefully, "When everything gets taken from you, you get like that. Minorities ain't got nothing *but* a culture. All we got is 'cool.' We got braids and locs. We got dance moves. But most of us ain't got anything else to go home to. White people made us insecure, for real for real."

Taylor tagged in seamlessly with her more volatile friend. "Kay talked about gang members on the corner claiming the block. It's because they have nothing else *but* the block. Nothing but their reputation. People of color can be that way with"—she looked at the board—"*cultural elements*. We're *insecure* because if white people take something that we think is ours, we might not have it anymore." She thought a little more, and added, "Also, when they take it, it makes it less cool sometimes. I mean when a white guy raps"—she made a rapid faux b-boy hand gesture—"it looks silly. And we're like, *Do we look like that?*"

Ariana, from across the room, added, "And we don't know if they're doing it ironically. Like on some hipster stuff. They might just be having a good time, but we think they are laughing at us." She paused. "Bigger feels that way." She was pointing to an early section of the car ride scene, when Bigger first meets Mary's radical boyfriend:

> "We may as well get to know each other," Jan said. "I'm a friend of Mary's."
>
> "Yessuh," he mumbled.
>
> "First of all," Jan continued, putting his foot upon the running-board, "don't say *sir* to me. I'll call you Bigger and you'll call me Jan. That's the way it'll be between us. How's that?"
>
> Bigger did not answer. Mary was smiling. Jan still gripped his hand and Bigger held his head at an oblique angle, so that he could, by merely shifting his eyes, look at Jan and then out into the street whenever he did not wish to meet Jan's gaze. He heard Mary laughing softly.

> "It's all right, Bigger," she said. "Jan *means* it."
>
> He flushed warm with anger. Goddamn her soul to hell! Was she laughing at him? Were they making fun of him? What was it that they wanted? Why didn't they leave him alone? He was not bothering them. Yes, anything could happen with people like these. His entire mind and body were painfully concentrated into a single sharp point of attention. He was trying desperately to understand. (66)

I praised the students for their honest conversation. Something about Reggie's fixation thesis and the girls' responses brought Sara Baartman's tragedy to mind. Quickly, I went to my computer to see if I could find an old slide show from my days teaching African American Literature to seniors. Briefly, and with visual accompaniment, I told Baartman's story:

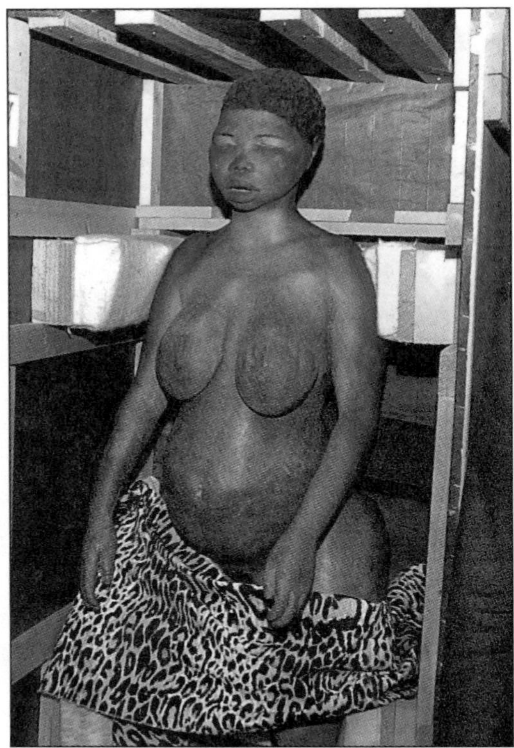

FIGURE 7.2
This plaster cast was made from Sara Baartman's body.

Taken in 1810 from South Africa, she was displayed as a circus act in London, then Paris. Her full-hipped body was the attraction. When she died at twenty-six, she was dissected by world-renowned racial scientist George Cuvier. Her genitals were pickled, put into jars, and displayed in a French museum until the 1970s. Figure 7.2 shows a plaster cast that was made of Baartman's dead body and displayed alongside her skeleton.

My students were stunned.

I reminded them about the racialized violence that had, along with Jim Crow laws and poor economic prospects, driven families like Bigger's from the South in the Great Migration. They knew about the lynchings. Fewer knew that lynch mobs routinely cut souvenirs from the murdered men's bodies to display in their houses. None knew that Cuvier's pseudo-scientific peers showed off preparations of male genitalia in most of London's anatomical museums. It's little wonder why, after generations of witnessing such an unholy blend of brutality, fascination, and exploitation, black people may have developed a certain insecurity about *their things*. It's little wonder why the well-intentioned white people that Mary Dalton represents face a steep climb to legitimacy in the eyes of Demi, Leah, Taylor, Ariana, and Bigger Thomas—who only a few pages after this ride, takes Mary's life.

Her death is even more tragic because Mary could have been an ally, if only she had come to terms with the truth of her relationship with Bigger. Her father, students soon learn, is slumlord of the apartment complex where Bigger's family lives—yet Mary cannot sense how her privilege is related to Bigger's stagnation. She can conceptualize neither the depths of his fresh-out-of-Jim-Crow-Mississippi pain, nor the acuteness of his fear—and these forces kill her before she has a chance to remedy her ignorance. (Afraid to be caught in a bedroom with a drunken, vulnerable white girl, he suffocates Mary with a pillow. Then, in a Baartmanesque defilement, Bigger decapitates and burns her corpse in her family's furnace.)

In my early days teaching this text, before allowing time for this conversation, Mary's murder was mostly unmourned. Students railed at Bigger's stupidity in committing the crime, and his foolhardy plan to cover it up, but few considered Mary's death any great loss. It was as if, with a couple of appropriated songs and a taste for fried chicken, she had committed a crime for which she had received an appropriate—if not utterly just—punishment. Ironically, I noticed a significant uptick in empathy for Mary's murder after the class started teasing out why they dislike her so much. They seemed to realize the pointlessness of thinking, as Bigger does after the crime, that the murder "was more than amply justified by the fear and shame she had made him feel" (114). It takes on a new heaviness not because students ever like, respect, or even know Mary, but because that night's interactions represent just how massive our collective racial lift is. As blind as Mary is, Bigger Thomas cannot see that she is trying to be a legitimate ally. There's no victory in her elimination, only a lost opportunity to develop what could have been a mutually beneficial relationship. This makes my students, sitting in one of the most racially diverse classrooms in the nation, measure just how much they are allowing stereotypes, past grievances, and myths to cloud their ability to see each other, to be fair with each other—so that they might eventually spend a little more time building relationships, and less time at each other's throats.

PUSHING PAST THE CHEAP VICTORIES

When accusing someone of cultural appropriation, the first instinct is to embarrass, to mock, to rage against, but rarely to understand. When answering such accusations, the first instinct is to equivocate, to justify, to dig in, but rarely to empathize. Unfortunately, when our students witness adults' engagement of this topic, their most unproductive habits are reinforced: accusation before questioning, vilification before education, defensiveness before humble reflection. Students learn that when emotions are high, it is permissible to suppress their analytical natures. Most destructively, both sides of the argument learn to celebrate cheap victories in inconsequential battles over would-be allies. These "victories" sate people's thirst for justice just as temporarily as a bag of chips might satisfy one's hunger for steak and potatoes.

Chapter 4 offers three propositions to ensure that our race conversations serve more nourishing purposes. The second of these propositions asks that teachers encourage new lines of inquiry. This chapter's *Native Son* conversations used the lens of cultural appropriation to point students toward one of life's most necessary—and difficult—lines of inquiry: the quest to more authentically see one another through a mist of cultural separation. Through his characters, Richard Wright forces readers to appreciate the blindness that this separation causes. Fueled by ignorance of each other's lives, and relying on stereotypes as source material, Bigger, Gus, Jan, and Mary are reduced to *playing the other,* a game they are drawn to by both insecurity and voyeuristic perversion. It is difficult for these characters to evaluate the impact of such games on the people being imitated, just as it is hard for the imitated to understand *why* they are offended, and what should be done about it. These are the core struggles of America's cultural appropriation discourse. Through both encouraging a historical perspective and incisive sparring, the conversations highlighted in this chapter tried to push students to engage these struggles, instead of settling for the trading of accusations and excuses. They didn't tarry in easy answers: that stereotypes are incomplete representations, that "Society" (my students' favorite catchall term) makes troubling use of them. Instead, the conversations push them to start the work of understanding each other's motives and sensitivities, while taking the time to unpack their own.

Professional Practice: "Put This in Your Pocket"

1. As argued in Chapter 3, teachers should commit to diversifying their conversational packages, blending various whole-class, SLC, and one-on-one structures. Success is not about choosing any one magic structure, it's about reliably mixing them up. For those of us who teach our students the humanities, it is equally helpful to consider the different ways that we can have students consume information. In this chapter, I ask students to dramatize the different selections that we are discussing. This approach was already in my conversational package, but the humbling exchanges from my drama class mentioned in the last chapter's "Pocket" notes have inspired me to let kinesthetic acting-out have more prominence in our discussion time. This has the benefit of scrubbing off the dryness that some students associate with reading aloud. A companion activity helps with analysis:

asking these characters to sit for an interview, go on a date, sit on a therapist's couch, and so on. All of these activities encourage students to make entertaining inferences about the characters' motivations. These inferences provide an influx of fresh perspectives to our conversations.

2. I interrupted one of this chapter's dramatic reviews to take a straw poll: *Who likes Mary? Who doesn't?* Such polls have proven very useful. Trained by testing culture, many students are conditioned to look at texts as a whole, which can lead to a skimming style of reading devoid of personal investment. Peppering our whole-class reading of texts with reminders that they've just passed something about which they might have an opinion (then encouraging them to track that opinion as it morphs) makes it easier for students to plug in to texts emotionally.

3. So often, English class is just a survey of novels. But this approach unnecessarily constricts our students' understanding of what writing skills can be used for. In this chapter, I use selections from Jabari Asim's *The N Word* to shed light on conversations about minstrelsy in *Native Son*. Doing so allows my students to see an adult version of the analytical essays that I make them write so often. Whenever prudent, I show them where traditional five-paragraph essay skills (Thesis/Evidence/Analysis) are used by professionals in the real world. Teachers should encourage students to thoughtfully engage nonfiction, especially (1) the critical literary reactions to the fictional texts they are discussing and (2) the historical context of the same. Though "interdisciplinary" collaboration between history and English teachers is wonderful, that phrase often evidences an unintentionally myopic view: English teachers deal in language. Language is bigger than novels. History teachers analyze the past. The past is bigger than dates and names. Let's not put ourselves in boxes.

CHAPTER 8

POP-UP CONVERSATIONS: THE 2016 PRESIDENTIAL ELECTION

Chapter 4 described pop-up race conversations as "risky outliers." Pop-up conversations, by my definition, have little to do with the conversational threads students are currently following. They exist outside the curriculum, which usually means they were designed quickly if at all, and meant to last only for a short amount of time. They normally root themselves in a singular current event, with few, if any, contextual sources. This current event itself, naturally, is evolving in real time, which means that yesterday's pop-up discussion can easily bleed into today's classroom with unanticipated complications. Finally, they are generally high-emotion affairs, involving topics about which students and teachers have not had time to compose themselves.

Pop-up conversations terrify me for two reasons. First, I have to consider the demotion in value that they impose on my regular curriculum: *Mr. Kay thinks this is more important than whatever we were talking about*. If students disagree with this assessment, I might have to face a justifiable *Why are we talking about this?* that I normally have little trouble answering. Second, and perhaps more important, the lack of discussion planning leaves me too many blind spots. I've not checked and rechecked the wording of my prompts for implicit or explicit bias. I've not anticipated possible conflicts between students. I've not gathered up sources to contextualize various points that might be made. Essentially, I am flying blind. I've heard that when rookie pilots fly into a cloud, they can get so confused that they don't trust their instruments. In such cases they've been known to fly out of clouds completely upside down. Or worse, they instinctively keep climbing to avoid hitting the ground, which causes their plane to stall out—then crash. When a conversation crashes, teachers waste important capital with students. Or end up in the newspapers.

Yet, for everything, there is a season. Occasionally, a moment's urgency is real, and not just a by-product of a teacher's impatience. Occasionally, an issue seems to suck up all the air in the classroom, and requires significantly more effort to ignore than acknowledge. We know that if we refuse to address this event, our students will consider us either too afraid to touch it, so out of touch that we don't see it, or arrogant enough to think that our curriculum is more important. The first makes us seem cowardly. The second heedless. The last selfish. All three erode our students' willingness to trust us when we ask them to be vulnerable, to take risks. We want our students to consider our classrooms relevant to their world and responsive to their needs, so when world events dredge up new discussion needs, we shouldn't inadvertently signal that students should save them for the hallway, the lunchroom, and their social media.

Dialogic teachers are bouncers deputized to decide which noncurricular issues get to supplant, or supplement, our students' current discussion threads. Just because a controversy is outside making a fuss doesn't mean we have to open the doors to it. When we're at our best, we ignore its noise, size it up, judge whether it should be admitted as is—or if it needs to go home and change. This discernment challenge is hardest in turbulent times, and no one day made this clearer in my classroom than November 9, 2016.

THE MORNING AFTER

Like many Philadelphia public school teachers, I spent most of Election Night of 2016 hurriedly trying to submit end-of-term grades by the district-imposed 11:59 p.m. deadline. As my family gathered in my aunt's living room for our Election-Night watch party, I was upstairs squinting at essays on my iPad. Focusing, however, was made more difficult by a stream of student text messages popping up on the screen. A freshman: *Mr. K I'm scared*. A sophomore: *Are you watching this! What's happening?* Later, my senior basketball captain: *This blog says he's gonna win, Kay*. As the night drew closer to a raw political reality—and heartbreak for many—more messages poured in and I wondered why my students were reaching out. I sure didn't want them to. I had my own bewilderment, my own piercing, indiscriminate anger to deal with, and I was not on the clock. Stewing, I powered down my phone. For the first time in a long time, I regretted not keeping my political leanings a secret from my students. I regretted my reluctance to equivocate when students asked for my opinions. I wished that my classroom wasn't dialogic, that we never talked about race in any depth, that we just read abridged canonical texts and filled out worksheets. Now, if the text messages were any indication, students would be expecting tomorrow's class to help them figure out *what was happening*.

I frightened myself. Normally, my round (enough) knowledge of America's racial history allows me to recognize precedent, to coolly analyze the deeper connections between now and then. When I'm functional, race issues are presented to students as puzzles to solve, organisms to dissect, symphonies to appreciate. If students come to an issue hot, this approach cools them down enough to consider race more rationally than many of their adult counterparts. Most students respect this composure. They generally do not respect a teacher's hyperbolic anger, a teacher's bewilderment, or a teacher's despair. I lay in bed on November 8 feeling all three—and no night's rest was going to cool me down. I wanted to answer Hispanic students' confusion with, *Don't overthink it. They want you gone*. I wanted to answer black students' confusion with, *Don't overthink it. They want to lock you up*. And that was more than I could say to my girls, who'd seen the nation shrug at their bodies' crude objectification. Or to my Muslim students, whose families' travel the new president had promised to ban. I didn't want to encourage detached analysis, for it seemed like counseling self-deception. I, like many colleagues around the country, closed my eyes that night thinking blasphemously, *There's no way I'm going to teach tomorrow*.

Morning came. I taught. Because it's what we do.

I had a free first period, which gave me time for an extra cup of bracing coffee. I took the long route to school, using the seven-block walk from city hall to mock out conversations. I hastily created discussion prompts that related the election result to *The Odyssey* and *Lord of the Flies*, the texts that my ninth and tenth graders, respectively, were studying. Both seemed forced, and I dropped them. Approaching the school, I noticed a massive sign posted over our school's windows that read as follows:

> To our School Family:
>
> As an inquiry-based school, SLA believes in asking questions, challenging assumptions, and working together to better understand each other and the world. We are a diverse group, and we embrace every member of our community, regardless of their identity. We also refuse to insult, threaten, exclude, disempower, or vilify others based on who they are or what they think. Instead, we listen before we speak. We see each other as complex individuals, not stereotypes. We protect and defend each other when needed. And when we disagree, we treat each other with decency. To us, that is the ethic of care. We will continue to work and act in this way, each and every day that we walk through these doors.
>
> Most important, we believe in you, our students—your ideas, your passion, and your ability to make the world a better place. Today, like every day, we hold out our hope that you strive to do just that.
>
> Love,
>
> The teachers of Science Leadership Academy

Later, I found out that my colleagues had collectively drafted this message as Election Night had drawn to a close. I relaxed a bit, reminded that whatever happened in my classroom today, it would not be happening in isolation. It would be ridiculous for any teacher to shoulder this load alone—in my case, try to rush-design a magic, home-run conversation that made everyone feel whole. I only had to remind students that I cared. With this reminder, I knew exactly what to do.

On the way to my classroom, I passed our main office. There I saw a black junior sitting on our principal's couch. He was crying. Knowing better than to attempt conversation, I approached him and offered a hand. He took it and pulled me in for a brief hug. I mouthed, "I'll talk to you later," and he nodded. I shook my head and mouthed, "Love you." He nodded again. I backed out, turning away before he could see my eyes watering. Upstairs, I was in my classroom only for a minute before a senior girl opened the door. I knew her schedule, knew she was supposed to be in another class. When I playfully asked why she was cutting class, she started smiling, incongruously. Her class had been discussing the election, and since "everyone" was crying, she'd gone for a walk.

We chatted as I straightened up my room. Then, in a preview of what I was about to hear from my own classes, she started narrating her election experience. She, like me, had gone to bed before it was officially called. In the morning, her mom had awakened her with the results. Then she started in on analysis: She had grown up with a black president. In her elementary school, she had designed projects about him and his family. She paused before asking me, "Who are my little brothers going to look up to?" I inhaled, thinking of the delightful young twins she was mentioning, interposed with the image of the young man I'd just consoled downstairs. She cried against my shoulder for a minute before I ushered her back to class. My freshmen were about to arrive, and I didn't want to put her grief on display. When she was gone, I walked over and erased the board, thinking, *What if, by the time they get to my class, they have already discussed this too much? What if they just want to sit down and talk some* Odyssey*? Is this more for me than them? Where is my ego in this—am I showing a hero complex?* Pop-up conversations are often undermined by faulty catalysts.

If I wasn't engaging this topic for the right reasons, it would be better to retreat for the day and plan something patiently.

As I debated, the freshmen started to file in. They were jostling each other and laughing just like any other day, which made me chuckle. Had I been expecting a funeral procession? A quick realization sobered me up: Most of the students in this group were Latino. The students travel from class to class in cohorts that we call "streams." Some accidental by-product of rostering had created a class of Dominicans, Puerto Ricans, Venezuelans, and Mexicans. They, of course, had noticed this quickly, and started pridefully calling themselves the *Latin* stream. As they sat down, I considered the implications of this demographic. I remembered the previous year, during the campaign, when a Mexican American freshman had used her journal entry to ask me if today's result was possible. I'd responded that she shouldn't worry. Now, I'd be seeing her sophomore class next period. Would she remember?

Always one of my more energetic classes, these freshmen took a while to get settled. I burned the first few minutes, answering their good humor with a few jokes. Soon enough, however, a student asked me, "Are we going to talk about the election?"

"Do you want to?"

"We were waiting to get here to talk about it." A couple of classmates agreed; others stayed silent.

"Yeah, but I don't want to if you've already gone there."

Many students spoke at once, saying whether they wanted to discuss the results. I listened, until someone griped about former teachers who had spent a year avoiding the topic. In this student's opinion, too many teachers were afraid to discuss Donald Trump. When I asked why, she said that teachers were probably afraid of students from different backgrounds fighting. I asked for other opinions, and a girl posited that teachers realized their great influence over students, and they didn't want to get in trouble for using it. The last volunteer, Layla, didn't so much answer my question as share a frustration. "Teachers don't know how to check kids when they say something racist. Teachers don't know what to do. It's easier not to talk about politics."

These all brought to mind my favorite section of James W. Loewen's *Lies My Teacher Told Me* (1996), which I paraphrased for them, and quote here.

> Many African societies divide humans into three categories: those still alive on the earth, the *sasha*, and the *zamani*. The recently departed whose time on earth overlapped with people still here are the *sasha*, the living-dead. They are not wholly dead, for they still live in the memories of the living, who can call them to mind, create their likeness in art, and bring them to life in anecdote. When the last person to know an ancestor dies, that ancestor leaves the *sasha* for the *zamani*, the dead. As generalised ancestors, the *zamani* are not forgotten but revered. Many, like George Washington or Clara Barton, can be recalled by name. But they are not the living-dead. There is a difference. (239)

And,

> Authors of American history textbooks appear all too aware of the *sasha*—of the fact that teachers, parents, and textbook adoption board members were alive in the recent past. They seem uncomfortable with it. Revering the *zamani*—generalized ancestors—is more their style. By definition, the world of the *sasha* is controversial because readers bring to it their own knowledge and understanding, so they may not agree with what is written. Therefore, the less said about the recent past, the better. (239)

I told students that teachers are probably less eager to discuss the *sasha*, or living history, for the same reasons that textbook authors are hesitant to write about it. The further back one goes—for example, discussing English literature's mostly white male canon, discussing the Founding Fathers' contributions—the less likely it is that students, or their parents, will care enough to make a fuss. But any teacher who talks modern politics, even within the context of state standard-driven curriculum, risks . . . *what?* I asked them.

Getting in trouble was the consensus answer; however, no student was entirely sure what that meant. Nor were they, after thinking about it, sure that the threat was real, or that it had ever been codified—and if it had, by whom. The School District of Philadelphia's policy on discussing political candidates had been emailed to every teacher on October 5, 2016. It read, in part, as follows:

> All School District personnel, while on duty or in contact with students, shall maintain complete neutrality with respect to all candidates. While on duty or in contact with students, School District personnel may not wear buttons, pins, stickers, articles of clothing, or any other items advocating a candidate, candidates, or political group. School District personnel may wear union paraphernalia so long as it does not advocate a particular candidate, candidates, or political group.

I'd imagine many districts have similar policies, as well. My students agreed that the possibility of getting into trouble had silenced many of their teachers over the past election cycle, which was the first that most had been old enough to pay attention to. I then addressed Layla's comment specifically, saying, "This campaign blurred lines between debate and hate speech."

"But teachers are afraid to call it that, Kay."

"I am too, to be honest." I paused, wanting to choose my next words carefully. A few students playfully encouraged me by shouting, "Go on!" After demurring for a few seconds, I tried to explain. "If one of you came in here shouting, 'One plus one is seven!' I'd tell you that you were *wrong*. I don't care how passionately you believe it, it would be my job to show you that the actual answer is two. Even if you don't believe me, I wouldn't want your classmates thinking, 'Hey, Mr. Kay can't count.'" As some of them tittered, I continued, "Kindness works the same way. There are ways to treat each other, and there are ways *not* to treat each other. If someone comes in here threatening, belittling, and stereotyping—*they are wrong*. No matter how passionately they think that such behavior has just been justified." I looked directly at Layla. "I don't know how it feels for students. But for me, it feels like the whole world just leaned on the other side of the seesaw. That's scary . . . Now I have to be that much better at my job." I continued in this fashion for another minute or so, asking students to empathize with their teachers as much as possible. None of us had any training in how to deal with days like today, and we would be doing the best that we could.

As we transitioned from the informal part of class, I asked students to put everything away. Tables completely clear. Cell phones, in particular, were to be put "behind something that zips." After waiting for everyone to comply, I reminded them why it was so important to *listen patiently*, *listen actively*, and *police our voices* during moments of high emotion. On a normal day, glancing down at your cell phone while someone is speaking might signal a mild disinterest. Today, it could be taken as an arrogant dismissal. On a normal day, raising your hand while someone is speaking might signal slight impatience. Today, it might be taken as an assault. Today we were predisposed to misunderstand each other. The easiest answers would be even more enticing than usual. In this moment, we had to be better than anything we'd seen on TV and social media over the past year. They agreed.

I thought back to my colleagues' sign: *We are a diverse group, and we embrace every member of our community.* Patting my chest in what I hoped read as an earnest gesture, I said, "*My* only goal today is to check in. So . . . how are you doing?" As students started to raise their hands, I remembered my classroom visitor from earlier, and her longish narration of the previous night. Such long stories would tax the sustained listening focus that I had just demanded from the kids. Especially in this stream, which had perhaps the most focus issues of any I taught. I had a better idea. "Give me one word." I gestured to the student who normally writes on the board for me. "Can you help me keep track?" She nodded and came up to get a dry erase marker. After handing it off, I asked for volunteers.

For the next couple of minutes, students shared their words. Some required little immediate explanation: *heartbroken*, *depressed*, *anxious*, *ashamed*, *confused*, *intrigued*, *numb*, and *without a home*. One word led to especially powerful exchanges. A black boy said, "*Afraid*." I completely misread him, and in the process, showed why listening patiently isn't just for students. When I asked what he was afraid of, he said, "Of what's going to happen." Unfortunately, this sparked an unnecessary heroic teacher moment. I assumed that his fear was based on what he thought the new president would do. Over the year, many students had approached me with legitimate fear based on myth and viral rumor: *I heard he'll put all Muslims in concentration camps. I heard that he'll make black people slaves again. I heard he'll deport all Latinos.* These students had often been comforted by a basic reminder about America's separation of powers. Because presidents were not kings, they couldn't do whatever they wanted, I had assured them. Thinking that this young man needed similar assurance, I launched into an extensive bit on governmental checks and balances. I ended with my customary, "Make sense? Or am I way off?"

He told me that I was way off. "I'm not talking about that. I'm talking about . . . I heard about this store in South Philly—it had Nazi graffiti on the window. In the hallway this morning, someone told me that her cousin got her hijab ripped off last night."

I understood immediately. "You aren't afraid of the president."

"I'm afraid of what some of his people will do."

"I'm sorry. I get it now." Sobered, I asked if anyone else shared his fear. It was not lost on me that a black boy had openly admitted vulnerability, too often a cultural taboo. I didn't want him to feel alone. This decision cracked the dam wide open, and students began tearfully sharing their trepidations. I stepped back from this, just calling on people and nodding, making sure that everyone in room showed complete focus, which they did. Chapter 1 argued that we build community *before* we hold meaningful conversations about race, and this moment proved the merit of these priorities. Students' eyes were latched onto whoever was speaking, for as long as they were speaking—which for some was quite a long time.

This is not to say that the conversation was conflict-free. One normally spirited black girl named Telah had spent most of the period with her head down. She brought it up only to theatrically check her phone. When this would happen, I would discreetly wave my fingers in a gesture that means *put that away*. She would roll her eyes, grudgingly comply, then put her head back down. On the surface, this behavior would seem to show a regression in our improving relationship. She had only recently realized that I wasn't the type to fuss at her for minor insubordinations. She displayed, in fact, my favorite young personality—sweet, opinionated, with developing impulse control. I knew well enough, however, that her current reticence wasn't to be taken personally. I remembered my own where's-the-nearest-exit moments, one of which I described earlier in this book (recall the professional development meeting moment from Chapter 4). As long as Telah stayed remotely respectful, I'd let her be. However, it soon became apparent that she couldn't keep it together. After another classmate named Ray shared his fear, she picked up her head and attacked. "Don't you act all serious now! Y'all been joking about this all year!" The room froze.

Ray, stunned, started to respond in kind before I cut him off. I asked Telah gently, but firmly, not to yell at her classmates. Then, I directed everyone's attention to the whiteboard, which was now covered with words. "When you all came in today, I was surprised by how playful you were. A part of me teased myself for expecting anything else. Y'all are goofy. But look at this." I paused, so they could read the words. "As silly as y'all are, some of you've been carrying a lot around with you. I mean, look at this list. Some of us seem to be . . . grieving." I gave them time to scan and think. (Figure 8.1 shows the whiteboard full of my students' words.)

"You know how there are different stages of grief? Some people get really analytical. Some people want to tell jokes. Others want to cry. Some people are ready to go out there and protest, and some of you don't have

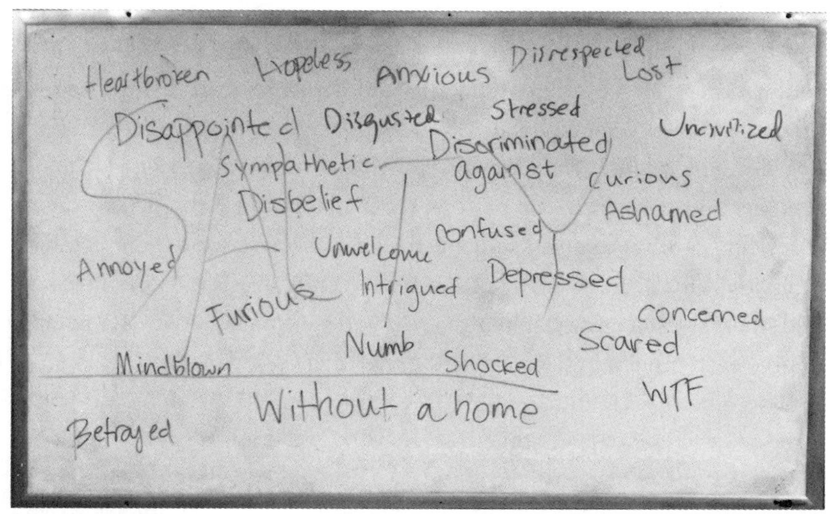

FIGURE 8.1
These are the words that my students shared.

the energy for all that. We have to remember that there is no one right way to process this. And it's not fair to make other people do it your way." I turned to Telah, whose grumpy yet open stare any veteran teacher would recognize as an olive branch. I took it. "We are all good people in here. There's no reason to try to score points on each other. That's what the bad guys want us to do."

A girl in the front of the room raised her hand. "Can I add a word?" I nodded, very grateful, for I didn't really know where to transition from my impromptu lecture. She smiled, and said, "Yo, I am so *salty*!" The class erupted in tension-busting laughter as my assistant scrawled the word as big as possible on the board. There was a chorus of snaps as classmates signaled their agreement. I'd held back my *Me too!* instinct throughout most of the word association, but this comment broke my resolve. In Philly, *salty* doesn't mean "angry" as much as it means "embarrassed for being wrong." Or "regretful." I told the students that probably my biggest problem today was that I was *salty*. I liked to think that I was smart enough to sniff out BS, but apparently I wasn't. I'd listened to the polls, I'd trusted our national conscience. I'd lampooned the cynicism of people who were wary. This was especially embarrassing as a black man moving in black circles, where everyone seemed ready to hit me with a *told you so*. Yes, *salty* was a perfect word.

There was only one way to end this conversation. I promised that, in cooler times, we would be dissecting the result, as it fit different units' Essential Questions. I could already see connections for my tenth graders' case law unit, while my ninth graders would certainly appreciate using our rhetoric unit to explore the various speech techniques that led to such a surprising result. I thanked students for being honest, for being open with each other, for keeping each other safe. Then, in an effort to summarize, I told students to take one last look at the board before I erased it. "Remember to give each other a break today." Most of them nodded.

Then, before I could even say it, a student asked, "Can we do High-Grade Compliments?" I smiled, seeing that we'd left nearly a half hour for the activity. They settled right in, walking up to each other one by one to share their appreciation. It was perfect. Kids of different ethnicities reaffirmed their friendship. Christian kids told Muslim kids that they had their back. Latino kids publicly admired each other's strength amidst their shared struggle. Over the day, more than one white student assured a black classmate that they were going home to have hard conversations about tolerance. One student even came out to her classmates, then thanked them for affirming her identity. I noticed that a few students had never really stopped crying, and I made a mental note to check in with them after class. However, as they were leaving, I quickly realized how little time I had to catch my breath before another class walked in. I sent each of them an email when I got home. Here are some of the replies:

> Hi Mr. Kay,
>
> I feel a little better. Thanks for checking in. How are you doing?

> Evening Mr. Kay,
>
> I went straight to sleep as soon as I got home but of course I'm not okay but I'm dealing with this to the best of my ability as we all are. I don't feel as alone as I did before but I am still scared for my family and I. Thank you so much for class today it was very needed and thank you for checking on me. I hope all is well with you and your family too.

> Hello Mr. Kay,
>
> I'm doing well thank you for asking, I just started crying because it had just hit me that he was president.

> Kay,
>
> Yes I'm ok thanks for checking on me. I really just want to have a future and honestly i believe that will be something that will be taken away from me thanks to trump. So I still believe that its just crazy that he is our future president. So yes I am still a little hurt and in pain but i believe I will get through this and I will

> just have to think about what i can do to keep my brother and my dad and all of my friends and other family safe. But thanks for checking up on me kay. Are you holding up??

These showed we were all a long way from healing. However, few pop-up conversations outside of Hollywood end with thorough healing. On November 9, 2016, my goals were much more realistic: My students were to know, beyond any shadow of a doubt, that they were loved. They would know that their teacher's priorities were in order. This was as good a platform as any. We'd continue the good work tomorrow.

"SOME PEOPLE CALL ME RACIST"

Late in the spring of 2017, I awoke to the following email from a former student named Alex:

> Is there a time that I can talk to you about some stuff I have been dealing with because I really need someone other than my parents to talk to. I think you would be the most understanding.
>
> Thanks.

Though I had taught Alex years earlier, I'd not considered our relationship especially close. I'd teased him about as much as I teased any student, asked for high fives in the hallway, celebrated some personal victories. All of our social interactions had been initiated by me, and we'd not spoken since he'd moved on to the next grade; it was unexpected for him to reach out first—especially with what had the tone of a deeply personal problem. We arranged for him to visit my room during a shared lunch period the next day.

When he walked in, I asked everyone to leave my classroom. After sitting down and thanking me for making time, he got right into it: As a person with politically conservative views, Alex had been feeling unsafe at school over the past few months. I asked immediately what he meant by unsafe. Were people threatening him? *No.* Were people making fun of him? *Sometimes.*

Was this happening in class or outside of class? *Not so much in class, but in the hallways and lunchroom. That's why I eat lunch in the hallway or the engineering room.* I paused, chastising myself for asking too many questions before acknowledging his vulnerability. "I'm sorry this is happening, bro. And I appreciate your checking in with me. You didn't have to." After he nodded, I returned to my checklist. Have you told your adviser? *No.* After we are done talking, would it be okay for me to tell your adviser, just so you can feel more supported? He paused, but not for long. *Yes, thank you.*

Now that we had worked through the essentials, I relaxed a bit. "So what have they been saying about you?"

Nervously, slowly, he said, "Some people call me racist. And other things." He didn't seem eager to elaborate on the name-calling. "And it makes me feel like I can't talk in class now, because whenever I open my mouth, they roll their eyes and . . ." He pantomimed an annoyed scoff. "When we leave class, I can hear them talking about me." I fought the temptation to ask Alex to itemize the beliefs that had gotten him into hot water. I didn't want to position myself as a judge of their rightness, nor did I trust my teaching instincts to focus on his troublesome social interactions—what he had come for, after all—and not to problematize his conservatism.

When recounting the N-word conversation in Chapter 5, I mentioned the far-reaching social consequences of our race conversations. We may try to contain controversies with guidelines like *Whatever happens in this classroom stays in this classroom*, but our best intentions are little match for the interconnectivity of our students' social lives. Yes, we hope that practicing healthy debate in a controlled environment will prepare students to be kinder when they are on their own. But pop-up race conversations stress this dynamic. Because the race conversation originated in their world, not the classroom, students feel even less inclined to think the classrooms' walls are a boundary. The farther their conversations stray from the classroom—and our immediate influence—the more likely our students will be to settle for the simplest, most cathartic answers. The more unbalanced a school's racial and political diversity, the more likely a pop-up race conversation will push the Alexes to sit alone in the hallway or hole themselves up in their favorite teachers' rooms, hiding from unintended social repercussions.

As he talked, I imagined how Alex might have experienced my class's November 9 pop-up conversation. For instance, what if, unlike a majority of his classmates, he was celebrating the outcome? When I asked students to share words, what would have happened if he had suggested *elated*, *vindicated*, or just plain *happy*? How might Telah have reacted? If she was ready to yell at Ray for clowning around, it's not much of a stretch to imagine her connecting Alex to every piece of racist rhetoric flung around during the presidential campaign. I was reasonably confident in my ability to manage that conflict, using the techniques outlined in Chapter 2. However, I am aware of my limited sphere of influence. I cannot say, with complete certainty, that the conversation wouldn't bleed into the hallway, or onto social media. Especially with students eager to break themselves into ideological camps. Questions like *Who believes what I believe?* and *Who do I feel safe around?* quickly become interchangeable and cause fissures that students feel licensed to discuss openly.

This thought brought me back to Alex, who was patiently waiting for my long introspection to end. I was happy that he'd come. My progressive politics are no big secret, particularly on race. As I am the sponsor of our school's Black Student Union, there was no way for him to know that rumors about his alleged racism hadn't already reached me (they hadn't) and that I hadn't already prejudged him. Our school is small, so it is difficult for any such issues to remain inconspicuous. Yet, Alex bet that I was still going to listen to him patiently. As we spoke, his intention became clear; he had not come to justify, clarify, or even explain his political beliefs. He wanted only to improve his dialogue with classmates. To this, I explained the bunker psychology that the political season had stirred up. I mentioned that when people are afraid, they often find security in labels and "othering." They are also less likely to entertain the nuances of an ideological opponent's argument. He could not productively engage his classmates without acknowledging the depth of their hurt, nor did his hurting classmates probably share his desire for fruitful political dialogue. This last bit hit hard, but he seemed to appreciate my honesty.

So what then? Should he just shut his mouth when class conversations turn to race and politics? Considering social risks, he (and all of his classmates) should certainly not be pressured to speak. But if he opts in to the discourse, he must take special care with his words, for political statements are rich with connotations that he may not have anticipated. For instance, Alex may wish to discuss the difficulty of creating sensible immigration policy. His stance might be that America's borders are too porous, a position that is not inherently racist. Or, he might question the efficacy of naming a movement Black Lives Matter, which would be a thoughtful challenge to an ideological opponent's messaging. Again, not racist. Any student who claims so might be trying to duck a good sparring session, and should be checked for applying the easy label. But if Alex uses the "illegal alien" label to make his immigration point, he has shifted the conversation—intentionally or not—into the realm of personal attack and transfer propaganda. Or if he, in questioning the Black Lives Matter movement, broadens his attack to call activists "thugs" and lawful protests "riots," he has shifted the conversation—intentionally or not—into the realm of stereotypes and post hoc fallacy. Words matter always, but during race conversations, these shifts can be deadly. Alex then asked, with a blend of fear and exasperation, if this meant that conservative white kids had to tiptoe their way around race conversations.

"No . . . Yes. It depends. You shouldn't just bulldoze your way through, blindly parroting silly people's phrases. Or at least you shouldn't do it without expecting some social consequences. But it comes down to what happens when a mistake is pointed out. That moment brings two choices: You can pump your brakes and make it clear that you didn't mean to offend—then actually listen to why your words were hurtful. Or, you can keep plowing forward, blaming political correctness for silencing you." I thought up another option. "Or, I guess, you could retreat back into your corner and give up on sharing your point of view that day." I leaned in and smiled. "You are so smart. When you contribute, everyone gets stretched. Again, no pressure to speak—but you should know that no class conversation gets better just because you shut up."

A rapidly ending lunch period forced an abrupt end to our conversation. I'd not been checking my watch. Before he left, I reminded him that I'd be letting his adviser know that we'd spoken, and that he could expect a follow-up. Until then, he knew where to find me. We hugged, and he thanked me for my time. Throughout the rest of the school year, he checked in with me occasionally to let me know that things were getting a little better.

It's tempting for us to be flattered when our students ask us to help them process a traumatic current event. This is not entirely wrong, because in every human relationship it feels good to be needed. Teachers are especially uplifted by this sort of validation—we feel important, trusted. We should, however, be careful to learn the right lesson: It's not about us. Our students should feel safe because of the classroom culture we've inspired, not because of our personality or politics. When they are vulnerable with us, it is not to feed our egos. If we allow our egos to be fed, we might stop crediting the processes that are actually working. When we do this, we might eventually define ourselves according to what generous students said about us years ago, without realizing that our current students no longer find our classrooms safe.

Professional Practice: "Put This in Your Pocket"

I have only one "pocket" suggestion for this chapter, because I don't wish to encourage quick-fix thinking about pop-up conversations. However, I must address the possibility of conflict that might have arisen had Alex been in the same class that held the November 9 discussion. Then, in this hypothetical situation, what would have happened if he had expressed joy? Chapter 2 described four different types of conflicts: over *Facts or Data*, over *Process or Methods*, over *Purposes*, or over *Values*. This situation would seem to present a *values* conflict—the most intractable of the four. In the case study, I did not preclude the conversation by reminding students that it was okay to both "agree to disagree," and to "disagree without being disagreeable." Nor did I patiently remind them what "disagreeable" would mean in this political context. So, admittedly, I didn't set myself up well for such a conflict, as any post-spat reminder would seem more reactionary plea than bedrock principle. And as we all know, teachers stand the greatest risk of losing their capital with students when we appear reactionary.

If, hypothetically, Alex had expressed joy on November 9, I would have had to—as explained in Chapter 2—quickly nudge everyone to the center of the Venn diagram: *What do we agree on?* We agree that nobody deserves to be hurt by their peers in our classroom community. We agree—as an axiomatic truth backed up by *hours* of house talk activities—that each other's hopes, anxieties, and vulnerabilities are worth both our attention and our empathy. So the chief focus of our discussion then was not the election of Donald Trump, or an evaluation of his proposed policies. (These, of course, can be categorically discussed during *planned* curricular threads.) It was an exploration and validation of our communities' feelings, so that we could better do our jobs as classmates and teachers. Specifically, Alex and his would-be antagonist, possibly Telah, would first have to understand that attempts to bury each other were not to be tolerated. This would have to be spoken unequivocally—to both parties—regardless of my own political frustrations and hurt.

EPILOGUE

Professional development practitioners often deemphasize struggle and promise ease. Their guaranteed gains are seismic, not incremental. According to most, teachers are perpetually one step away from the smoothness and efficiency that they, their superiors, and their students desire. Few tell us that growth will always be hard and that our lessons (and techniques) will always *just* be catching up to relevancy when our students' world changes again.

In writing this book, I have tried to never lose sight of the grind. Discussing race in the classroom will never be easy. We will make mistakes, most of which we will not notice. We will misjudge the capital we've banked with students. While chipping away at generational biases, we will unintentionally wound students' psyches. Parents will send emails, not all of which will be encouraging. Certain conversations will strike a nerve with those invested in our students' silence, which will spark bitter consequences. Time after time, we will be tempted to retreat from the edge, to lay before our students what has already been discussed ad nauseum. We will want to avoid the *sasha* in favor of the much safer, February Soup–inducing *zamani*. This book opened by citing Frederick Douglass's 1852 antislavery speech, in which he contrasted easy *light* with strenuous and productive *fire*.

In pushing for the latter, I've no choice but to put struggle at the forefront, to not offer teachers snake oil.

Douglass, in 1857, spoke to an audience in Canandaigua, New York, celebrating the twenty-third anniversary of the emancipation of the West Indies from British rule. He shared the following truth:

> If there is no struggle there is no progress. Those who profess to favor freedom and yet deprecate agitation are men who want crops without plowing up the ground; they want rain without thunder and lightning. They want the ocean without the awful roar of its many waters.

He knew the stubbornness of the status quo, how it dies an ugly death—flailing violently at every last possible foothold, emerging countless times in different forms before being laid to rest. Colonialism and antebellum slavery were buoyed by the most intractable ignorance; it took centuries of disruptive conversations to destabilize racism's most basic tenets. History remembers Douglass, but not the countless teachers, parents, and mentors, both enslaved and free, who kept the toughest conversations alive under the bleakest circumstances. These people had scant encouragement. They could more readily count on cynicism, apathy, or threats from power structures that benefited from their silence. Yet they conversed, either with pamphlets or through spirituals, in packed auditoriums or in lonely cookhouses. They did not leave us a legacy of quick fixes. And as teachers, we would do well to remember Douglass's curt dismissal of easy roads.

LET THEM IN

We are tempted down many easy roads with our dialogic professional development. The first involves our collection of data. One of the early questions that I ask colleagues when leading a professional development session is, "How healthy is your classroom culture?" This is important, considering the reminder in Chapter 1 that community must come before conversation—and must be maintained throughout the year. Teachers journal on the prompt for a while before I offer a follow-up: "How do you know?" At this, I can count on thoughtful nods and audible "hmms" before the teachers start to write. When asked to share, teachers tend to be cathartically honest, zeroing in on anything they've identified as a problem. *Kids from different backgrounds have been teasing each other. My kids are cliquey. They don't listen very well.* In the too-rare occasions where teachers don't jump reflexively to a deficit stance, they might say, *My classroom is a real safe space. My students are sweet to each other.* Answers to my second question, however, are seldom as clear. Teachers who focus on problems usually cite specific classroom incidents (which, if not checked, can devolve into a half-hour purgative storytelling session). Teachers who share that things are going well tend to recount anecdotal conversations with individual students. The group hears stories about quiet students who've found their voices or alumni who came back to visit years later to tell teachers how influential they were. Both sides, however, tend to qualify their statements with something like, "Now that I think of it, I don't really know."

Anecdotal evidence deserves neither the trust nor the power that we teachers have given it. It's naive to consider my classroom community healthy because one of my basketball kids likes me. Or because a student happened to be rostered with a bunch of her friends. Or because a certain problem student happened to discover a love for writing in ninth grade. Or because a wistful alumnus has realized that high school wasn't so bad after all. I call this "starfish" data, after Loren Eiseley's famously uplifting allegory called *The Star Thrower* about a man who throws starfish into the sea to save them one by one, because it focuses on the one kid for whom I've "made a difference." Starfish data could skew the other way, too, if teachers focus on the one student whose personality they've yet to understand, while gathering no information about how anyone else is doing. Either way, individual anecdotes masquerade as comprehensive data, which gives us false impressions about both the state of our classroom community and what we need to work on.

One solution can be seen on nearly every college campus. At the end of the semester, college students complete course evaluations. Not doing so in secondary school signals that students have not yet reached the age where they can be trusted to reliably articulate their needs. This doesn't jibe with our language about empowering youth. Some of our students realize this. More of them, sadly, don't even register the disconnect. It's easy to understand why we teachers might be hesitant to offer course evaluations. We might think that our students find our discourse exhilarating, only to find out that we've bored them. We may have added certain activities to our conversational package and noticed some anecdotal success among a few students. But a thorough evaluation might reveal that we leaned too heavily on it and alienated an entire learning style. Our best-intentioned strategies can fail spectacularly without our even knowing it. It's happened to me often: I've tried directing more loquacious students toward "leadership" positions in class conversations, until some of them told me that it came off as an attempt to quarantine their voices. For about half of one ill-fated semester, I decided to have an assistant teacher list volunteers' names on the board, then call on students in the order of their raised hands. Students told me, quite reasonably, that this practice led to disjointed conversations. *By the time it's my turn to speak, what I'm saying is no longer relevant. And when I want to respond to what someone says, or ask them a question, I have to wait ten minutes.* Unmitigated disaster.

The most piercing criticisms are personal. We dialogic teachers often cultivate a vision of ourselves based on our relationships with students. These relationships depend, as much as any, on setting and maintaining healthy boundaries. We can quickly assume a familiarity with our students that spends capital that we've not earned. This is especially harmful when discussing race. We might share a joke or make the kind of throwaway racial observation that friends might share with friends: *I've noticed that many white students have raised their hands; let's wait for someone else.* Students might be wildly uncomfortable with this and never tell us. My freshmen open every year with a project in which students describe a previous educational experience. They tell many stories about overfamiliar teachers. When asked if they ever redrew boundaries, students often look at me quizzically, asking, *When was I supposed to do that?*

Dialogic teachers must, systematically, ask their students how things are going. It is the only way to get good data on what we need to work on. As professionals, we should be trusted to craft our own prompt language. I like to keep curriculum questions simple: *What was your favorite discussion?*

What worked about it? What was your least favorite discussion? What would you change about it? Then a few about classroom community: *What made you feel safe? What made you feel unsafe?* Some personal questions: *How could I have better helped you meet your goals? What habit of mine needs to go away right now?* Then I ask for text recommendations and general suggestions. I normally give students the option to remain anonymous; however, the most detailed feedback tends to come attached to names. I attribute this to a culture of frequent check-ins—after every project, unit, quarter, and semester, almost always informal. By the time we get to the end of the year, many students own their role as my most important critics. Without their intel, we must lean on infrequent administrator observations for an outside perspective. These, when we think about it, are of dubious value. Whether we get observed on a good or bad day, their data is woefully lacking in context, which sets unreliable foundations for our professional development. The students, as the people forced to endure your conversations, can offer the most useful opinions on your execution. We should never stop imagining ways to better gather these opinions, as painful as the process might be.

One last student evaluation note: Whenever reasonable, invite students to participate in your staff's professional development. In every *Not Light, but Fire* PD, I try my best to arrange for a student to come along. They have one important role: When I group teachers, and prompt them to design mock discussions, students are to respectfully describe how they would feel as a student in those discussions. At the conclusion of such activities, teachers constantly thank my students for their candor. We shouldn't seek to improve our dialogic skills in complete isolation from our students. When it's appropriate, let them in the room! We could all benefit from the occasional student panel as PD. Sure, we should share our best practices with each other, but why not occasionally hear these practices described from students' perspectives? Many of our growth processes should remain private, but we could all stand to benefit from our students' frankness.

TRACK IT

I often invite students from the University of Pennsylvania's Reading, Writing, and Literacy graduate program to observe my students' conversations. One of the grad students' assignments is to write a descriptive review of the class, the first step being a minute-by-minute chronicling of a class period. Below is a snippet of one of these observations from my third year in the classroom. It covers the last thirty-five minutes of a freshman English class. I've retained most of my observer's shorthand:

- T {Teacher} asks students to read EQs (essential questions)—asks them all to read at once, tries to do it like spoken word—students end up reading out over top of one another—T laughing and joking with students—trying to coordinate their reading of the EQ.
- 1:26 starts discussing the book.
- Student comments about some {graffiti} writing in a book—T jokes around with students about the things written in one of their books.
- Side note: Classroom atmosphere is very relaxed.
- T mentions an incident from the news, a professor suing students for disagreement—a student makes a comment (inaudible to me) that causes lots of oohs from students—T teases one of them "When do grades go in?" More oohs.
- T talks to students about Essential Questions: talks about new ideas—equates new ideas to racism (in past) and gay marriage (currently)—this causes a lot of discussion among students—asks for people to quiet down after a minute of chatter—asks students to raise hands to answer this part of the discussion and they do—talks through the EQ (which is "what gets in the way of new ideas")—many hands are up—T praises by saying: "take a snapshot—i love all the hands!"
- Acknowledges everyone's answers positively—most students answer with thoughtful comments—all seem engaged in the discussion.
- T points out a theme of the class—says: i hope you have noticed that there is a theme—respect for your ideas—i respect your ideas & you need to respect the ideas of others—now as you go to 10th grade and start thinking of systems—i want you to think a little revolutionary—i want you to think about your individual ideas—

how many of you have revolutionary ideas? (students want to know what he means)—gives deeper description—many students raise hands to say they have revolutionary ideas.

- Transitions to reading aloud from text.
- T has a student start reading—they hit a word that they do not know—(*assuage*)—T encourages them to raise hands (it seems that they are forgetting a system used in the classroom of raising hands if they encounter a word they do not know in the reading)—they do and ask what *assuage* means—T has other students give answers.
- Same thing happens at *apothecary* and *piety*.
- There is a lot of talking and laughing as they read & when someone stumbles—there is light jeering—does not seem to bother those who are reading.
- T is walking around room as students read.
- The reader notes that someone should have raised their hand for *chattel*—T says well, that is because they know it—calls on a student who it turns out doesn't know what *chattel* means—a couple take a stab at it and then the T tells them what it means.
- T ends class by giving them HW reading and then dismisses them by saying "bye."

I was amazed when this observer first showed this to me. I flashed back to hours spent breaking down film as a student assistant football coach at West Chester University. I didn't remember half of the incidents that her running observation had caught—much like a player might not remember how he ended up flat on his back hearing the other team celebrate. *Even though I was joking, had I really threatened to lower a student's grade? That's probably not a good idea. Did I really not hear kids laughing at a slow reader? That's very bad.* There was a section before this excerpt where I asked kids to put their technology away. My observer noted that three kids opened laptops every time my back turned, and one texted throughout the entire class. Then there was this gem: *T walks to a person who is sleeping and says*

"How can you sleep with my voice that loud?" (I cannot see if the student picks up his head.)

To any passing observer, this class period might seem phenomenal. My students were loose, engaged, asking good questions. They were diving into the book with great energy, using an essential question to connect it to the outside world. Even though my veteran self cringes at the vague, rookie-ish discussion prompts—*How many of you have revolutionary ideas?*—I would generally be proud of this young teacher's approach. The detailed observation, however, encouraged another level of reflection. Just in this excerpt, I can see how my vocabulary approach stilted my students' reading process. And worse, I apparently was so focused on vocabulary skills that I missed my students' making fun of a classmate's lack of fluency. And why would I have instinctively put a student on the spot for not knowing the definition of *chattel*? These moments, exposed raw on paper, persuaded me to reconsider how I approached in-context vocabulary. These deficits were now harder to tuck between my already-determined strengths: *Classroom atmosphere is very relaxed / Acknowledges everyone's answers positively—most students answer with thoughtful comments—all seem engaged in the discussion.*

Neither our administrators nor our colleagues should be expected to consistently offer this level of observation (which shouldn't be much of an excuse, as some of my best tracking has come from current students, student teachers, senior assistants, etc.). But if we wish to get better at leading conversations, we must find ways to see the granular details we wouldn't ordinarily notice. The chance to track our classrooms even twice a year might spark seismic change. Different tracking activities have exposed gender and racial patterns in my calling on students, my inconsistency with "wait time," and just how many minutes are lost to shiny tangents.

There are specific benefits to tracking race conversations:

1. We lack the capacity to remember any more than a few highlights and lowlights of any one class conversation. It is dangerous to put too much stock in either.

2. There's no better way to develop our classroom awareness. It's hard to teach listening skills when our focus on one student exchange causes us to miss other students' distractions.

3. We can more easily see the impact of our personal habits on the discourse.

Most of us are no more able to see our conversational quirks than we can see our own noses. We need a mirror, which tracking provides. With a mirror, we might notice that we shift violently away from a topic every time we anticipate student conflict, even if the kids aren't actually fussing. Or we might notice our reflexive defensiveness when students disagree with us. The possibilities are as varied as our complex personalities. It's well worth the time investment.

OLYMPIA ACADEMY, PART 2

Among professionals, true community building is hard, but it is always preferable to heroic isolation. The perceived riskiness of meaningful race conversations makes it more tempting for teachers to nudge our classroom doors shut from both our colleagues and administrators. But we need each other. We should try our hardest to form Olympia Academy–styled relationships with like-minded teachers. This includes *any* fellow teachers at *any* school who are willing to authentically invest their time in our development.

Some of the advantages of these relationships are immediately clear. Feedback from student evaluations is best reviewed with like-minded colleagues, who can help us sift out the most useful information. Also, colleagues can occasionally track each other's classroom conversations. While the data from student evaluations or discussion tracking can be good for solitary reflection, it's even more useful when used to spark a discussion among like minds. It is common for teachers to be encouraged to share best practices, but it's even better to mix that in with the tougher conversations sparked by either student feedback or granular tracking. We can ask, *Why do you think my student said this about my discussion prompts? What do they say about yours?* or *Where do you think this conversation went off the rails? I don't know how we got here.*

However, the most important opportunity that an Olympia Academy-inspired professional learning community can provide is the chance to *practice*. And by practice, I do not mean the mock teaching that some of us had to survive as undergrads, as our classmates pretended to be high school students with classroom management problems. I mean that we should actually engage in meaningful race conversations within these small communities, and that the practice should be fully legitimized by our bosses as PD. Chapter 2 discusses how important it is for teachers to express ourselves clearly. Racial issues require even more careful articulation as terms go in and out of favor, and as newer labels and expectations appear (*microaggression*, *trigger warning*, etc.), it helps to develop one's fluency without students present. We dialogic teachers can help ourselves hunt for possible hard problems to explore. We can search out solutions. We can practice *listening patiently* to one another. We can *listen actively* by citing one another, then pushing one another through questions. Finally, and this is perhaps hardest for passionate dialogic teachers, we can practice *policing our voices*. And if, after practicing all three skills, we disagree, we can spar with the same good intent and trust that we expect of our students.

The best growth is aided by community. Yes, we teachers should study our craft vigorously. We should take classes. We should attend conferences. But, in truth, without discussion practice, we will never see our fullest potential. Here, teaching is no different from other pursuits: Lasting improvement requires dedication to the humbling cycle of practice and reflection. And, try as we might, we cannot practice facilitation by ourselves. It's best to practice with colleagues, regardless of whether they teach in our building. This book, if anything, has been an earnest attempt to step from the old inertia of *why we should talk about race* into the urgent struggle of *how to do it*. And in doing so, maybe build a community of like minds that can offer fresh ideas, steadfast support—and most importantly—the opportunity to practice.

A FINAL NOTE ON MAGIC

I began this book criticizing the myth of the magical teacher. Iconoclastic, young, and blessed with a preternatural interpersonal intelligence. Rich in the immeasurable, unteachable "stuff" that all greats were born with. A teacher who, with a stirring speech or *Rocky*-esque training montage, can cause the most disinterested students to morph into streetwise scholars. I wrote about how this pervasive myth separates teachers into *haves* and *have-nots*, pushing the former toward hubris and the latter toward stagnation. Neither road leads our students to better conversations about race. We must always struggle to find, then maintain, a sturdy and self-assured humility. This humility will inspire inquiry—we will never credit conversational successes to our general awesomeness. We will try to figure out what made things work. We will never blame conversational failures on our lack of charisma, our race, or our age. Instead, we will examine our techniques, isolate and develop our relevant communication skills, add to our conversational packages.

It's hard to get better. Many of us work in school systems that use a barrage of empty platitudes to mask their fixation with our imperfections. With our confidence under such assault, risks are disincentivized. We don't want parades thrown to celebrate our missteps. And while we can teach dates, names, formulas, and vocabulary without inspiring opposition, resistance to meaningful race conversations is passionate, organized, and stubborn. Many systems have a great deal invested in our students' silence. They've persuaded too many of us to doubt our capability, so we settle for ladling out February Soup. I hope this book has provided a countervision—one that, while acknowledging our inherent challenges, respects our universal ability to overcome them. Guided by humility, we *can* lead race conversations infused with consequence, conversations that motivate our students to push forward, to build more honest cross-cultural relationships. Together, we *can* encourage a generation to be unwilling to waste their time, ever dissatisfied with half measures and repetitive "light." We, as teachers, *can* answer Douglass's challenge to deal instead in "fire"—in truth, there are no professionals better equipped for the job.

REFERENCES

Adichie, Chimamanda Ngozi. 2006. *Half of a Yellow Sun*. New York: Knopf.

———. 2009. "The Danger of a Single Story." Filmed July 2009 at TEDGlobal 2009. www.ted.com/talks/chimamanda_adichie_the_danger_of_a_single_story.

———. 2013. *Americanah*. New York: Knopf.

Alexander, Michelle. 2010. *The New Jim Crow: Mass Incarceration in the Age of Colorblindness*. New York: New Press.

Asim, Jabari. 2008. *The N Word: Who Can Say It, Who Shouldn't, and Why*. New York: Houghton Mifflin.

Brooks, Gwendolyn. 1960. *The Bean Eaters*. New York: HarperCollins.

Butler, Octavia E. 2009. *Kindred*. Boston: Beacon Press.

CBS6 Albany. 2013. "'Think Like a Nazi' Homework Controversy." Published May 9, 2013. www.youtube.com/watch?v=HTowfwjdfeo.

Chase, Zac. 2011. "Things I Know 44 of 365: Positivity Can Be Viral." www.autodizactic.com/things-i-know-44-of-365-positivity-can-be-viral.

———. 2016. "Can You Take a Compliment?" www.autodizactic.com/can-you-take-a-compliment.

Dilg, Mary. 1999. *Race and Culture in the Classroom: Teaching and Learning Through Multicultural Education*. New York: Teachers College Press.

Douglass, Frederick. 1852. "What to the Slave Is the Fourth of July?" Oration to Rochester Ladies' Anti-Slavery Association. Rochester, New York. July 5.

Du Bois, W. E. B. (1903) 2014. *The Souls of Black Folk*. Millennium Productions.

Dumas, Firoozeh. 2004. *Funny in Farsi: A Memoir of Growing Up Iranian in America*. New York: Random House.

DuVernay, Ava, dir. 2014. *Selma*. Paramount.

Edwards, Gavin. 2015. "Billboard Cover: Kendrick Lamar on Ferguson, Leaving Iggy Azalea Alone and Why 'We're in the Last Days.'" *Billboard*, January 19, 2015. www.billboard.com/articles/news/6436268/kendrick-lamar-billboard-cover-story-on-new-album-iggy-azalea-police-violence-the-rapture.

Eiseley, Loren. 1979. *The Star Thrower*. New York: Harcourt Brace.

Evanski, Jerry. 2009. *Classroom Activators: More Than 100 Ways to Energize Learners*. Thousand Oaks, CA: Corwin.

Farley, Christopher John. 2005. "Dave Speaks." *Time*. May 14. http://content.time.com/time/magazine/article/0,9171,1061512-6,00.html.

Foner, Philip S., ed. 1950. "West India Emancipation." In *The Life and Writings of Frederick Douglass, vol 2, 437.* Novato, CA: New World Library.

———. 1999. *Frederick Douglass: Selected Speeches and Writings*. Chicago: Lawrence Hill.

Friedman, Jonathan C. 2002. *Speaking the Unspeakable: Essays on Sexuality, Gender, and Holocaust Survivor Memory*. Lanham, MD: University Press of America.

Hansberry, Lorraine. 1959. *A Raisin in the Sun*.

Haygood, Wil. 2016. *Showdown: Thurgood Marshall and the Supreme Court*

Nomination That Changed America. New York: Vintage Books.

Helgeland, Brian, dir. 2013. *42: The Jackie Robinson Story*. Burbank, CA: Warner Home Video.

Isaacson, Walter. 2008. *Einstein: His Life and Universe*. New York: Simon and Schuster.

Isenberg, Nancy. 2016. *White Trash: The 400-Year Untold History of Class in America*. London: Atlantic.

Jay-Z [Shawn Carter]. 2003. "Moment of Clarity." CD. Track 8 on *The Black Album*. Roc-A-Fella.

Jefferson, Thomas. 1999. *Notes on the State of Virginia*. New York: Penguin.

Kauffman, Caryl. 2002. "Iverson Unapologetic During Confrontational Press Conference." www.thereporteronline.com/article/RO/20020508/SPORTS/305089975.

King, Jamilah. 2016. "The Improbable Story of How Kendrick Lamar's 'Alright' Became a Protest Anthem." Mic. February 11. https://mic.com/articles/134764/the-improbable-story-of-how-kendrick-lamar-s-alright-became-a-protest-anthem#.v4K8k49D0.

King, Martin Luther. 1965. Address at the Conclusion of the Selma to Montgomery March. http://kingencyclopedia.stanford.edu/encyclopedia/documentsentry/doc_address_at_the_conclusion_of_selma_march.1.html.

Kwok, Jean. 2010. *Girl in Translation*. New York: Riverhead.

Lebedun, Jean. 1998. *Managing Workplace Conflict*. Virginia Beach, VA: Coastal Training Technologies.

Lee, Harper. 1960. *To Kill a Mockingbird*. New York: HarperCollins.

Lee, Spike, dir. 2000. *Bamboozled*. New Line Cinema.

Lehmann, Chris, and Zac Chase. 2015. *Building School 2.0: How to Create the Schools We Need*. San Francisco: Jossey-Bass.

Lipsyte, Robert. 1967. The Contender series. Harper and Row.

Loewen, James K. 1996. *Lies My Teacher Told Me: Everything Your American History Textbook Got Wrong*. 1996. New York: Touchstone.

Lubrano, Alfred. 2017. "The 'Imposter' Syndrome of First-Generation Penn Students: Uneasy Among Privileged, Distanced from Family." *Philadelphia Inquirer*. October 3. www.philly.com/philly/news/university-of-pennsylvania-working-class-college-education-freshmen-family-20171004.html.

McLeod, Lea. 2014. "3 Smart Ways to Keep Yourself from Rambling." April 27. http://www.leamcleod.com/3-smart-ways-keep-yourself-from-rambling.

Meek Mill [Robert Williams]. 2012. "Real Niggas Come First." CD. Track 14 on *Dreams and Nightmares*. Warner Bros.

Mosely, Walter. 1990. Easy Rawlins series. New York: W. W. Norton.

The Notorious B.I.G. [Christopher Wallace]. 1995. "Real Niggaz." CD.

Obama, Barack. 2008. "Barack Obama: 'A More Perfect Union' (Full Speech)." Filmed March 18, 2008 in Philadelphia, PA. www.youtube.com/watch?v=zrp-v2tHaDo.

Paik, Carol Q. 2008. "I'm Not Who You Think I Am." *Newsweek*, February 8.

Rock, Chris, prod. 2009. *Good Hair*. HBO Films.

Rock, Chris. (1996) 2017. "Chris Rock: Bring the Pain." Published August 22, 2017. www.youtube.com/watch?v=tNLQfKs5sFQ.

Sando, Mike. 2016. "Rooney Rule in Reverse: Minority Coaching Hires Have Stalled." ESPN. July 19. www.

espn.com/nfl/story/_/id/17101097/staggering-numbers-show-nfl-minority-coaching-failure-rooney-rule-tony-dungy.

Saturday Night Live. "Black Jeopardy—Saturday Night Live." Filmed March 2014 in New York. www.youtube.com/watch?v=VWuJHbVZBQg.

Shakur, Sanyika. 1993. *Monster: The Autobiography of an L.A. Gang Member*. New York: Grove.

Sharpley-Whiting, T. Denean, ed. 2009. *The Speech: Race and Barack Obama's "A More Perfect Union."* New York: Bloomsbury.

Silberman, Mel, and Freda Hansburg. 2000. *PeopleSmart: Developing Your Interpersonal Intelligence*. San Francisco: Pfeiffer.

Singleton, Glenn E., and Curtis Linton. 2006. *Courageous Conversations About Race: A Field Guide for Achieving Equity in Schools*. Thousand Oaks, CA: Corwin.

Spielberg, Steven, dir. 1985. *The Color Purple*. Warner Bros.

Stenberg, Amandla. 2015. "Don't Cash Crop on My Cornrows." YouTube. April 15. www.youtube.com/watch?v=O1KJRRSB_XA.

Stewart, Jon. 2014. *The Daily Show*. "The Daily Show—Race/Off." Published August 28, 2014, by Comedy Central. www.youtube.com/watch?v=T_98ojjIZDI.

Taylor, Mildred. 1976. *Roll of Thunder, Hear My Cry*. New York: Penguin Random House.

———. 1981. *Let the Circle Be Unbroken*. New York: Penguin Random House.

———. 1990. *The Road to Memphis*. New York: Penguin Random House.

Teaching Channel. "Conver-Stations: A Discussion Strategy." www.teachingchannel.org/videos/conver-stations-strategy.

Troutwine, Chad, Chris Romano, and Dan O'Meara, prods. 2011. *Freakonomics: The Movie*. Toronto, ON: Mongrel Media.

Twain, Mark. (1884). 1965. *The Adventures of Huckleberry Finn*. New York: Bantam Books.

Vento, Joey. 2007 "Order in English: Joey Vento of Geno's Steaks on Glenn Beck." December 17. www.youtube.com/watch?v=MeNHJCQDyIA.

Walker, Alice. 1982. *The Color Purple*. New York: Houghton Mifflin Harcourt.

Weir, Peter, dir. 1989. *Dead Poets Society*. Burbank, CA: Touchstone Pictures.

Wiggins, Grant P., and Jay McTighe. 2005. *Understanding by Design*. Alexandria, VA: Association for Supervision and Curriculum Development.

Wilson, August. (1985) 2010. *Fences*. New York: Samuel French.

Wright, Jeremiah. 2008. "God Damn America" sermon. YouTube. April 25. www.youtube.com/watch?v=Ix-AMYos0Js.

Wright, Richard. 1998. *Black Boy*. New York: HarperCollins.

———. 1999. *Native Son*. New York: HarperCollins.

X, Malcolm. 2012. "Chickens Coming Home to Roost." Published July 21, 2012. www.youtube.com/watch?v=oD6aX3dHR2k.

X, Malcolm, and Alex Haley. (1965) 2007. *The Autobiography of Malcolm X, as Told to Alex Haley*. London: Penguin.

Zimmerman, Jonathan, and Emily Robertson. 2017. *The Case for Contention: Teaching Controversial Issues in American Schools*. Chicago: University of Chicago Press.

Zinn, Howard. 1980. *A People's History of the United States*. New York: HarperCollins.

Zusak, Markus. 2005. *The Book Thief*. New York: Knopf.

INDEX